CHRONOLOGY OF CHAOS

THE MISTAKES, MISSTEPS, MISHAPS, AND MISSED OPPORTUNITIES DURING DONALD TRUMP'S REIGN AS POTUS

ROBERT SANTUCCI

Chronology of Chaos
The Mistakes, Missteps, Mishaps, and Missed Opportunities
During Donald Trump's Reign As POTUS

ISBNs
978-1-7346412-0-2 (hardcover)
978-1-7346412-1-9 (softcover)
978-1-7346412-2-6 (E-reader)

Library of Congress Control Number: 2020902826

Facebook: Chronology of Chaos
Twitter: @ChronologyChaos
Website: Chronologyofchaos.com

CONTENTS

FOREWORD

I began this journey as a bit of catharsis after Trump was elected to run the country in November, 2016. It was indeed a dark day for me, as it was for many Americans.

However, in every dark tunnel, there is light at the end. So I decided to use this light to document and record everything during the Trump administration that like-minded people would see as detrimental to the health of our nation, and by extension, the world.

This is a compilation (along with chapter commentaries) of information I have gleaned from various news sources with dates of each story. Although it is a selective list of events (I did not write about every action taken by the administration or reproduce each tweet), it is a true document of the "chaos" perpetrated by Trump and his associates. Overall, it is not attractive.

I'd like to thank my wife Monika for putting up with me as I continued to write about Trump on a daily basis, and for good friend Kevin Schwab for suggesting I write chapter summaries to make my book more readable.

Lastly, you'll notice I never put the word "president" before Donald Trump's name (unless it was quoted by someone else). Although some may see this as a sign of disrespect, I view it as a symbol of respect that may never be earned......... Enjoy.

SOURCES

- ✓ Associated Press
- ✓ Axios
- ✓ Washington Post
- ✓ CNN
- ✓ ABC News
- ✓ NBC News
- ✓ CBS News
- ✓ Chicago Tribune
- ✓ NY Times
- ✓ Huffington Post
- ✓ Canada Today
- ✓ Britain Times
- ✓ Indianapolis Times
- ✓ Wall St. Journal
- ✓ Syracuse Post Standard
- ✓ Time Magazine
- ✓ Newsweek
- ✓ NPR
- ✓ USA Today
- ✓ FOX News
- ✓ NorthJersey.com
- ✓ MSNBC
- ✓ The Resistance (web)
- ✓ Independent Journalism Review
- ✓ TheHill.com
- ✓ Al Jazeera
- ✓ Reuters
- ✓ Yahoo
- ✓ Leftscoop.com
- ✓ NY Daily News
- ✓ Forbes
- ✓ Twitter
- ✓ Daily Mail
- ✓ New Yorker
- ✓ Ecowatch

CHAPTER 1

DONALD JOHN TRUMP WAS sworn in as the 45th president of the United States on January 20th, 2017. He wastes no time in creating controversy. Trump immediately begins claiming that his inaugural ceremony was attended by far more people than any in recent history (although we all know it wasn't). Thus begins the presidency of "mine is bigger, better, and more fabulous than yours." Trump makes claims that his address to the CIA was one of "the greatest speeches ever," and that he would have won the presidential popular vote if he had simply "tried." And so we have the second coming of Harold Hill from the *Music Man*, and there's about to be trouble in River City once again.

Trump's demonization of the press starts early on after the swearing-in ceremony. He blames the media for failing to back up his crowd size claims, (it's always about "size" with him, 'right?) and for not reporting that millions of illegal immigrants voted for his opponent (qué pasa, Hillary?). This begins the "truth-be-damned" pattern of the newly-minted president, who seems hell-bent in creating his own reality. It's also the time that Trump mouthpiece Kellyanne Conway created the now-famous concoction of "alternative facts." She'll soon be joined by a whole host of other Trump sirens who will make Conway's act pale by comparison.

Meanwhile, Trump's inauguration is not well received by the public at large. Thousands of rallies against the president spring up world-wide. Trump finally gets the massive crowds, but they're not wearing red "MAGA" hats. And, we're just getting started.

- Former President Obama, who stated that he would only comment on the current administration if he felt that America's "core values" were being challenged, makes a statement against Donald Trump's immigration ban less than two weeks after leaving office. **1/19/17**

- The president's inauguration speech is an extension of his campaign remarks; dark and full of despair. It paints the U.S. as a nation in danger, decline, and in need of Donald Trump to save it. **1/20/17**

- The Department of the Interior/Parks Department is ordered not to use Twitter to reference crowd size at the inauguration by order of the White House. **1/21/17**

- There are women's marches protesting Trump's inauguration in 266 U.S. cities, and two to three million marchers join protests worldwide. **1/21/17**

- Donald Trump claims his inaugural ceremony had 1.5-2 million people attending. Reports show that number to be between 250,000 and 300,000. Trump then has White House Press Secretary Sean Spicer complain to the press about the low estimates. **1/21/17**

- The president addresses the CIA by airing grievances about the inauguration crowd size estimates, and how the media is lying. Because the site of the speech was in an area dedicated to fallen CIA officers, many members of the bureau feel it shows a lack of respect. **1/21/17**

- The Department of Justice, on the second day of Trump's administration, issues a writ stating that Trump's son-in-law, Jared Kushner, could serve in the presidential cabinet, despite anti-nepotism laws that are in place against such appointments. **1/21/17**

- Kellyanne Conway spars with CNN anchor Chuck Todd, claiming that Trump's information about the inauguration was based on "alternative facts." **1/22/17**

- The first legislation signed into law by the Trump administration cancels a drop in rates for FHA insured homes, which will cost low-income home buyers an additional $500-$1,000 per year. **1/21/17**

- Donald Trump decides not to release his tax returns, even though throughout the presidential campaign, he stated that he would do so after an audit by the Internal Revenue Service. Spokesperson Kellyanne Conway explains that, "No one would be interested in them, except the press." **1/22/17**

- The White House places a gag order on the Environmental Protection Agency to prevent them from delivering press releases, or commenting on social media. The Agriculture Department, and Department of Health and Human Services are also covered under this order. **1/24/17**

- The White House website deletes all references to LGBTQ rights and global warming. **1/24/17**

- Donald Trump advocates the use of torture and other "enhanced interrogation" techniques for political prisoners, and drafts an executive order to re-open so-called "black site" prisons. **1/25/17**

- The president claims in an ABC News interview that his speech to the CIA was one of "the greatest speeches ever," and that FOX News reported the applause after the address was equal to or better than the ovation given to Peyton Manning after winning the Super Bowl. He also states that if a poll had been taken of the 350 people in attendance, it would have been, "350-to nothing" in his favor. **1/25/17**

- During the same interview, Trump claims he could have won the popular vote in the 2016 U.S. presidential election if he had simply "tried." He also mentions that a meeting with a former combatant in the presidential race resulted in the vanquished candidate saying that their meeting was, "The single greatest meeting I've ever had with anybody." **1/25/17**

▪ During a tour of the White House as part of the interview, Trump stops at a framed picture of the inauguration to once again address the issue of crowd size. He then takes Muir to another image, a panoramic photo by a local Washington artist, to prove the point that his inauguration audience was larger than President Obama's. No other photos are shown to compare and contrast his claim. **1/25/17**

▪ Donald Trump pushes his border wall agenda with Mexico, calling for Mexico to fund the project. Based on this, Mexican president Enrique Peña Nieto cancels his scheduled trip to the U.S. to meet with Trump. **1/26/17**

▪ Trump complains to members of Congress during a White House dinner that he would have won the presidential popular vote if between 3 to 5 million illegal immigrants hadn't voted for Hillary Clinton. There is no proof to support this claim. **1/26/17**

▪ Press Secretary Sean Spicer says that Mexico will have a 20% import tax on their exported goods to help fund the border wall. He then says that the tax is only "one way" to finance payment for it. The tax would most likely be borne by U.S. consumers, who would be stuck paying higher prices for goods from Mexico, as prices would be raised to compensate for the tax. **1/26/17**

▪ Steven Bannon, Trump's senior cabinet advisor, tells the media to "shut up," because he disapproves of their criticism of the president. **1/26/17**

▪ Trump signs an executive order that temporarily prohibits migrants from seven predominantly Muslim nations from entering the U.S. The order has little clarity, and also seems to ban those with green card visas from entering the country, even though they are permanent legal residents of the U.S. **1/27/17**

▪ During the annual "Walk for Life" March held annually by right-to-life advocates, Vice President Mike Pence at the urging of the president, directly addresses the crowd during the Washington, D.C. rally. This is the first time a member of the Executive Branch of the U.S. Government has ever done so. **1/27/17**

- Reince Priebus, Trump's chief of staff, tries to walk back the green card issue, stating that the ban did not apply to holders of that particular form of visa, even though the White House said that it did just a day earlier. Federal judges issue rulings to temporarily halt the travel bans. Tens of thousands of Americans protest against the ban across the country in over 300 cities. A group of 16 state attorneys general claim they believe the travel ban is unconstitutional. The Trump administration says the order was written largely to protect the U.S. against a terrorist attack, such as those that occurred on 9/11, even though those hijackers came largely from Saudi Arabia-a country not on the ban list. The executive order was not vetted with any government agencies outside of Donald Trump's inner circle. **1/28/17**

- The president restructures the National Security Council to include Steve Bannon, who will now hold a spot on the Principals' Committee-a spot usually reserved for the nation's most senior military advisors, including the secretaries of Defense and State. The reorganization also states that the director of national intelligence and chairman of the Joint Chiefs of Staff will sit on the Principals' Committee only when issues to be discussed pertain to their "areas of expertise." In the previous two presidential admin-istrations (Under Obama and Bush), the persons in these two positions attended all meetings, not only when invited. **1/29/17**

- Donald Trump fires acting Attorney General Sally Yates after she orders the Justice Department not to defend his immigration order to ban entry into the U.S. for citizens of seven Muslim-majority countries. **1/30/17**

- More than 100 State Department diplomats sign a memorandum arguing that the immigration ban will not deter attacks on American soil. The memos amount to what is called a "dissent channel." Press Secretary Sean

Spicer says that diplomats who disagree with the immigration ban should, "either get with the program, or go." **1/30/17**

∎ Donald Trump accuses Sen. Chuck Schumer of shedding "fake tears" while speaking about the plight of immigrants affected by the U.S. travel ban. **1/30/17**

∎ Donald Trump's "voter fraud" expert, Gregg Phillips, is found to be registered to vote in three states simultaneously. **1/30/17**

CHAPTER 2

DONALD TRUMP HITS THE ground running in his first full month as president. He continues legitimizing his presidential victory (a theme played out nearly every month) by repeatedly referring back to the size of his Electoral College win, like an aging former football star recounting the score of the city championship in his youth.

Immigration also plays a large role in Trump's first month in the White House, as great acrimony is displayed with Trump's travel ban, and the subsequent overturning of the ban in court. This game of high-stakes ping pong pits Trump with one paddle, the courts with the other, and immigrants are, well, the "ball."

More of the Trump Administration's "dubious" claims become apparent during February, including reports of terrorism not being covered by the press, news of attacks in Sweden, and the famous "Bowling Green Massacre" (thank you, Kellyanne Conway), which were false, more false, and falser.

Distain for the Trump Administration surfaces on many levels, with more protests on (Not My) Presidents' Day, with anti-Trump rallies featured across the nation, and increasing anger at Republican Congressmen who fail to hold town hall meetings with their constituents (even though most meetings were cancelled because constituents begin showing up with pitchforks, lit torches, and a hangin' rope).

February also reveals that DJT refuses to appoint anyone to a government position who has spoken ill of him. That leaves the population of Idaho and some guy named "Vinnie" left to pick from.

■ National Security Adviser Michael Flynn, issues a statement that Iran is being "put on notice" for test firing ballistic missiles, even though the firings do not violate the Nuclear Weapons Treaty. **2/1/17**

■ Donald Trump says that he may have to send U.S. troops to Mexico to control the "bad hombres." **2/1/17**

■ The president advises Senate Majority leader Mitch McConnell to "go nuclear" (change the established voting rules in the Senate) if his nominee for the Supreme Court, Neil Gorsuch, is filibustered by Senate Democrats. **2/1/17**

■ During a scheduled one hour telephone conference with Australia's Prime Minister Malcolm Turnbull, (which the president abruptly ends after 25 minutes), Trump blasts an agreement signed by the Obama administration to send Australia's Syrian refugees to the U.S. (he also boasts about the size of his Electoral College win once again during the call). At one point, Trump states that out of four calls he has had with world leaders (including Russia's Vladimir Putin), Turnbull's was, "the worst by far." **2/2/17**

■ The White House states that they are considering ways to allow Americans to opt out of federal laws and regulations, based on religious beliefs. It is commonly believed that such actions could open the door to widespread discrimination, based on religious values and practices. **2/2/17**

■ Donald Trump vows to "totally destroy the Johnson Amendment," which would then allow churches and other non-profits to endorse political candidates. The amendment has been in place since 1954. **2/2/17**

■ The president uses a prayer breakfast to comment on the supposedly poor ratings of Arnold Schwarzenegger on *The Apprentice*, a program that Trump previously hosted, by mockingly asking the audience to "pray for his (Schwarzenegger's) ratings." **2/2/17**

▪ The White House delivers a message honoring African-Americans, which seems to infer that former abolitionist and social reformer Fredrick Douglas is still alive. He died in 1895. **2/2/17**

▪ Kellyanne Conway says during an interview on MSNBC that Donald Trump's immigration ban is similar to former President Obama's ban on Iraqis, because of the "Bowling Green Massacre," an event which never happened. **2/3/17**

▪ Trump's immigration ban is overruled by a federal judge in Seattle. Trump tweets that U.S. District Judge James L. Robart, who made the ruling, is a "so-called judge." **2/4/17**

▪ The president once again tweets attacks on Judge Robart by saying that his ruling against the immigration ban, "put our country in such peril," and "If something happens, blame him and the court system. People pouring in. Bad." **2/5/17**

▪ Trump threatens to defund the state of California by withholding federal dollars if they continue to advocate for sanctuary cities within their borders. **2/5/17**

▪ In an interview with FOX News's Bill O'Reilly, Donald Trump is asked why he respects Russia's President Vladimir Putin, since he is widely thought of as a being a killer. Trump replies, "Oh, you think our country's so innocent?" **2/6/17**

▪ Trump also states during the same interview that terror attacks have gotten so bad in Europe, that it's no longer being reported, because a "very dishonest" press doesn't want to report it. White House spokesperson Sean Spicer concurs with the president's comments, but could offer no specific incidences where terror attacks weren't being reported. **2/7/17**

■ The White House issues a statement that shows 78 supposed acts of terrorism committed around the world where the media either did not report on, or "underreported them." Included on the list were attacks on San Bernardino and Paris, which were extensively covered by world-wide media outlets. The hastily-prepared statement is riddled with misspellings, including the words "attack" or "attackers," which are written several different ways. **2/7/17**

■ The president claims that violence and crime in the United States is higher now than it has been in the past 47 years. This was immediately denounced as a false statistic, with crime rates actually dropping in the U.S. in recent years. **2/7/17**

■ Donald Trump tweets on his personal account about how unfairly Nordstrom is treating his daughter Ivanka, due to the fact that the retailer is dropping her clothing line from their stores. He then re-tweets the criticism on the Twitter POTUS account. Press Secretary Sean Spicer states that Nordstrom is dropping the line in order to undermine her father, Donald Trump. It is a "direct attack on his policies and her name," Spicer says. **2/8/17**

■ Trump again criticizes Judge James Robart, who overruled his controversial immigration ban, by stating, "Even a bad high school student" could comprehend the meaning of his executive order. Trump later says that his own personal comprehension skills are "outstanding," stating that he "comprehends better than almost anyone." **2/8/18**

■ Donald Trump criticizes Sen. Richard Blumenthal (D-CT) because he released information from a meeting he had with Supreme Court nominee Neil Gorsuch. In that interview, Gorsuch stated that Trump's attacks on the federal judiciary were, "disheartening and demoralizing." Trump tweets, "Sen. Blumenthal, who never fought in Vietnam when he said for years he had (major lie), now misrepresents what Judge Gorsuch told him?" Sen. Blumenthal stands by his comments, as he points out that

White House staffers were in the same room during the interview, and could verify what was said between the two men. **2/8/17**

∎ Trump claims that Democrats are delaying his cabinet choices, and that this is the longest delay in U.S. history. A fact check proves this to be incorrect, with several previous administrations having had cabinet approvals as late as March or April of their first terms. **2/9/17**

∎ Kellyanne Conway, White House adviser, tells *Fox and Friends* viewers to "Go buy Ivanka's stuff," a comment in response to Nordstrom's recent decision to pull Ivanka Trump's line of clothing from their stores, due to poor sales. Conway's remarks are widely seen as a violation of laws prohibiting federal employees from using their position to endorse products. The White House later states that Conway was "counseled" on her statement. **2/9/19**

∎ The 9th Circuit Court of Appeals rules 3-0 to retain suspension of the administration's immigration ban. Trump tweets, "SEE YOU IN COURT, THE SECURITY OF OUR NATION IS AT STAKE!" Trump follows up with another tweet, stating that the judges' ruling is, "a political decision." **2/9/17**

∎ Trump tweets, "Trump administration seen as more truthful than news media." He bases this claim on a poll from Emerson College. No other national polls support the Emerson findings **2/9/17**

∎ National Security Adviser, Michael Flynn, is accused of discussing the rollback of sanctions against Russia, before Donald Trump took office. Flynn first denies the claims, and then says he can't recall if he did discuss sanctions with Russian authorities. Under mounting pressure, Flynn resigns his post on February 13th. **2/9/17**

∎ Senior presidential aide Stephen Miller says on several Sunday network news programs that there were "busloads" (thousands) of voters brought into New Hampshire to vote illegally during the presidential election. When pressed, Miller offers no proof regarding his claim. **2/12/17**

■ During a joint press conference with Canada's Prime Minister Justin Trudeau, Donald Trump once again brings up his Electoral College victory in the presidential election. **2/13/17**

■ While hosting a State dinner at Mar-a-Lago with Japanese Prime Minister Shinzo Abe, Donald Trump receives documents detailing the most recent missile launch by North Korea. Instead of moving to a private room, Trump looks over the documents in full view of the public. He then discusses the information while allowing guests to use their cell phones to illuminate the documents for a better view. Numerous guests post the scene on their Facebook accounts. **2/13/17**

■ Stephen Miller, Senior White House Adviser, states in an interview on CBS's *Face the Nation* that Trump's national security actions "will not be questioned." **2/13/17**

■ Major developments surface after National Security Adviser Michael Flynn resigns his position on the Cabinet. It is reported that Donald Trump asked for his resignation. Reports from the *Washington Post* confirm that Flynn spoke with Russian Ambassador Sergey Kislyak in late December regarding lifting U.S. sanctions against Russia once Trump took office. It was also discovered that Russia decided against expelling U.S. diplomats from their country in response to President Obama's expulsion of 35 Russian nationals from Washington. Phone intercepts with Kislyak seem to indicate that Flynn suggested Russia hold off on any quid pro quo by expelling U.S. diplomats, which Russia agreed to. **2/13/17**

■ Michael Flynn apparently lied both to the Justice Department and Vice President Mike Pence, by stating he did not discuss lifting sanctions against Russia. The president was notified in late January (2 weeks prior to Flynn's forced resignation), by the Department of Justice that Russia had compromising information on Flynn which could have been used to blackmail him. Leading Democrats, as well as some Republicans, call for a full investigation of the matter. **2/13/17**

▪ U.S. Department of Labor Secretary nominee Andrew Pudzer withdraws his name from consideration amid reports of previous spousal abuse against his wife, and failure to pay taxes (until December 2016), on the wages of an undocumented domestic worker he employed in his home. **2/15/17**

▪ Donald Trump uses Twitter to attack supposed White House leaks of information, which he says are crippling his presidency. He tweets, "Information is being illegally given to the failing @nytimes and @washingtonpost by the intelligence community (NSA and FBI?). Just like Russia." **2/15/17**

▪ The MSNBC *Morning Joe* program announces that it will no longer book White House spokesperson Kellyanne Conway on their program. CNN also announces that they will no longer book Conway as well. **2/15/17**

▪ Donald Trump announces plans to hold a campaign rally event, to highlight his 2020 re-election bid. Trump files to run for president on the same day he is sworn in (1/20). This is the earliest filing in presidential history. **2/15/17**

▪ Donald Trump holds a 77 minute press conference in the East Wing of the White House. The original purpose was to announce a new nominee for Labor Secretary, Alexander Acosta, but quickly turns into an attack on the press, media, and anyone who disagrees with the president. Among Trump's claims are that he "inherited a mess" when he took office, that his new administration was not in chaos (as had been widely reported), but instead was "operating like a fine-tuned machine." He also states that his immigration ban was "perfect." Trump then says that his Electoral College win in November was the largest victory since Ronald Reagan's. When it is pointed out by a member of the press that Clinton, Bush, and Obama had larger E.C. victories than he did, Trump responds by saying,

"I was given that information." As his press conference continues, he denies being anti-Semitic, even though no one accuses him of it. Also at the event, Trump re-introduces false claims about Hillary Clinton authorizing the State Department to sell 20% of U.S. uranium production to Russia, and states that, "There has never been a presidency that has done so much in such a short period of time." During the news conference, he once again calls reporting from the *New York Times* and *Wall Street Journal* as "fake." Donald Trump then accuses Democrats of posing as supporters, and holding up signs at his rallies designed to smear him. At that same conference, he suggests to April Ryan, a black reporter from the American Urban Radio Network, that she should schedule a meeting between himself and the Congressional Black Caucus. An exasperated Ryan tells Trump that she would be unable to do so, as she is a reporter, and not connected to the Black Caucus. The president then responds by stating that he had planned a meeting with Elijah E. Cummings, an African-American Democrat from Maryland, but was turned down. Rep. Cummings later states that Trump's claim was false. As the press conference is winding down, the president takes a swipe at the circuit court that overruled his immigration ban by saying that the court was "in chaos..... and frankly, in turmoil." **2/16/17**

■ Donald Trump's replacement for National Security Adviser, Bob Harward, turns down the position, citing family obligations. Unconfirmed reports however, cite Harward's unwillingness to work in what he calls the White House's "shit sandwich." **2/16/17**

■ Other reports surface that Donald Trump refuses to appoint anyone to a government position who has ever said anything disparaging about him. Due to this fact, the administration has been having problems finding applicants who meet those specific criteria. **2/16/17**

■ The president signs an executive order allowing coal companies to dump their mining waste directly into local rivers and streams. The repeal of an Obama-era order called the "stream protection rule" is immediately criticized by environmental groups. **2/16/17**

▌ Donald Trump says on Twitter that the Democrats are making up allegations that Russia interfered with the 2016 presidential election. "The Democrats made up and pushed the Russian story as an excuse for running a terrible campaign. Big advantage in Electoral College and lost," Trump tweets. **2/16/17**

▌ In a press conference with Israeli Prime Minister Benjamin Netanyahu, the president declares his affinity for a "one-state solution, or two-state solution, whatever the leaders want." This position involving the tense relationship between Israel and Palestine veers sharply from past U.S. policy, which strongly favors a two-state solution in Israel. During the press conference Donald Trump once again references his victory in the Electoral College over Hillary Clinton in the presidential election. **2/17/17**

▌ Reports by the Associated Press, which are denied by the White House, show that there was some consideration to use as many as 100,000 National Guard troops as part of a nationwide illegal immigrant deportation force. **2/17/17**

▌ In the wake of ever-troubling rhetoric by Donald Trump, Vice President Mike Pence, Secretary of Defense Jim Mattis, Homeland Security John Kelly, and Secretary of State Rex Tillerson arrive in Europe to meet with European allies in an effort to re-assure NATO members that Trump's policies will not be in deference to them. **2/18/17**

▌ Donald Trump holds a campaign rally in Melbourne, Florida, and dedicates most of his speech to railing against the press. He also comments on a terrorist attack that happened, "last night in Sweden." There was no such attack in the Scandinavian country, and Trump was roundly criticized by the press and the Swedish Government. Trump later explains that his comments were based on reports from a FOX News program he recently watched. **2/18/17**

- Thousands of US citizens turn out on Presidents' Day (2/20), to hold rallies across the country. The rallies, labeled "Not My President's Day," are organized to show contempt for Donald Trump and his policies. **2/20/17**

- During the February Congressional recess, Republican Congressmen who hold town hall meetings in their home districts are met with large crowds of angry constituents who are opposed to the president's executive orders, Cabinet appointments, and other policies and actions. The White House issues a statement, claiming that protests at these meetings are being infiltrated by "paid activists." **2/21/17**

- Donald Trump rescinds protections for transgendered students, who were previously able to use restrooms consistent with their gender identity, by issuing an order that overrides Education Secretary Betsy DeVos, who opposes the action. **2/22/17**

- The president states that deporting undocumented immigrants is a "military operation." Homeland Security Secretary John F. Kelly, speaking in Mexico, clarifies that there will be "no use of military force in immigration operations." **2/23/17**

- The White House blocks CNN, the *New York Times*, *Politico*, and the *LA Times* from attending a press briefing with Press Secretary Sean Spicer, directly contradicting statements from Trump's press team that the media would not be banned from such briefings. This is in line with Trump's ongoing feud with media outlets that he considers oppositional. **2/24/17**

- The FBI, asked by the White House to publically refute reports of collusion between Donald Trump's campaign and Russian intelligence, refuses to do so. Direct communication between the White House and U.S. intelligence agencies during pending investigations is prohibited by law, preventing the agency from doing so. Trump then attacks the FBI for failing to do his bidding. **2/24/17**

∎ Due to the widespread nature of the Trump business interests and residences, there are increasing costs associated with protecting Donald Trump and his family. From Trump Towers (wife Melania and son Barron), to Mar-a-Lago (Trump himself), and business trips for sons Eric and Donald, Jr., Secret Service and local enforcement budgets are being stretched to unhealthy limits. It is estimated that the overall costs of protection for Trump and his family during this administration could reach into the hundreds of millions of dollars. Also, since Trump is not fully divested from his business interests, reports surface that he may be profiting from payments to host government events at his properties. **2/24/17**

∎ Donald Trump, in a tweet directed at newly-elected Democratic National Committee Chairman Tom Perez, sends his "congratulations" to him, and then follows up by tweeting, "I could not be happier for him, or for the *Republican* Party." **2/25/17**

∎ The Trump administration announces that it will more aggressively enforce the nation's immigration laws, unleashing the full force of the federal government to find, arrest, and deport those who are in the country illegally, regardless of whether or not they have committed any crimes. The Department of Homeland Security announces that it will publicize crimes committed by immigrants, enlist local police as enforcers, strip immigrants of privacy rights, discourage asylum-seekers, and ultimately, speed up deportations. **2/27/17**

∎ Reports of dozens of Jewish cemeteries being desecrated across the country are revealed. Some sources blame the culture of hate being fostered during the Trump tenure as president. White House Press Secretary Sean Spicer calls the reports, "incredibly wrong." **2/28/17**

▌ Donald Trump delivers his first full address to Congress on 2/28. In his 1 hour and 42 minute address, he focuses on his policies on immigration and domestic terrorism, along with other topics. Upon review, his speech is found to contain numerous lies and half-truths included in the body of the address. However, others praise the speech for its clarity and "presidential" tone. **2/28/17**

CHAPTER 3

MARCH IS THE BEGINNING of a contentious relationship between the President and Attorney General Jeff Sessions, a man with a severe "Russian meeting memory disorder," who recuses himself from the Russian investigation because of his self-induced affliction. This creates a void that will later be filled when Robert S. Mueller steps into the breach later in the year.

Always a fan of poppycock, Donald Trump ushers in his own claims of illegal conduct in government, as he accuses former President Obama of "tapp-ing" his phones at Trump Tower. Even Kellyanne Conway joins in on the fun by claiming, "microwaves turned into cameras" could have been used to spy on her boss. After pressure from Congress and nearly every other sane person in the country, this nonsense dies a quick and embarrassing death.

One of Trump's signature campaign promises, to repeal and replace the Affordable Healthcare Act (aka "Obamacare"), starts to skid off the road in March, as Republicans, with a majority in both houses, can't reach an agreement as to what a new plan should look like. "Who knew healthcare was so hard?" Uh, we all did.

This month features a look into Trump's vision of reshaping government, with budget plans that would slash funding for many vital agencies, (like the Department of Education) while increasing others, (like the military). Less books, more bombs.

The president also tries to give Germany's Angela Merkel a bill for NATO, to which she says, "Nein." HUD Secretary Ben Carson calls slaves brought to America "immigrants." And, alliteration aside, the Russia investigation heats up as "Flynn Flips." Enjoy March!

∎ Attorney General Jeff Sessions was discovered to have had two meetings with Russian ambassador Sergey Kislyak during July and September 2016, at the height of supposed Russian cyber campaigns to influence the U.S. presidential race. During his Judiciary Committee confirmation hearing on January 10th, Sessions, after being questioned by Sen. Al Franken (D-MN) about contacts with Russian officials, denies any such summits occurred, stating, "I'm not aware of those activities….I did not have any communications with the Russians." Due to the accusations, and his close ties to the Trump administration, there have been calls to have Sessions recuse himself from any investigation revolving around Russian involvement in the November election. **3/2/17**

∎ After calls for his resignation by members of Congress, including Nancy Pelosi (D-CA) and Charles Schumer (D-NY), Attorney General Jeff Sessions officially recuses himself from any U.S. investigation related to the 2016 presidential campaign, which would include Russian interference in the electoral process. Donald Trump, angered with the move, gives his full support to Sessions, stating that the Democrats "are overplaying their hand" by criticizing Sessions, and that their attacks are a "total witch hunt." **3/2/17**

∎ More Trump fallout occurs, as it is reported that Marco Rubio's (R-FL) lease on one of his Florida government offices is not being renewed by his landlords. This is mostly due to repeated protests by anti-Trump demonstrators marching in front of the building, causing disruption. **3/2/17**

∎ *USA Today* reports show that two other Trump advisers, J.D. Gordon and Carter Page, spoke to Russian ambassador Sergey Kislyak at a diplomatic conference revolving around the Republican National Convention in July, 2016. This meeting raises questions about the RNC platform changing to delete support for supplying Ukraine with weapons, which would aid in their fight against Russian aggression. Trump's supporters within the RNC deny that any changes were made. **3/2/17**

▮ Donald Trump claims that former President Barack Obama ordered wiretaps of Trump Tower before the 2016 election. He offers no proof of the accusations, which appear in multiple tweets on March 4, including one that states, "How low has Pres. Obama gone to tapp (sic) my phones during the sacred election process?" Some observers claim that Trump based his allegations (which he compared to a "Nixon/Watergate" plot), on reports from Breitbart, and from radio talk host Mark Levin. **3/4/17**

▮ Donald Trump tweets that Arnold Schwarzenegger was fired by producers of *The Apprentice*, and that he did not resign, as previously stated, because of poor ratings. Schwarzenegger had claimed that the show's decline stemmed from anti-Trump backlash. **3/4/17**

▮ The Trump administration officially asks the Congressional Intelligence Committees to investigate supposed wiretaps on Trump Tower phones by the White House, under former President Obama. FBI Director James Comey asks officials to refute Donald Trump's unproven wiretapping claim. **3/5/17**

▮ The White House releases a revamped travel ban that reduces the number of countries (Iraq is deleted) affected, and eliminates language that seemed to favor minority Christians. **3/6/17**

▮ Housing and Urban Development secretary Ben Carson refers to slaves being brought to America in the bottom of slave ships as "immigrants" who came to the United States to seek "opportunities." **3/6/17**

▮ Donald Trump tweets (incorrectly) that "122 vicious prisoners released by the Obama Administration, from Gitmo, have returned to the battle-field. Just another terrible decision." Records show that George W. Bush released 500 prisoners from Guantanamo Bay, with 113 confirmed to have returned to the battlefield. President Obama released 144 prisoners, with only nine having been reported to have returned to fight. **3/7/17**

■ Scott Pruitt, head of the Environmental Protection Agency, states on record that he disagrees with the idea human activity on Earth is a contributing factor to global warming. This statement flies directly in the face of the EPA's own previously documented position. **3/9/17**

■ As reported by *Time Magazine*, Donald Trump's chief strategist Stephen Bannon claims that the administration's aim in Washington is to have the "deconstruction" of the administrative state. He also says that a "deep state" exists, in the U.S., which has become a de-facto fourth branch of government. **3/9/17**

■ The Trump administration moves to remove 46 federal prosecutors who were holdovers from Pres. Obama's term in office. Although such terminations are considered routine with an incoming administration, Trump's mass firings were done suddenly, and without warning, which causes widespread outrage. In related news, Manhattan federal prosecutor Preet Bharara refuses to step down, causing him to be fired. Bharara defends his refusal, stating that Donald Trump had previously asked him to stay in his position, before he was sworn in, and that Trump had now reneged on that promise. **3/10/17**

■ Kellyanne Conway in an allegation aired on *NorthJersey*.com says that the president may have been spied on in unconventional ways, as operatives had been known to turn "microwaves into cameras." MSNBC's *Morning Joe* program, which had previously banned Conway due to the inaccuracies of her information in the past, immediately denounce her comments, as do numerous other news outlets. **3/13/17**

■ The March 13th deadline set by Sen. John McCain (R-AZ) for the Department of Justice to present proof that Trump Towers had been wiretapped by the Obama administration, passes with no information or proof being offered by the White House. A week's extension is then given by McCain. White House Press Secretary Sean Spicer tries to walk back Trump's accusations, claiming that the word "wiretap" (used by Trump in three different tweets), actually refers to various surveillance techniques, as opposed to the physical actions of having his phones tapped. **3/13/17**

■ The Congressional Budget Office issues its findings on the GOP's American Health Care Act (a replacement for the Affordable Care Act, also known as "Obamacare"), claiming that 24 million Americans would be uninsured by 2026 if the legislation passes. **3/13/17**

■ Host Rachael Maddow releases two pages of Trump's 2005 tax returns during her program, *The Rachel Maddow Show*, on MSNBC. The returns show that Trump paid 38 million dollars in taxes, but had scant other information on the billionaire's business dealings. Trump claims that the tax documents were obtained illegally, but there are those who believe that Trump himself leaked the returns in order to once again recapture the news cycle. **3/14/17**

■ House Intelligence Committee chairman Devin Nunes (R-CA), who was a member of Donald Trump's transition team, reports to the press that there was no evidence that Trump Tower was wiretapped while Trump was a presidential candidate. The president follows up this announcement by saying that he has new information on the supposed wiretapping, promising to release it "soon." **3/15/17**

■ A federal judge in Hawaii issues a sweeping freeze of the president's new executive order banning immigrants from certain Middle Eastern countries, hours before it could take effect. U.S. District Judge Derrick K. Watson cites Trump's campaign statements about banning Muslims from entering the country to support the hold, which the judge believes is unconstitutional and discriminatory. In a campaign rally in Nashville after the order was issued, Trump cites "political reasons" by the judge as an excuse for his actions. **3/16/17**

■ Donald Trump accuses the British spy agency GCHQ of helping the Obama administration wiretap phones in Trump Tower. The agency quickly issues a rare public statement, saying that the report was, "utterly ridiculous, and should be ignored." Britain's ambassador to Washington, Kim Darroch, also denies the charges, and confronts White House spokesman Sean Spicer, who apologizes for the comments. British Prime Minister Theresa May's office reports that it had been assured by Trump associates that the White House would no longer repeat the allegations. **3/16/17**

■ In a related budget story, White House Budget Director Mick Mulvaney justifies cutting Meals on Wheels by insisting it is a program that doesn't show "results." He also doubles down on another cut of after-school programs that feeds poor children because their overall academic test scores hadn't "improved." **3/16/17**

■ In a joint press conference with German Chancellor Angela Merkel, Donald Trump seemingly refuses to shake her hand during a photo opportunity between the two world leaders. Merkel announces hours before the meeting that she had taken a phone call from Chinese President Xi Jinping, where they discussed a joint trade venture between the countries, which may have caused Trump's snub. **3/17/17**

■ Donald Trump's first budget plan is greeted with controversy, as deep cuts to social programs are suggested. Agencies such as the Departments of Agriculture, Commerce, Education, Energy, Health and Human Services, Housing and Urban Development, Interior, State, and the U. S. Agency for International Development would see significant budget cuts under Trump's budget proposal. The effects of the proposed deep cuts in domestic spending would be felt in such programs as job training in rural areas, mine and safety oversight, home heating for low-income families, the Appalachian small loan business program, Meals on Wheels, after-school lunch programs, and many others. The proposed budget does not address the federal debt, and adds 54 billion dollars to the Defense Department. **3/17/17**

■ Treasury Secretary Steve Mnuchin, appearing at a gathering of economic ministers and central bankers from the largest 20 world economies, rebuffs multiple requests from German officials to include language stressing the importance of free trade, and how it should be considered in a "rules-based" manner, following existing standards and agreements. By rejecting language that would have said that the U. S. is opposed to protectionism, the White House sends a clear signal that it would not accept existing trade norms, and could pursue a more antagonistic approach with trading partners around the world going forward. **3/18/17**

■ In an interview with Erin McPike, the only journalist allowed to accompany Secretary of State Rex Tillerson on a diplomatic trip to Asia, it is revealed that he had never met Donald Trump before being asked to serve as the secretary, and that he was "stunned" when the offer was made. He also reveals in the interview that he didn't want the position, and had only taken it at the urging of his wife, who said that, "I'm supposed to do this." **3/18/17**

■ FBI Director James Comey, testifying before the House Intelligence Committee during a public hearing, said that there is "no information" that supports Donald Trump's claims that former president Obama ordered surveillance of Trump Towers during the presidential campaign. **3/20/17**

■ Trump's daughter Ivanka Trump receives an office in the West Wing of the White House and a security clearance, as she serves as an unpaid advisor to her father. **3/20/17**

■ Donald Trump tells a crowd in Louisville, Kentucky that "your San Francisco quarterback" wouldn't be picked up by an NFL team because the owners don't want to get a nasty tweet from him. This was a reference to free agent Colin Kaepernick, whom Trump criticized over his refusal to stand for the National Anthem during NFL games. **3/21/17**

▪ House Intelligence Committee Chairman Devin Nunes holds a news conference in which he discloses information from a confidential source (which appears to be classified) about intercepted communications involving Trump associates. His news conference is held outside the White House, after he briefed the president on the intercepts, even though the committee he chairs is supposed to be investigating the Trump campaign's possible links to Russia. Democrats serving on the committee, including ranking member Adam Schiff, strongly criticize Nunes for revealing information that had not been presented to the committee. The president, after hearing the information, tells *Time Magazine* that he felt "vindicated" from the charges of Russian involvement in the presidential election. **3/22/17**

▪ A group of Democratic members of Congress propose new legislation to create more openness in the Trump administration. The bill, called "Making Access Records Available to Lead American Government Openness Act, is an acronym which names the legislation the "MAR-A-LAGO" Act. **3/24/17**

▪ The Affordable Health Care Act (AHCA) is wrapped up in negotiations with members of the House of Representatives which leads to numerous changes and compromises to the bill. House Speaker Paul Ryan and the president engage in a week's worth of meetings and negotiations to sway votes and pass the bill. The House Freedom Caucus, a group of conservative congressmen, led the fight to kill the bill, because they believe that it didn't go far enough to lower costs of the program. Ryan continues to press for votes beyond the first scheduled vote, originally scheduled for 3/23, but the White House calls for a vote the next day. Faced with a possibility that the bill had no chance of passing the House, it is withdrawn. Donald Trump then posts on Twitter, blaming Democrats for not supporting the AHCA as the main reason it fails. **3/25/17**

▪ It is reported that during the healthcare negotiations, Senior Adviser Steve Bannon told gathered members of the House Freedom Caucus, "Guys, look. This is not a discussion. This is not a debate. You have no choice but to vote for this bill." **3/25/17**

∎ One day after the cancelled House vote on healthcare, Donald Trump tweets that his followers should watch the *Judge Jeanine Pirro Show* on FOX News, that night at 9 pm. He offers no other explanation. Viewers who tune in see Pirro calling for House Speaker Paul Ryan to resign his position for failing to deliver the votes to pass the AHCA. Both Pirro and Trump's aides claim there that there was no collaboration between the president and television judge in the matter. **3/26/17**

∎ German Chancellor Angela Merkel is reportedly handed an invoice from Donald Trump for 300 Billion (Euros) to cover Germany's shortfall of NATO contributions, which was supposed to have been 2% of that nation's GDP. **3/26/17**

∎ Published reports surface that Donald Trump has been golfing 13 times (8 consecutive weeks) at his golf courses since taking office. **3/26/17**

∎ Frustrated with the inactivity of the House investigation into the Trump campaign's potential involvement with Russia, the Senate Intelligence Committee announces their intention to put together a bi-partisan investigation of their own, to move ahead on the Russian influence issue. **3/26/17**

∎ It is announced that former Trump campaign manager Paul Manafort and senior Trump adviser (and son-in-law) Jared Kushner have both agreed to make themselves available for interviews with the House and Senate Intelligence Committees, to answer any questions pertaining to Russian ties. **3/27/17**

∎ The president signs a sweeping executive order rolling back rules limiting carbon emissions and regulating fuel producers. One section of the order turns back a temporary ban on coal mining, and a stream protection rule, imposed by the Obama administration. Trump states that he will "put our miners back to work." Critics of the order point out that coal mining jobs have been declining steadily since 1990, as more companies choose to use natural gas and clean power alternatives. **3/28/17**

▌ Officials of Palm Beach, Florida, home of Trump's Mar-a-Lago resort, plead with the federal government to help reimburse them for costs associated with his frequent weekend golf visits. Since the beginning of his term, costs of time-and-a-half being paid to members of the Palm Beach Sheriff's Department have totaled over 1.5 million dollars. **3/28/17**

▌ Former Attorney General Sally Yates, who was scheduled to appear in front of the House Intelligence Committee's probe of Russian meddling in the 2016 U. S. presidential election, is informed by the Department of Justice that she would need to contact the White House before testifying. The Trump administration considers her possible testimony, including the resignation of former National Security Adviser Michael Flynn, to be off-limits in a Congressional hearing. The reason cited is that Yates's testimony is covered by attorney-client, or presidential communications privileges. White House spokesman Sean Spicer denies that the White House tried to prevent Yates from testifying. **3/28/17**

▌ Donald Trump, still stinging from his defeat on healthcare, tweets that voters should try to defeat members of the Republican Freedom Caucus as well as Democrats in the 2018 elections. Rep. Justin Amash (R-MI), responds to Trump's tweet with a taunting reference to the president's promise to "drain the swamp" in Washington. He also states that Trump's election tactic would be, "constructive in the fifth grade." **3/30/17**

▌ Former National Security Adviser Michael Flynn offers to cooperate with congressional investigators, in exchange for immunity from prosecution, in the Russian influence investigation. **3/31/17**

CHAPTER 4

APRIL IS "BOMB" MONTH for Trump. He begins by taking a hard line on Syrian President Bashar-al-Assad, and ultimately bombs a Syrian military base with a "fire and fury" (more on that later), that sends Trump's message of strength to the world. Not to be outdone however, the president uses the "bigger" approach to warfare by ordering the military to drop the MOAB (Mother of All Bombs) on Afghanistan. If the FOAB (Father of All Bombs) had existed, someone would have been pulverized by it as well.

Trump begins to rack up time on the golf course, a trend that continues throughout his presidency. Despite his previous mocking of former Pres. Obama for taking some time to enjoy the links, and comments about how he'd "never have time to play" the game if elected, Trump manages to squeeze in far more rounds than most PGA touring pros. In fact, "putting" might be the only activity he engages in more than "tweeting."

April also brings a new round of protest marches (Tax Day and the Marches for Science), gaffes from Press Secretary Sean Spicer (remember the doozie he told about Hitler not using poison gas against his people?), and court case losses keep piling up like an embarrassing pile of aging firewood.

It is also a month that foreshadows National Security Chief Strategist Steve Bannon's eventual demise, as he is booted from the National Security Council's Principals Committee. The Conservative firebrand will be reduced to a "foot-nut" (not footnote) in the Trump saga, as he is one of many who are used, abused, and "screwed" by 45.

▪ Donald Trump's Director of Social Media, Dan Scavino Jr., tweets that voters should defeat Rep. Justin Amash (R-MI), who is running in an upcoming primary election. Amash, a member of the House Freedom Caucus, had previously clashed with Trump over healthcare reform. There are claims that Scavino's comments could violate the Hatch Act, which prevents government officials from using their position to sway elections. **4/1/17**

▪ After it is revealed that FOX News paid out over 13 million dollars to settle sexual harassment allegations against host Bill O'Reilly (*O'Reilly Factor*), Donald Trump claims that O'Reilly is "a good person" and should have fought the claims against him instead of reaching settlements. **4/1/17**

▪ Donald Trump tells an audience at a CEO TOWN Hall event that, "When you look for a job, you can't find it and you give up, you are now considered statistically unemployed. But I don't consider those people employed, and 100 million people are seeking jobs." The Bureau of Labor Statistics website shows both claims to be completely false. **4/4/17**

▪ After chemical weapons attacks on Syrian citizens, which may have been carried out by the Syrian Government under orders from President Bashar-al-Assad, White House spokesman Sean Spicer blasts former President Obama by stating that, "These (acts) are a consequence of the past administration's weakness and irresolution." Interestingly, in 2013, Donald Trump issued a series of tweets urging then-President Obama not to use military force in Syria against Assad. **4/4/17**

▪ It is revealed that former Obama national security adviser Susan Rice obtained names of Trump associates while reviewing information from surveillance conducted by the NSA. Rice asked that several members' names be "unmasked" (identity revealed) as part of the Russian influence investigation. Rice and others claim that her actions were consistent with the role of National Security Adviser, while Trump and the White House accuse her of intentionally spying on him and his aides. Trump states, "It's such an important story for our country and the world. It is one of the big stories of our time." **4/4/17**

▮ White House Chief Strategist Stephen Bannon is removed as a member of the National Security Council's Principals Committee. Although the White House claims that the move is not a demotion, skeptics question the action. **4/5/17**

▮ House Intelligence Committee Chair Devin Nunes (R-CA) recuses himself from any activity surrounding Russian involvement with Donald Trump, or his associates. Nunes was under fire after he met with White House officials who provided him with information on supposed surveillance of the Trump campaign that occurred before the 2016 U.S. presidential election. **4/6/17**

▮ Donald Trump claims that his first 13 weeks in office have been some of the "most successful" weeks of any U.S. presidency in history. **4/6/17**

▮ It is reported that China grants three trademarks for Ivanka Trump's company on the same day she dined with Chinese president Xi Jinping at her father's Mar-a-Lago resort. **4/6/17**

▮ The president, in response to reported chemical gas attacks on Syrian nationals, orders a Tomahawk cruise missile strike on a Syrian military airbase. 59 missiles hit airplanes, bunkers, etc. The strikes however, cause limited damage to the base and Syrian warplanes resume bombing civilians just 24 hours later from the same compound. It is also widely reported that the U.S. informed Russia of the strike before it was carried out. **4/7/17**

▮ The *Washington Post* reports that Attorney General Jeff Sessions is preparing the government to return to a hard line strategy against illegal narcotics which will effectively create a new "War on Drugs." **4/8/17**

■ Trump Press Secretary Sean Spicer has two serious gaffes in the span of two days. First, he claims that severe action would be taken against the Syrian Government if they were to drop chemical weapons or barrel bombs on their citizens. However, in light of the fact that Bashar al-Assad's military has dropped over 12,000 barrel bombs during the Syrian civil war, and did so the same day of Spicer's comments, the White House walks his comments back. The second misstep occurs on the Jewish holiday of Passover, when Spicer compares al-Assad to Hitler, claiming that, "even Hitler didn't use poison gas against his own people," which totally ignores the fact that he gassed millions of Jews, Gypsies, and others in concentration camps during WWII. Spicer refers to the camps as "Holocaust Centers." Criticism is swift, and Rep. Nancy Pelosi (D-CA) calls for Spicer's resignation. After several attempts at revising and explaining his remarks, Spicer retracts them, issuing a full apology. **4/9/17**

■ It is reported that at the current pace of Trump's golf vacations, the cost to taxpayers in Trump's first term would exceed that of Pres. Obama's entire eight year presidency. The cost is estimated to be at least $20 million dollars at present. **4/11/17**

■ Donald Trump abandons a number of his key campaign positions. He announces that he will no longer consider China to be a "currency manipulator" (which he said he would do on his first day in office). Trump also announces that he now embraces the Import-Export Bank, an institution he soundly mocked while on the campaign trail. The president also reverses field on the validity of the North Atlantic Treaty Organization (NATO), stating that is no longer "obsolete." In another stunning about-face, Trump announces that he is open to re-appointing Federal Reserve Board Chair Janet Yellen to her position, months after saying she should be "ashamed" of what she was doing to the country financially. **4/12/17**

■ Paul Manafort, former Trump campaign chairman, announces that he will register as a foreign agent, due to his business ties with interests in Ukraine. **4/12/17**

■ The president hints that he may not authorize payments of the Affordable Care Act subsidies, which helps policyholders to pay deductibles and co-pays, in order to force Democrats to negotiate with him on health care. **4/12/17**

■ The president, during an interview with FOX News, tells the host that he ordered bombs dropped on Iraq after eating a "beautiful piece of chocolate cake" with China's President Xi at Mar-a-Lago. The host corrects him, saying that the bomb was dropped on Syria, not Iraq. **4/12/17**

■ Donald Trump signs legislation which allows states to withhold family planning dollars from clinics that provide abortion services. The legislation would effectively deprive Planned Parenthood and other such organizations significant sources of funding. **4/13/19**

■ The Trump administration says that records of visitors to the White House will stay secret for at least five years. Trump's team's decision follows a lawsuit which was filed against the administration, demanding the release of visitor logs to the White House, Trump Tower in New York, and Mar-a-Lago resort in Florida. **4/14/17**

■ The U.S. military drops a 21,000 lb. munition on a supposed ISIS position in Afghanistan. The bomb, which is identified as the GBU-43B, or *MOAB* (Massive Ordinance Air Blast), has been nicknamed the "Mother of All Bombs." It is reportedly the largest non-nuclear weapon ever used in military action. **4/14/17**

■ Trump defender and CNN commentator Jeffrey Lord calls Trump "the Martin Luther King of healthcare." He is roundly criticized by numerous press outlets for the statement. **4/14/17**

■ April 15th brings renewed protest marches and rallies across the U.S. The Tax Day events in over 120 cities across the nation are aimed at forcing the president to release his tax returns. **4/15/17**

- Donald Trump takes to Twitter to respond to thousands of protesters who marched against his unwillingness to release tax returns. "The election is over" Trump tweets. He also suggests that the protest rallies were financed by outside political organizations, and are not the efforts of grass-roots protesters. **4/16/17**

- While hot spots are burning in Syria, Afghanistan, and North Korea, Donald Trump tweets about the "fake media," and how "We have to hold them to the truth." A second tweet tells supporters to read the book entitled, "REASONS TO VOTE FOR DEMOCRATS," which is filled entirely with blank pages. He follows up by posting, "The first 90 days of my presidency has exposed the total failure of the last eight years of foreign policy! So true!" **4/17/17**

- Tensions rise between the U. S. and North Korea, as joint South Korean and American military exercises are held in and around the Korean Peninsula. North Korea, through a spokesman offers, "We will go to war if they (U.S.) choose." Donald Trump, confident that the North Korean situation can be handled, states, "North Korea is a problem. The problem will be taken care of." **4/17/17**

- Sarah Palin, Ted Nugent, and Kid Rock tour the White House as guests of Donald Trump, and they pose mockingly for photos in front of a portrait of Hillary Clinton. **4/20/17**

- More than 600 marches occur around the globe to support science and evidence-based research pertaining to climate change, a protest partly fueled by opposition to the president's threats of budget cuts to agencies funding scientists' work. **4/20/17**

- Donald Trump takes to Twitter to demand funding for building the border wall between the U.S. and Mexico. Later, he seems to soften his stance in order to avoid a government shutdown, by indicating that he might be open to a system of border surveillance, coupled with a wall in certain areas. **4/24/17**

■ The president proposes a drastic cut in the corporate tax rate, from 35% to 15%, as part of his budget proposal. Budget analysts predict that this could negatively impact the federal debt. Trump reasons that the tax cuts would stimulate the economy, and spur growth. **4/24/17**

■ The State Department removes a blog post that touts Donald Trump's privately owned club, Mar-a-Lago. It is removed in response to accusations that the post is a conflict of interest, and could benefit Donald Trump's bottom line, as he profits from the resort. **4/24/17**

■ The *Washington Post* reports that Donald Trump made 488 false or misleading claims in the press or by Twitter during his first 100 days in office, an average of 4.9 per day. **4/24/17**

■ Donald Trump, for the 14th time, makes a false claim about saving 725 million dollars on the F-35 Joint Strike Fighter planes. Price cuts on the planes were sought and received by the Defense Department long before he began meeting with manufacturer, Lockheed Martin. In the same interview with the Associated Press, Trump either outright lies, makes deceiving or conflicting claims about: the border wall, number of U.S. jobs created, China as a currency manipulator, WikiLeaks, proposed savings on proposed tax cuts, NATO, the 100 day presidential milestone, the Electoral College, NAFTA, his ratings on *Meet the Press*, quotes from Rep. Elijah E. Cummings (D-MD.) about Cummings' potential presidency, crime statistics, and other issues. **4/25/17**

■ A federal judge in San Francisco deals the Trump administration another legal blow, as he temporarily halts the president's executive order to withhold federal funding from cities and towns that declare they are Sanctuary Cities, (which means that they refuse to cooperate with immigration officials trying to deport illegal immigrants from the country). Trump responds with a tweet stating, "See you in Supreme Court." **4/25/17**

■ Ivanka Trump draws catcalls, boos, and hisses from an audience attending a women's empowerment gathering in Germany, when she states that her father, Donald Trump, is an advocate for women and families. **4/25/17**

■ The House Oversight Committee reports that former National Security Adviser, Michael Flynn may have broken the law by not reporting payments from Russia and the government of Turkey for services rendered. **4/25/17**

■ Donald Trump in an interview with Reuters states that the presidency is "more work than in my previous life. I thought it would be easier." He also uses the interview as an opportunity to talk about his election win, by handing out copies of the latest figures on voting maps. **4/27/17**

■ The president issues a one-page tax plan outline which drastically cuts taxes for corporations and higher income individuals, which experts say could balloon the federal deficit by more than four trillion dollars over the next decade. Treasury Secretary Steven Mnuchin defends the plan, stating that it will create economic growth to cover the loss of tax revenue. **4/27/17**

■ Donald Trump holds an election rally in Harrisburg, Pennsylvania instead of attending the annual White House Correspondents' dinner in Washington. He spends a great deal of time assailing the media during his event, once again calling out CNN and MSNBC as "fake news." He also tells his audience that the Correspondents' dinner was, "A large group of Hollywood actors and Washington media consoling themselves in a hotel ballroom." **4/27/17**

■ Donald Trump signs an executive order to open up oil drilling in the Arctic and Atlantic oceans. Environmental groups widely condemn the order, which reverses President Obama's restrictions on drilling, and is damaging to whales, walruses, and possibly contributes to global warming. **4/28/17**

■ During a speech to the National Rifle Association (NRA) the president once again touts his election victory over Hillary Clinton. He then continues by slurring potential Democratic presidential candidate Sen. Elizabeth Warren (D-MA), referring to her as "Pocahontas," a term he used against her during his presidential campaign. **4/28/17**

■ Donald Trump uses Twitter to complain about presidential expectations in the first 100 days of a first term in office. "No matter how much I accomplish during the ridiculous standard of the first 100 days, and it has been a lot (including S.C.-Supreme Court), media will kill." **4/30/17**

CHAPTER 5

WHEN HISTORIANS WRITE ABOUT the foibles of Donald Trump, they may point out May 2017 as either the beginning of the end, or perhaps the most discombobulated month of his only term in office. Why? Because May is the month when Trump admits to NBC's Lester Holt that he canned Comey because of "this Russian thing with Trump." The "tip of the spear" that begins with Comey, will continue to reverberate throughout the Trump presidency because..........

The issue of Russian "collusion" begins to bubble up. May is the month that Donald Trump openly consorts with Russian diplomats in the White House Oval Office by bragging about classified military operations against ISIS. Although history may not record this as genuine cooperation with Mother Russia, Sergei Lavrov and Sergey Kislyak certainly must have received an "attaboy" from Russian intelligence folks when they returned to Moscow.

A Twitter-weary Donald Trump creates a new word in May, tweeting about something called "covfefe." Pundits from around the globe rush to read meaning into this new combination of letters, but alas, it's just added as another example that the president "knows more about spelling than anyone."

And rounding out the month, who could forget "Shrubgate," the panicked retreat from the media that then-White House press secretary Sean Spicer had while hiding in the bushes in order not to answer questions about the firing of FBI director Comey? If nothing else, the episode made for great fun, especially when Melissa McCarthy parodied "Spicey" that week on NBC's *Saturday Night Live*.

▮ Donald Trump tells an interviewer that he would be "honored" to meet with North Korean leader Kim Jong un. This revelation comes on the heels of Trump's praise of Philippine President Rodrigo Duterte, whose extrajudicial killings of thousands of citizens accused of drug trafficking, and insults of then-president Obama (calling him a "son of a whore," among other things), have drawn harsh criticism. **5/1/17**

▮ Donald Trump espouses that the American Civil War might not have happened if President Andrew Jackson had been able to intervene and negotiate with both sides. Jackson, an avowed slave owner (with more than 150 slaves), died 16 years before the War Between the States began. After some blowback on his comment, Trump later tweets that he was aware that Jackson was dead before the Civil War began, but that Jackson was "angry" about the war. **5/1/17**

▮ Donald Trump, frustrated with his inability to meet his administration's legislative goals, tweets that a government shutdown might be necessary for progress to be made on his agenda. He also suggests that Senate rules should be changed to eliminate future filibusters. Trump's suggestions are roundly criticized by members of Congress on both sides of the aisle. **5/1/17**

▮ While being interviewed by an ABC News reporter about issues he supports, a furtive Trump tells a reporter, "I don't stand by anything." **5/1/17**

▮ Donald Trump signs an executive order relaxing enforcement rules of the Johnson Amendment, (named for then-Senator Lyndon Johnson) which are prohibitions against tax-exempt churches contributing to political campaigns, or endorsing candidates. **5/4/17**

▮ With plodding from the president, House Republicans pass their second version of the American Health Care Act (AHCA) by a slim margin of 217-213. The bill, which goes to the Senate, faces numerous challenges due to controversial language in the legislation. Donald Trump claims that there will be "insurance for everybody, lower premiums, and lower deductibles."

The bill is not scored by the Congressional Budget Office before the House vote is taken, making Trump's claims subject to question. **5/4/17**

∎ The president, during a meeting with Australia's Prime Minister Malcolm Turnbull, praises his country's health care system by saying, "You have better health care than we do." Australia's system is partially government funded, which Republicans oppose. **5/4/17**

∎ Former acting attorney general Sally Yates testifies before a Senate sub-committee about alleged Russian interference in the 2016 U.S. presidential election, as well as then-national security adviser Michael Flynn's involvement with Russian authorities. Donald Trump fires off several tweets at Yates, accusing her of being complicit in the release of classified information, and also lambasting the Russia-Trump collusion story as a "total hoax." **5/9/17**

∎ Donald Trump issues an order to fire FBI Director James Comey. The administration's contention is that Comey damaged the reputation and credibility of the Bureau by his handling of the Hillary Clinton email case. Leading Democrats and some Republicans in Congress however, call for a special prosecutor to lead the investigation of Trump associates colluding with Russia during the 2016 U.S. presidential election. **5/9/17**

∎ More fallout from the James Comey firing surfaces. It is reported that Comey had recently sought greater funding from the Department of Justice to widen the Trump-Russia probe. Also reported was the involvement of Attorney General Jeff Sessions in the firing, when Sessions had previously recused himself from any involvement in that investigation. Finally, Trump's letter of dismissal to Comey references three occasions when he directly spoke to Comey about the ongoing probe, which could have been a violation of Justice Department policies prohibiting the discussion of such matters between the DOJ and White House. Trump also claims that then-FBI Director Comey stated during these meetings that he (Trump) was not being directly investigated-a claim that could not be verified. **5/10/17**

▮ A reporter for the Public News Service is arrested by the Capitol Police in Washington after he was found to be too aggressive in his questioning of Health and Human Services Secretary Tom Price. Although reporter Dan Heyman is charged for "aggressively breaching" the Secret Service agents protecting Price, the complaint filed against him notes that, "the defendant was causing a disturbance by yelling questions at Ms. (Kellyanne) Conway and Secretary Price." **5/10/17**

▮ In a related series of events, Trump administration spokesman Sean Spicer retreats behind shrubbery on the White House grounds after being hounded by the press for more information on the firing of FBI Director James Comey. Spicer answers questions (with TV cameras off), and takes a leave of absence to honor his National Guard commitment for several days afterwards. He is temporarily replaced by Sarah Huckabee Sanders. **5/10/17**

▮ During an NBC News interview, Donald Trump tells Lester Holt that he fired James Comey partially due to the fact that he was thinking of "this Russian thing with Trump." The statement flies in the face of previous reports that Trump only went along with Department of Justice recommendations by Attorney General Jeff Sessions and Deputy Attorney General Rod J. Rosenstein to remove Comey. Trump also calls Comey "a showboat" and "a grandstander." **5/11/17**

▮ During an interview with *The Economist* magazine, Donald Trump makes a claim that he invented the term "prime the pump," while referencing ways to move the economy forward. This is a patently false statement, as the term has been widely used for hundreds of years. **5/11/17**

▮ Donald Trump tweets that fired Director of the FBI James Comey should "be careful" of what he leaks to the press, because there may be "tapes" of their conversations. **5/12/17**

▪ The *Washington Post* reports that during a White House visit with Russian Foreign Minister Sergei Lavrov and Ambassador Sergey Kislyak, Donald Trump revealed highly classified information pertaining to the fight against ISIS. The information had previously been provided by a U.S. intelligence sharing partner, and was not authorized to be shared with Russia or any other nation. The release of the highly-sensitive "code-word" data, while not illegal by a president, could prevent future cooperation from an ally who has access to the inner-workings of the Islamic State (ISIS). The White House rushes to issue statements that Donald Trump did not release classified information, only to have the president tweet that he did; a stunning confirmation of the *Washington Post's* initial report. **5/15/17**

▪ In an unrelated Trump missive, the hosts of MSNBC's *Morning Joe* program allege that White House councilor Kellyanne Conway complained extensively about Donald Trump during the 2016 U.S. presidential campaign, and while off camera, she said, "Blech, I need to take a shower," after defending Trump during the program. Conway also reportedly tells hosts Mika Brzezinski and Joe Scarborough that she had only taken the Trump job for the money, and would soon be done with him. Conway later refutes the claims, saying that she fully supports Donald Trump and his administration. **5/15/17**

▪ In a major development, the *New York Times* reports that the president asked then-FBI Director James Comey to drop the bureau's probe of former National Security Adviser Michael Flynn, and instead, turn his focus on stopping leaks to the media. The discussion between Trump and Comey occurred in private, at Trump's request, after a national security meeting at the White House. Trump supposedly told Comey, "I hope you can let this go," referring to the Flynn investigation. Comey reportedly took notes of the meeting, resulting in two pages of information of discussions between them. Although the Justice Department and FBI decline to comment on the matter, a White House spokesperson vehemently denies that the president asked Comey to interfere with the probe. **5/16/17**

■ Donald Trump addresses 195 U.S. Coast Guard cadets during their commencement, and airs grievances about how he feels he is being treated while in office. Trump states, "No politician in history-and I say this with great surety-has been treated worse or more unfairly." Following applause from the audience, Trump once again references his election win by saying, "I guess that's why I won-Thank you. I guess that's why we won." **5/17/17**

■ Deputy Attorney General Rod. J. Rosenstein appoints a special counsel to investigate possible coordination between Donald Trump's associates and Russian interests. Robert S. Mueller, a former federal prosecutor who served as FBI director from 2001-2013, will lead the investigation. The appointment of Mueller signals a concession by the Trump administration to Democrats' demands for the probe to be run independently of the Justice Department, and free of partisan politics. The following day, Donald Trump unleashes two tweets to show his displeasure. The first; "With all of the illegal acts that took place in the Clinton campaign and Obama Administration, there never was a special councel (sic) appointed." He then adds: "This is the single greatest witch hunt of a politician in American history!" **5/18/17**

■ The president asks two of the country's top intelligence officers to help him push back against possible collusion between his campaign and the Russian government. Trump's appeals are to Director of National Intelligence Daniel Coats, and Admiral Michael S. Rogers, Director of the National Security Agency. He asks that they both publicly deny the existence of any connections between his associates and Russia during the 2016 U.S. presidential campaign. Coats and Rogers refuse to comply with the requests, which they deem inappropriate. **5/22/17**

■ The former national security adviser under Donald Trump, Michael Flynn, refuses to comply with a Senate Intelligence Committee subpoena, as information is revealed that he lied about his ties with Russia to federal investigators. Flynn invokes his Fifth Amendment rights, leaving the committee to decide if they will hold him in contempt of Congress in order to secure his testimony. **5/22/17**

■ Donald Trump, in an address to Israeli President Reuven Rivlin, announces that, "We just got back from the Middle East. We just got back from Saudi Arabia." Trump, seemingly unaware that Israel is geographically part of the Middle East, makes these comments shortly after publically proclaiming to Israeli Prime Minister Benjamin Netanyahu that he had never mentioned the word "Israel" to Russian diplomats visiting the White House, which would have linked their country to sensitive intelligence information, revealed by Trump during the visit. **5/22/17**

■ In testimony before the House Intelligence Committee, former FBI director John Brennan testifies that he became increasingly concerned that Trump associates were being manipulated by Russian intelligence services, in order to help disrupt the 2016 U.S. presidential election, and deliver the victory to Trump. **5/23/17**

■ The *New York Times* reports that Russian officials schemed during the summer of 2016 to influence Donald Trump through Michael Flynn and then-campaign manager Paul Manafort. **5/24/17**

■ The president's travel ban once again fails to pass muster with the 4th Circuit Court of Appeals, which rules that the ban, "drips with religious intolerance, animus, and discrimination." The White House pledges a Supreme Court showdown on the matter. **5/25/17**

■ Donald Trump returns to the U.S. after a nine-day trip to the Middle East and Europe, embroiled in more controversy. While in Europe, Trump has harsh words behind closed doors for German trade practices, blasts European leaders at NATO for failing to spend enough on defense, and refuses to endorse the Paris Agreement on global warming in meetings with the Group of Seven (G-7). In response to Trump, German Chancellor Angela Merkel comments that, "Europe must, really take our fate into our own hands," a clear reference to a fading relationship with the United States. **5/25/17**

▌ Department of Justice investigators announce that White House adviser and presidential son-in-law Jared Kushner is a "target" in the continuing probe of Trump/Russia connections. Kushner is not accused of wrong-doing, but the FBI is looking into his contacts with Russian officials after the 2016 U.S. presidential election. **5/26/17**

▌ News reports arise with accusations of Jared Kushner attempting to set up a Russian "back channel" of communication, while he worked for the Trump presidential transition team. The discussion allegedly involved Kushner and Michael Flynn, and included contact with Russian ambassador Sergey Kislyak. **5/26/17**

▌ White House Communications Director Mike Dubke resigns his position, after serving for three months in the Trump Administration. **5/30/17**

▌ White House spokeswoman Hope Hicks, responding to a *Washington Post* editorial about the negative attitude of Donald Trump towards his staff, issues the following statement: "President Trump has a magnetic personality and exudes positive energy, which is infectious to those around him. He has an unparalleled ability to communicate with people, whether he is speaking to a room of three or an arena of 30,000. He has built great relationships throughout his life, and treats everyone with respect. He is brilliant with a great sense of humor…and an amazing ability to make people feel special and aspire to be more than even they thought possible."**5/30/17**

▌ Comedienne Kathy Griffin posts a photo online, depicting her holding the severed, bloody head of Donald Trump. Media and political criticism is swift, condemning Griffin's stunted attempt at comedy. She is removed from hosting CNN's New Year's Eve program, and has numerous appear-ances cancelled. Griffin issues a tearful apology, but the negative comments continue from all sides of the entertainment and political spectrum. **5/30/17**

- In a move that has members of the intelligence and justice communities concerned, Donald Trump urges world leaders to call him directly on his personal cell phone whenever they need to reach him. This raises security and secrecy issues on numerous levels. **5/31/17**

- In a late-night tweet, the president posts the following: "Despite the constant negative press covfefe." Later that morning, Trump tweets, "Who can figure out the true meaning of covfefe??? Enjoy." **5/31/17**

- Donald Trump, in response to a Hillary Clinton interview with the Recode Code Conference in California on how Russian influence potentially caused her loss in the 2016 U.S. presidential election, tweets, "Crooked Hillary Clinton now blames everybody but herself, refuses to say she was a terrible candidate. Hits Facebook & even Dems & DNC." Clinton's Twitter response is: "People in covfefe houses shouldn't throw covfefe." Jumping into the fray, Donald Trump, Jr. responds with a tweet of his own, stating: "What house is he in again???That's what I thought. You're trying too hard." **5/31/17**

- Donald Trump tells the Russian delegation visiting the White House that he fired FBI Director James Comey because he was "crazy," and a "real nut job." Trump goes on to say that firing Comey eliminated a "great pressure" on him, caused by the investigation. **5/31/17**

CHAPTER 6

BY TRUMPIAN STANDARDS, JUNE was almost like a hall pass. There was limited action and acrimony from 1600 Pennsylvania Avenue, and most of what transpired was an extension of previous battles and the extending of grudges by the president. But there were moments of audacity, including the U.S. withdrawal from the Paris agreement (joining stalwart countries like Nicaragua and war-torn Syria), which started the march away from natural power generation.

The Trump travel ban also garners attention, as he criticizes the courts time and again, only to be met with limited success. But just to show he means business, the president tweeted that our country is practicing "EXTREME VETTING" of people coming to the U.S. The all-caps delivery was made, we're sure, to show that the POTUS means business.

In June, Trump continues his ongoing war of words with fired-director of the FBI James Comey, by stating that he is "100%" willing to testify that he didn't ask him to "take it easy" on former national security adviser Michael Flynn. Trump then suggests there are tape recordings of his private White House meeting with Comey, but alas, no.

But, on a slightly less-impactful note, June also provided us with some eye-opening events to chew over. There was the "presidential fawning" cabinet meeting, where Trump appointees fell all over themselves heaping praise on 45. The political "revival" only lacked a tent and toll-free number in order to qualify as a full-fledged "come to Jesus" (Donald) meeting.

■ The president announces that the U. S. will be withdrawing from the Paris Climate Agreement, a move that is highly criticized by environmental groups, foreign leaders, and members of Congress. Trump claims that the agreement kills U.S. jobs. The country now joins Nicaragua (who didn't sign because they didn't think it was stringent enough), and Syria (engaged in a civil war), as the only nations on earth not involved with the effort to slow or reverse the effects of global warming and climate change. Trump, in an effort to appease those who oppose his decision, agrees to re-negotiate the terms of the pact, an idea that was swiftly rebuffed by other world leaders. The decision by Trump shows a divide in the White House between Ivanka Trump and Rex Tillerson (who favored staying in the agreement), and Stephen Bannon and EPA chief Scott Pruitt (both advocated withdrawal). **6/1/17**

■ Donald Trump uses a vicious ISIS-inspired attack in London as a platform to push his travel ban by tweeting, "We need to be smart, vigilant and tough. We need the courts to give us back our rights. We need the Travel Ban as an extra level of safety!" Trump also criticizes the mayor of London, Sadiq Khan, because he stated on Twitter that London's citizens had "no reason to be alarmed." Khan, in his tweet, was referring to the number of extra police officers on the streets of the city, and that citizens should not panic due to their increased presence. Trump's response to Khan is, "Pathetic excuse by London Mayor Sadiq Khan who had to think fast on his "no reason to be alarmed" statement. MSM (mainstream media) is working hard to sell it!" A spokesperson for Khan later says that the mayor "Has more important things to do than to respond to Donald Trump's ill-informed tweet that deliberately takes out of context his remarks." Trump, doubling down on his comments, then takes a swipe at gun control efforts, tweeting, "Do you notice we are not having a gun debate right now? That's because they (the London terrorists) used knives and a truck." **6/4/17**

■ The president, in a series of tweets expressing exasperation about his inability to push travel restrictions against various Middle Eastern countries, fires off a tweet on June 5th stating, "People, the lawyers and the courts can call it whatever they want, but I am calling it what we need and what it is, a TRAVEL BAN. The Justice Department should have stayed with the original Travel Ban, not the watered down, politically correct version they submitted to S.C. (Supreme Court)." He also says, "The Justice Department should ask for an expedited hearing of the watered down Travel Ban before the Supreme Court-and seek much tougher version!" and, "In any event we are EXTREME VETTING people coming into the U.S. in order to help keep our country safe. The courts are slow and political." **6/5/17**

■ The No. 2 diplomat at the U.S. embassy in Beijing, China resigns from his post in the wake of Donald Trump's withdrawal from the Paris Agreement. David H. Rank, a career foreign services officer for 27 years, had been acting ambassador. He tells his staff that as, "a parent, a patriot, and a Christian," he could not play a role in implementing Trump's decision to withdraw from the accord. **6/5/19**

■ The *New York Times* reports that the day after Donald Trump asked James Comey, the fired FBI director, to end an investigation into his former national security adviser Michael Flynn, Comey confronted Attorney General Jeff Sessions after his meeting with Trump and said he did not want to be left alone again with the president. **6/6/17**

■ Fired FBI Director James Comey testifies in front of the Senate Judiciary Committee for three hours, answering questions about his dealings with Donald Trump while he was with the government. Comey testifies that the president, during a private dinner with him in the White House, repeatedly asked him for his loyalty, and also told him that he (Trump) "hoped" that Comey could "let Flynn go" This was a reference to the Michael Flynn/ Russian investigation, being conducted by the Department of Justice. Comey also indicates that he felt the need to take copious notes of each meeting with Trump, because he strongly believed that the president would lie about what the two men discussed in private. Trump himself does not Tweet during Comey's testimony, but his surrogates, including son Donald Trump, Jr., take to Twitter to roundly mock Comey during the hearing. **6/8/17**

■ Donald Trump responds to James Comey on Twitter the following day, stating, "Despite so many false statements and lies, total and complete vindication…and WOW, Comey is a leaker." Trump's comments are in response to Comey's testimony that he disclosed information about his discussions with Trump to the press. Trump's lawyer, Marc Kasowitz, states that he will file a complaint over Comey's passing of information, claiming that such conversations are privileged communications. **6/9/17**

■ Donald Trump says that he is "100%" willing to testify under oath to dispute former FBI Director James Comey's testimony that Trump asked him to halt an investigation of former national security adviser Michael Flynn. Trump flatly denies all allegations made by Comey, including a supposed loyalty oath, by stating, "I didn't say that." Trump also leaves open the issue of producing taped recordings of his meeting with Comey, telling reporters he might provide more information, "maybe sometime in the future." In a related matter, the House Intelligence Committee asks the White House for any tapes, if they exist, by June 23rd. They also request that Comey turn over copies of any notes he produced as a result of his meetings with Trump. **6/9/17**

■ It is reported that the lawyer hired by Donald Trump to defend him in the Russian investigation has prominent clients with ties to the Kremlin. Marc E. Kasowitz's clients include Oleg Deripaska, a Russian oligarch who is close to Russian president, Vladimir Putin, and who has also done business with former Trump campaign manager, Paul Manafort. **6/9/17**

■ Donald Trump's director of social media is issued a warning by the Office of Special Counsel for violating the Hatch Act, which prohibits government employees from using their influence to sway public elections. Dan

Scavino, Jr. is cited based on his tweets involving the primary election of Rep. Justin Amash of Michigan, a member of the House Freedom Caucus, a group that opposed Trump's initial health care plan. **6/9/17**

▌ According to the *Guardian*, Donald Trump advised British Prime Minister Theresa May that he will not hold his planned State visit to the U.K. unless he has the support of its citizens. Trump is reacting to the possibilities of large protests against him if he visits. Press Secretary Sean Spicer counters by saying that the Guardian story is false, but he releases no information when (or if) Trump plans his visit. **6/11/17**

▌ The Attorneys General from the state of Maryland and the District of Columbia announce that they are filing suit against Donald Trump, alleging that he has violated anti-corruption clauses in the U. S. Constitution by receiving payments and benefits totaling millions from foreign governments, since assuming the presidency. The lawsuit contends that Trump failed to divest himself of business holdings when he took office, despite promising to do so. The action, which attempts to require Trump to release tax return information, is the second such lawsuit to be filed in the matter, following one from Citizens for Responsibility and Ethics in Washington, D.C. in January. It is also reported that a group of Democratic members of Congress plan to file a similar suit as well. **6/12/17**

▌ The president holds a cabinet meeting which begins with members of the body taking turns heaping praise on him while on camera. Trump starts his meeting by stating, "Never has there been a president, with few exceptions-case of FDR, he had a major depression to handle-who has passed more legislation and who has done more things than we've done." Following his opening remarks, Trump has his staff address him one-by-one with remarks about his presidency, flowing with praise. In response, Sen. Charles Schumer (D-NY.) creates a mocking video of his own staff praising him for how his tone was for a recent speech and how good his hair looked after a morning visit to the gym. **6/12/17**

■ Rep. Mike Quigley (D-Ill.) introduces a bill that would preserve tweets from Donald Trump's personal account into an archive as "presidential records." The measure, dubbed the COVFEFE ACT is not expected to gain much traction from the Republican-controlled House of Representatives. **6/12/17**

■ Attorney General Jeff Sessions testifies in front of the Senate Intelligence Committee about his role in the investigation of ties with Russia. Sessions refuses to answer questions about any conversations he had with the president on the matter, citing that revealing details of these discussions were a violation of a long-standing Justice Department policy which prohibits such disclosures. The Attorney General however, confirms earlier testimony from former FBI Director James Comey, who had previously testified that he was uncomfortable having private conversations with the president and asked that he not be left alone with him going forward. **6/13/17**

■ USA Today reports that since Donald Trump became president, more than 70% of buyers of Trump Co. properties were limited liability companies (LLCs), which allows purchasers to buy properties without revealing the owners' names. This compares to 4% ownership before Trump took office. The LLC arrangement would allow buyers to purchase Trump properties in order to curry favor with the president, without any public scrutiny. **6/13/17**

■ In a brazen act of violence, a deranged gunman opens fire on a group of Republican members of Congress who were gathered for an early-morning baseball practice in Alexandria, Virginia. The gunman, James T. Hodgkinson, from southern Illinois, posted his anger at Donald Trump on social media, and had written anti-Republican letters to his hometown newspaper. The shooter approaches the practice and asks a bystander if the men on the field are Republicans or Democrats. When they are identified as Republicans, he opens fire. Hodgkinson is killed during a shootout with Capitol Police, but not before firing significant rounds of ammunition, and wounding five. The most seriously injured is House

Majority Whip Steve Scalise, who is shot in the hip, and requires surgery at a local hospital. **6/14/17**

■ The *Washington Post* reports that the special counsel overseeing the Russian investigation is interviewing senior intelligence officials in an effort to examine if the president obstructed justice by interfering with the probe. The investigation, led by special counsel Robert S. Mueller III, is looking for evidence of a link between Trump campaign surrogates and Russian agents, will also delve into the possibility of financial improprieties among Trump's circle of associates. **6/14/17**

■ In a stunning rebuke to Donald Trump, the U.S. Senate votes 98-2 to block any attempts by the president to roll back sanctions against Russia. The vote displays a desire to prevent the Trump administration from scaling back any actions against Russia, as Trump refuses to accept intelligence assessments that point to Russian meddling in the 2016 U.S. presidential election. **6/15/17**

■ Donald Trump, responding to an article in the *Washington Post* that claimed the Obama administration failed to respond to intervention in the presidential election, fires off numerous tweets criticizing the former president. One such missive states, "The reason President Obama did NOTHING about Russia after being notified by the CIA of meddling is that he expected Clinton would win and did not want to rock the boat." He also tweets, He didn't 'choke,' he colluded or obstructed, and it did the Dems and Crooked Hillary no good." He then tweets, "The real story is that President Obama did NOTHING after being informed in August about Russian meddling." **6/15/17**

■ Donald Trump in a display of anger about the Russian investigations targets Deputy Attorney General Rod Rosenstein by tweeting, "I am being investigated for firing the FBI Director by the man who told me to fire the FBI Director! Witch Hunt." Trump also follows up by tweeting, "After 7 months of investigations and committee hearings about my 'collusion with the Russians,' nobody has been able to show any proof. Sad." And, in an attack on the media, Trump takes this Twitter shot, "The Fake News Media hates when I use what has turned out to be my very powerful social media-over 100 million people! I can go around them." **6/16/17**

▪ The White House announces a ban on video cameras during press briefings, allowing only off-camera presentations by press secretary Sean Spicer. When asked about the ban, Spicer comments that, "There are days where we decide that the president's voice should be the one who speaks for the administration." **6/19/17**

▪ Embattled Attorney General Jeff Sessions who has been under pressure in recent months for his contacts with Russian officials during the 2016 presidential election, retains an attorney to represent him during the Russia investigation. Charles J. Cooper, Sessions' longtime friend, confirms his position as counsel to the Attorney General. **6/20/17**

▪ Donald Trump reveals that he did not record private meetings with then-FBI Director James Comey. In a statement via Twitter, Trump states that he has no idea "whether there are any 'tapes' or recordings of my conversations with James Comey, but I did not make, and do not have, any such recordings." Although Trump's admission leaves open the possibility of someone else taping conversations in the White House, several Democrats claim that he may be guilty of witness intimidation against Comey. **6/22/17**

▪ Donald Trump reacts to reports that he is being investigated by special counsel Robert S. Mueller III by tweeting, "You are witnessing the single greatest WITCH HUNT in American history-led by some very bad and conflicted people. #MAGA." He follows up with another tweet, stating, "They made up a phony story, found zero proof, so now they go for obstruction of justice on the phony story. Nice." **6/24/17**

▌ The Supreme Court agrees to allow portions of Donald Trump's much-maligned travel ban to proceed, but stopped short of the full travel restrictions of citizens from six Muslim majority countries from the Middle East sought by the White House. **6/26/17**

CHAPTER 7

JULY, 2017

JULY BRINGS US (DRUMROLL, PLEASE)...The Mooch! Yes, Anthony Scaramucci, aka "The Mooch" is appointed as White House Communications Director, in order to bolster Trump's tarnished image. Although he is woefully unqualified to perform the duties of the office, his short but lasting effect on the president will be felt for months on end. Scaramucci's accomplishments (in a breathtakingly short time period) include; causing White House spokesman Sean Spicer to resign (much to the chagrin of Melissa McCarthy, whose deadpan send up of Spicer on *Saturday Night Live* was epically funny), the resignation of White House Chief of Staff Reince Priebus (based on Scaramucci's unkind depiction of him to a reporter which accuses Priebus of being somewhat crazier than Jack Nicholson's character in *One Flew Over the Cuckoo's Nest*), and finally, The Mooch's teardown of presidential adviser Steve Bannon, (whom he accuses of orally gratifying himself. Eww.). So much Scaramucci, so little time.

But wait, there's more. July brings us the Trump v. The *Morning Joe* MSNBC battle, where Donald Trump attacks television hosts Mika Brzezinski and Joe Scarborough by accusing them of; having a poorly rated show, possessing a low IQ, being crazy, bleeding from a botched face lift, and being dumb as a rock. He later said that they weren't "bad people." Huh?

July is also the month that brings us the first glimpses of the now-famous Trump Tower meeting with Russians looking to peddle dirt on Hillary Clinton. We now wonder if meeting attendee, Trump's son, Donald Jr., would have uttered that now-famous phrase, "If it's what you say it is, I love it," if he only knew of the brouhaha to follow.

▌ Donald Trump, reacting to criticism from MSNBC's *Morning Joe* talk show hosts, launches into a Twitter attack on co-host Mika Brzezinski. Trump's tweet states, "I heard poorly rated @MorningJoe speaks badly of me. (don't watch anymore)." He follows up with a second tweet which says, "Then how come low I.Q. Crazy Mika, along with psycho Joe came to Mar-a-Lago 3 nights in a row around New Year's Eve, and insisted on joining me. She was bleeding badly from a face lift." Trump's comments were immediately vilified by the press, and members of both parties, including House Majority Leader Paul Ryan (R-WI), Lindsey Graham (R-SC), and Ben Sasse (R-NE). The following day, Trump doubles down on his attack of Scarborough and Brzezinski by tweeting, "Watched low rated @MorningJoe for the first time in a long time. FAKE NEWS. He called me to stop a National Enquirer article. I said no! Bad show." The Enquirer reference revolves around Scarborough being asked to retract negative stories about Trump in exchange for the *National Enquirer* "spiking" a story on him they were about to publish. As the war of words continues into the second day, Trump tweets, "Crazy Joe Scarborough and dumb as a rock Mika are not bad people, but their low rated show is dominated by their NBC bosses." Trump also weighs in on host Greta Van Sustern's nightly show being cancelled on MSNBC by stating that she "refused to go along w/Trump hate!" **7/1/17**

▌ The Trump administration's newly-formed commission on voter fraud announces that it is seeking data from all 50 states on voters' first and last names, dates of birth, political parties (if available), and the last four digits of their Social Security numbers. Governors and election officials of numerous states announce that they will not comply with the commission, and others state that they will only provide information that is publically-available. **7/1/17**

▌ Donald Trump posts an old video clip on Twitter, showing his appearance in a WWE professional wrestling match, with a CNN logo superimposed on the face of his opponent. Trump is shown body slamming the wrestler (with the CNN logo on it) to the ground, and beating him with his fists.

Trump then adds the hashtags #FraudNewsCNN and #FNN (Fraud News Network) and retweets the video on the POTUS account. **7/2/17**

▪ The president, speaking at the G-20 Summit, once again reverses his stance on Russian hacking in the 2016 U.S. presidential election, stating that, "other people in other countries could have been involved." This stance flies in the face of U.S. intelligence reports which clearly state Russia's involvement under the orders of Vladimir Putin. **7/6/17**

▪ Donald J. Trump Jr., the president's eldest son, reveals that he met with a Russian lawyer in June 2016, because the attorney claimed to have damaging information about the Clinton campaign. The meeting, which included Trump son-in-law Jared Kushner, and then-campaign chairman Paul Manafort, revolved around Russian contributions to the Democratic National Committee and Hillary Clinton's campaign. The Russian lawyer, Natalia Veselnitskaya, supposedly did not have any significant information to report, and the meeting ended soon after it began. Trump Jr. gave conflicting explanations about the purpose of meeting after it was reported by the *New York Times*. **7/9/17**

▪ Twitter users who were blocked by Donald Trump go to court to have the blocks lifted, citing First Amendment violations. The defendants in the lawsuit claim that Trump's Twitter postings are "official statements," and as a "public forum," should not be blocked. **7/9/17**

▪ Responding to the uproar over supposed meetings between Donald Trump, Jr. and a Russian lawyer, Trump Jr. releases the email chain of conversations which preceded the meeting, on Twitter. In the emails, Trump confidant Rob Goldstone tells him that the meeting with the lawyer (Veselnitskaya), would provide incriminating information against candidate Hillary Clinton, which would be of value to Donald Trump Sr.'s election hopes. Goldstone tells Trump Jr., "This is obviously very high level and sensitive information, but is part of Russia and its government support of Mr. Trump." Trump Jr.'s response, "If it's what you say, I love it, especially in the summer." The president responds to the ongoing story by stating, "My son is a high-quality person, and I support his transparency." **7/11/17**

■ Marc Kasowitz, head of Donald Trump's legal team, lashes out at a stranger's email to him, with a series of profanity-laced threats and insults. Kasowitz tells the stranger that, "You are fucking with me now. Let's see who you are. Watch your back, bitch." He also says, "Call me. Don't be afraid, you piece of shit. Stand up. If you don't call, you're just afraid." Kasowitz's remarks become more personal when he writes, "I already know where you live. I'm on you. You might as well call me. You will see me. I promise bro." Kasowitz's firm issues an apology the next day, attributing the remarks to "long working hours and fatigue." **7/12/17**

■ The president, in a response to questions surrounding his son's meetings with a Russian lawyer, tells reporters that Donald Jr. is a "fine person," and that he was only doing "opposition research" when he sought damaging information on Hillary Clinton and her campaign. Trump also states that, "Most people would have taken that meeting," if offered. **7/13/13**

■ During a meeting with French President Emmanuel Macron and his wife Bridgette, Donald Trump awkwardly comments on Mrs. Macron's appearance, by stating, "She's in such good physical shape. Beautiful. Isn't she beautiful?" This exchange is in line with Trump's history of making forward and controversial comments on women's appearance throughout his life. **7/14/17**

■ The president kicks off "Made in America" week by touting the great manufactured products from America. It is pointed out however, that nearly all Trump Company business products (including Ivanka Trump's), are made in foreign countries. **7/16/17**

■ Also at the summit, Donald Trump makes two announcements on Russia. In the first, he states that during a meeting with Russian President Vladimir Putin, the Russian leader "vehemently denied" any involvement with the hacking of the 2016 U.S. presidential election. He then announces the formation of a joint U.S.-Russian "cyber-security unit" to address future hacking. This proposal by Trump is met with widespread criticism by members of his own party, including Sens. Marco Rubio (R-FL), and Lindsey Graham (R-SC). Following Trump's return to the U.S. after the summit concludes, he crafts a denial of his own program by tweeting, "The fact that President Putin and I discussed a cyber-security unit doesn't mean I think it can happen. It can't-but a ceasefire can, & did!" Trump then attempts to divert attention away from his remarks by tweeting about former FBI Director James Comey, stating "James Comey leaked CLASSIFIED INFORMATION to the media. That is so illegal." **7/16/17**

■ Donald Trump, while at the G-20 Summit also tweets the following, "Everyone here is talking about why John Podesta refused to give the DNC server to the FBI and the CIA. Disgraceful!" **7/17/17**

■ After learning that the U.S Senate didn't have enough votes to pass a healthcare bill, Donald Trump states that his new plan will be to, "let Obamacare fail; it will be a lot easier. And I think we're probably in that position where we'll let Obamacare fail." Trump also comments, "We're not going to own it. I can tell you the Republicans are not going to own it." **7/18/17**

■ It is reported that Donald Trump held an unscheduled meeting with Russian President Vladimir Putin during the G-20 Summit dinner in Germany. Trump signaled Putin during the dinner, and directed to meet him in an area adjacent to the main dining hall, where the two men spoke privately for an hour, with only Putin's translator present. The White House had no comments on what was said during the impromptu meeting. **7/19/17**

■ In an interview with the *New York Times* the president states that he would not have appointed Jeff Sessions to lead the Department of Justice if he knew Sessions would recuse himself from the Russian investigation of the Trump campaign. Trump also criticizes DOJ deputy Rod Rosenstein and special counsel Robert S. Mueller III for having conflicts of interest in the probe. And in an ominous warning to Muller, Trump states that if the special counsel looks into the Trump family finances as part of his probe, he would consider that to be a breach of the Russia investigation, which could lead to Mueller's removal. **7/19/17**

- Donald Trump unleashes a series of negative tweets criticizing the press, the Russia investigations, and Republicans who don't openly support him. After the *Washington Post* reports new meetings between then-senator Jeff Sessions and a Russian official in 2016, Trump tweets, "A new INTELLIGENCE LEAK from Amazon Washington Post, this time against A.G. Jeff Sessions. These illegal leaks, like Comey's, must stop!" **7/21/17**

- The president, in an effort to repair his damaged public image, appoints a new Communications Director. Anthony Scaramucci is hired, and White House spokesman Sean Spicer abruptly resigns. Sarah Huckabee Sanders replaces him. Scaramucci delivers a 37 minute initial press conference, outlining his devotion to Trump, stating that his political insincts might be among "the best in history." He also speaks of Trump's ability to "throw a tight (football) spiral through a tire, make consecutive foul shots on the basketball court while wearing a trench coat, and making three-foot puts on the golf course." **7/21/17**

- Donald Trump's criticism of his own party is outlined in a tweet which states, "It's very sad that Republicans, even some that were carried over the line on my back, do very little to protect their president." **7/23/17**

- Donald Trump delivers a controversial address during the annual Boy Scout Jamboree in West Virginia. Trump, weaving in his traditional campaign talking points during the speech, criticizes Washington, ("a swamp...a cesspool,") Democrats, (for losing the election), and fellow Republicans (for not supporting his healthcare initiative). Trump also opines on his Electoral College victory ("a beautiful red map"), holidays, ("people will now be saying Merry Christmas again"), and tells an off-color story about the debauchery of a rich businessman and a yacht in front of young boys attending the Jamboree. **7/25/17**

■ Donald Trump blasts Attorney General Jeff Sessions with consecutive Twitter attacks. In one post, Trump tweets, "Attorney General Jeff Sessions has taken a VERY weak position on Hillary Clinton crimes (where are emails and DNC server), and intel leakers." He also posts, "Why didn't AG Sessions replace acting FBI Director Andrew McCabe, a Comey friend who was in charge of Clinton investigation but got big dollars ($700,000 for his wife's political run from Hillary Clinton and her representatives). Drain the swamp!" **7/25/17**

■ Donald Trump announces (on Twitter), that there will be a ban on transgender people serving in the military. Citing the costs of gender-reassignment surgery, Trump claims that the military will no longer allow transgender soldiers to serve "in any capacity." The Pentagon is caught completely off guard by this announcement, and refers all questions on the new policy to the White House. **7/26/17**

■ The GOP leadership of the U.S. Senate tries to push across a "skinny" repeal of the Affordable Care Act (Obamacare). The vote does not pass (51-49), and Senate Majority Leader Mitch McConnell announces that the measure has gone down to defeat. Before the final vote however, Sen. Lisa Murkowski (R-AK), receives an unpleasant phone call from Donald Trump, threatening to withhold federal dollars earmarked for projects in her state if she did not vote for the bill. Murkowski is not swayed from his call, and votes against her party's healthcare plan. **7/27/17**

■ Newly appointed director of communications for the White House, Anthony Scaramucci, uses vile language with a reporter as he battles White House Chief-of-Staff Reince Priebus. Scaramucci accuses Priebus of leaking information to the press, and calls him a "fucking paranoid schizophrenic, a paranoiac." He also has unkind words for presidential adviser Steve Bannon, stating, "I'm not Steve Bannon. I'm not trying to suck my own cock. I'm not trying to build my own brand off the fucking strength of the president. I'm here to serve the country." **7/27/17**

■ Chief of Staff Reince Priebus resigns his position with the Trump Administration. Donald Trump appoints Homeland Security Secretary John F. Kelly, a four-star general, to replace Priebus. The official comment from the White House is that the president wants to go "in a different direction." **7/28/17**

■ Donald Trump during a speech to a gathering of police officers at Suffolk Community College tells law enforcement to use brutality when arresting suspects. Trump advises them to not protect a suspect's head while putting them in a squad car. Response from police organizations is swift and forceful in condemning Trump's remarks. **7/28/17**

■ White House Communications Director, Anthony Scaramucci, is fired by incoming Chief-of-Staff John Kelly. Scaramucci reportedly tells Kelly that he is going to report directly to the president, and is then fired by Kelly, who disagrees with Scaramucci's chain of command plans. He serves in the White House for just 10 days. **7/31/17**

CHAPTER 8

AUGUST WILL ALWAYS BE remembered as the "Fire and Fury" month, as Donald Trump makes his incendiary comments to North Korea's Kim Jong un in what will be a long tug-of-"war" (no pun intended), over Kim's nukes. Although no one realized it at the time, the words "fire and fury" turn out to be a godsend for author Michael Wolff, who spins that title into a household phrase with his bestselling novel on the president and his skullduggery.

Also in August, Trump begins to become more involved in Don Jr.'s meeting in Trump Tower with Russians, as he "weighs in" on an official statement, (which means "he wrote it") that begins to unravel almost as it soon as it leaves his pouty lips.

White House senior adviser Steve Bannon and National Security aide Sebastian Gorka reach mutual agreements with the White House that they have somewhat overstayed the nation's welcome, and need to go away. Unfortunately, they don't take Stephen Miller with them.

Donald Trump lies about his speech to the Boy Scouts (doesn't their oath begin with, "A scout is trustworthy?"), and also fibs that Mexico's president is onboard with his immigration policies ("No hay pared para ti"…No wall for you), and for good measure, he issues a pardon for everyone's (least) favorite retired sheriff, Joe Arpaio.

But the defining moment in Trump's rocky August, is his epic mishandling of the violence in Charlottesville, Virginia. Trump's knuckleheaded foot-in-mouth statements about white supremacists being "some fine people" will loom over him like low-hanging storm clouds for many months to come.

■ Donald Trump claims that the head of the Boy Scouts called him to say that his speech during the annual Boy Scout Jamboree was "the best ever given by a president to his organization. The Boy Scouts deny such a phone call or conversation ever took place. **8/2/17**

■ The president tweets during his vacation that his political base is "bigger and stronger than ever before," even as new poll numbers show his approval ratings sinking to a new low of 33%. Trump then tweets attacks on the media, posting, "Hard to believe that with 24/7 #Fake News on CNN, ABC, NBC, CBS, NYTIMES, and WAPO, the Trump base is getting stronger." **8/2/17**

■ Donald Trump reportedly calls the White House "a dump" while talking with members of his Bedminster, New Jersey golf course, and states that he spends so much time away from it due to its shoddy condition. Trump later denies he made such comments on Twitter. **8/3/17**

■ The president claims he had a phone conversation with Mexico's president, Enrique Peña Nieto, in which the Mexican leader supposedly praised Trump's immigration policies. Nieto denies that this call ever took place, and that he and Trump spoke briefly at the G-20 summit in Germany. A White House spokesperson confirms Nieto's account. **8/4/17**

■ The White House releases a statement contradicting a previous one saying Donald Trump Sr. did not have any input on crafting Donald Trump Jr.'s story about a meeting with a Russian lawyer in Trump Tower. Trump Sr. now claims he "weighed in" on crafting a response to the charges, and had "significant" input in creating the statement. **8/5/17**

■ The president unleashes a tweetstorm against Senator Richard Blumenthal (D-CT), after he voices support on CNN for the ever-widening Russia investigation. Trump tweets, "Interesting to watch Senator Blumenthal of Connecticut talking about hoax Russian collusion when he was a phony Vietnam con artist….Never in U.S. history has anyone lied or defrauded voters like Senator Richard Blumenthal. He told stories about his Vietnam battles and …conquests, how brave he was, and it was all a lie. He cried like a baby and begged for forgiveness like a child. Now he judges collusion." **8/7/17**

■ A published report in the *New York Times* states that Vice President Mike Pence's support staff has been probing a possible presidential run in 2020, based on Donald Trump's dismal performance in office. The vice president angrily issues a denial that he is planning to run and pledges loyalty to the president. **8/7/17**

■ Donald Trump issues fiery rhetoric aimed at North Korea in response to that nation's threats of firing nuclear weapons at Guam, which is a U.S. territory. Trump states that North Korean leader Kim Jong un "has been threatening beyond a normal state, and as I said, they will be met with fire and fury and frankly power, the likes of which this world has never seen before." **8/8/17**

■ The president makes an off-the-cuff remark during an impromptu press conference at his Bedminster golf course resort about Russia expelling 700+ U.S. embassy workers by saying that he's glad that Vladimir Putin did this so that "we could save money on our payroll." The White House later states that Trump was being sarcastic. **8/11/17**

■ The president claims that he is not ruling out a military option to confront the autocratic government of Venezuelan president Nicolas Maduro, due to the difficulties facing the South American country. **8/11/17**

■ Violence erupts in Charlottesville, Virginia, as white supremacists, protesting the removal of a statue of Confederate General Robert E. Lee clash with counter-protestors. Two police officers are killed in a helicopter crash while monitoring the protests, and 32 year old Heather Heyer is also killed when a white supremacist runs her over with his car which was driven directly into the crowd of counter protestors. Numerous others are injured before the two groups are separated. First Lady Melania Trump delivers an initial tweet from the White House, followed later by the president's own tweets, which condemn violence by "many sides." Trump draws criticism from numerous groups, including members of his own party, for not taking aim at the alt-Right movement, who initially scheduled the rally and protest march. **8/11/17**

■ In a stark reversal of comments he made only day before about the violence in Charlottesville, Donald Trump revises his position of placing blame for the violence on white supremacist groups. The president once again splits the between blame alt-Right and "alt-Left" groups. In a rambling impromptu press conference, Trump appears to defend the white supremacist protesters, saying that they were made up of "some fine people." He also poses the possibility that the statues of George Washington and Thomas Jefferson might be targeted for removal if the Confederate statues continue to be taken down. Trump is criticized by the press, and high-profile members of his own party, including Paul Ryan (R-WI) and Marco Rubio (R-FL). **8/14/17**

■ Under pressure, Donald Trump issues a prepared statement denouncing the violence in Charlottesville by naming the white supremacist movement, alt-Right groups, and the KKK as responsible for creating the situation. **8/15/17**

■ The president's Strategy and Policy Forum and the Manufacturing Council announce that they are disbanding due to the resignation of several top CEOs in the organization, based on Trump's comments about the violence in Charlottesville. Trump later announces that he had intended to disband the council before the resignations. **8/16/17**

■ Donald Trump, doubling down on his remarks about the violence in Charlottesville, tweets a defense of Confederate monuments, by saying that attempts to remove them would be an attack on America's "history and culture." Trump also tweets a long-debunked legend about General John Pershing shooting Muslim rebels in the Philippines a century ago, which supposedly stopped Islamic terror for 35 years. **8/17/17**

▪ White House senior adviser Steve Bannon issues his resignation from the Cabinet, after reports surface he had offended the president with remarks he made during an interview with the *American Prospect Magazine*. Bannon, who will reportedly go back to *Breitbart News*, tells an interviewer with the *Weekly Standard* that after his resignation/termination he feels "jacked up, and free." He also states, "I've got my hands on my weapons. Someone said it's 'Bannon the Barbarian.' I am definitely going to crush the opposition." *Breitbart* welcomes back Bannon by tweeting, "#WAR." **8/18/17**

▪ Fallout continues in the wake of Trump's remarks on the violence in Charlottesville, with billionaire adviser Carl Icahn announcing that he is stepping away from the White House to prevent "political bickering." **8/18/17**

▪ Donald Trump and his wife Melania announce that they will not attend the Kennedy Center Honors program, after it was announced that three of the recipients (Norman Lear, Carmen deLavallade, and Lionel Richie) would not appear at the event because they would have to be presented an award by the president. This marks the first time a U.S. president or first lady will not attend the prestigious event, since its inception in 1978. **8/19/17**

▪ The American Red Cross, Cleveland Clinic, American Cancer Society, Salvation Army, Susan G. Comen Foundation, Friends of David Adom, and the Preservation Foundation of Palm Beach, all announce that they are cancelling fund raising events at Trump's Mar-a-Lago resort. In a related story, members of the President's Committee on the Arts and Humanities resign their positions over Trump's incendiary comments on the events at Charlottesville. **8/20/17**

▪ The U.S. Secret Service announces that it will run out of money to protect Donald Trump and his family on September 30. The main reason for the financial crunch is overtime hours for agents protecting the president and family, who travel extensively for business and vacations. **8/21/17**

▮ Donald Trump holds a campaign rally in Arizona, where he lashes out at the "fake press" once again citing negative coverage of his response to the violence at Charlottesville. Trump spends 77 minutes of off-script attacks on his enemies, including Arizona Senators Jeff Flake and John McCain, whom he does not directly name. Police use tear gas outside the Phoenix Convention Center to hold back crowds angry at the president. **8/22/17**

▮ James R. Clapper Jr., a former national intelligence director who has served under previous administrations, dating back to John F. Kennedy, openly questions Donald Trump's capacity to act as president. Clapper shows concern about Trump's readiness to govern, with regards to access of the U.S. nuclear launch codes. **8/24/17**

▮ National Security aide Sebastian Gorka, a hard-line supporter of Steve Bannon, resigns from his position in the White House. Officials in the Trump administration say that Gorka did not resign, but that he "no longer works at the White House." **8/25/17**

▮ Donald Trump pardons former sheriff Joe Arpaio from his conviction for disobeying a judge's order in an immigration case. Arpaio faced constant criticism while in office for his stance on immigrants, and his treatment of immigrant prisoners under his watch. Arpaio was a strong supporter of Trump during the presidential campaign, and shared Trump's "birther" views on former president Obama. **8/25/17**

▮ Michael Cohen, attorney for Donald Trump, in a statement to the House Intelligence Committee, testifies that the president's company pursued a major building project in Moscow during the 2016 presidential election. Cohen claims that the Trump Organization entered into a letter of agreement with developers, but the project was ultimately dropped. **8/27/17**

CHAPTER 9

LOOKING THROUGH A TRUMP lens, September was more like a late-summer vacation month in which you try to kick back and tie up a few loose ends before the weather changes. There is the un-ceremonious departure of Health and Human Services Director Tom Price, (who probably should have been named head of the FAA, based on his love of frequent first-class air travel) and Trump's debut of a nickname for North Korea's Kim Jong un, by calling the notoriously unstable autocrat who possesses nuclear warheads, "Rocket Man."

Although "Lock (Hillary) Up!" was the number one chant at Trump campaign rallies, "On day one of my presidency I will repeal Obamacare" had to be credited as his #1 promise to the American people. Well, Hillary is still free, and thanks to the U.S. Senate, the Affordable Care Act (Obamacare's grown-up name) is still the law of the land, much to Donald Trump's chagrin. But he continues bellyaching that it should be replaced, with…..something……anything else that doesn't have "Obama" in the name.

The Donald spent part of his lazy month criticizing NFL players who kneel as the National Anthem is played ("fire the son of a bitch"), and the mayor of San Juan, Puerto Rico (who was apparently ticked off that Trump was playing golf while her constituents had no water or power….imagine that!). And in keeping with the golf theme, Donald Trump posts an animated GIF showing him lacing a Titleist off the noggin of poor, vanquished Hillary Clinton. Wonder if he took a penalty stroke? Welcome to a September to (feh), un-remember.

- Amid increasing threats of a nuclear weapon capable of striking the U.S. mainland, Donald Trump criticizes the South Korean Government for its policy of "appeasement" towards the North. Trump also picks this delicate time to question U.S.-South Korean trade agreements. **9/4/17**

- The president announces an end to the Obama-era DACA (Deferred Action for Childhood Arrivals) program, by sending the measure back to Congress, with instructions for them to put the immigration program into law, instead of implementing it as an executive order. Trump gives Congress six months to come up with a solution, or he will "revisit" the program at the end of that period. **9/5/17**

- Mr. Trump, frustrated by his inability to work with Republican congressional leaders, aligns himself with Democrats in that body, by negotiating a deal with them for short-term government funding, and hurricane relief aid. Republicans are understandably miffed by the president's actions. **9/17/17**

- Donald Trump retweets a GIF showing him hitting and knocking down former presidential candidate Hillary Clinton with a golf ball. **9/17/17**

- During a speech in front of the United Nations, Donald Trump threatens to "totally destroy" North Korea if necessary, and insults North Korea's leader, Kim Jong un, by calling him "Rocket Man." **9/19/17**

- Mr. Trump criticizes NFL players who protest the National Anthem by taking a knee during the song. Trump urges NFL team owners to "fire the son of a bitch" if a player takes a knee during the Anthem. Responding to Trump's comments, hundreds of NFL players kneel and show other forms of solidarity with teammates in stadiums across the country during the National Anthem. Nearly every team has some form of action, and many NFL owners criticize Trump's comments. **9/22/17**

- Jared Kushner, Donald Trump's son-in-law, reportedly uses a private email account while conducting White House business. Critics of the administration point out that this is the same behavior Hillary Clinton was attacked for during the 2016 U.S. presidential campaign. **9/24/17**

■ A last-ditch attempt by Republicans to repeal and replace the Affordable Care Act (Obamacare) fails in the U.S. Senate. The Cassidy-Graham bill did not garner enough support from Republicans, and is withdrawn without a floor vote. **9/28/17**

■ Roy Moore wins a Republican primary race against Luther Strange in Alabama. Strange was supported by Donald Trump, who then deleted all of his tweets supporting Strange after the election results were announced. **9/27/17**

■ Secretary of Health and Human Services, Tom Price, resigns his post in the Trump administration; amid reports that he spent nearly one million dollars in air travel (mostly First Class) while holding office. **9/29/17**

■ Donald Trump, in a series of tweets, criticizes Carmen Cruz, the mayor of San Juan, Puerto Rico, who had urged him to send more assistance to the people of her country, which was devastated by Hurricane Maria. Among Trump's tweets: "The mayor of San Juan, who was complimentary only a few days ago, has now been told by Democrats that you must be nasty to Trump." He also says via Twitter that local officials "want everything to be done for them when it should be a community effort." He also criticizes Cruz (while at his Bedminster golf resort), for "poor leadership." **9/30/17**

CHAPTER 10

A "SYMPATHETIC" DONALD TRUMP begins the month by telling residents of a hurricane-torn island to be happy because they weren't uprooted by a "real catastrophe" like Hurricane Katrina. Most Puerto Ricans weren't upset by the remark however, as they had no power to watch it on TV. Trump then doubles down on his seemingly endless lack of empathy by comforting the wife of a military hero (LaDavid Johnson) by saying that her husband "knew what he was signing up for." Mother Teresa he's not.

As Senators Jeff Flake and Bob Corker both announce they won't seek re-election, a cantankerous Trump sends them a heartfelt farewell by saying they couldn't win an election without his endorsement anyway. And, reports surface that Secretary of State Rex Tillerson may or may not have colorfully described his ex-boss as being a "moron" (oopsie).

October brings NFL football, and an opportunity for Trump to once again show his displeasure that NFL players are kneeling as the National Anthem is played, by diabolically sending Vice President Mike Pence to a pro football game with plans to walk out in protest as a handful of players knelt. Total cost to taxpayers? A cool $250,000! Perhaps that money could have been used to buy clean drinking water for the "should be happy" citizens of Puerto Rico.

And as Donald Trump enjoys the lowest approval ratings of any president in the past 70 years, millionaire businessman Tom Steyer launches a national television campaign to have him impeached. Happy Halloween to the Orange One!

▪ Donald Trump visits hurricane ravaged Puerto Rico, and during a press conference, states that island officials should feel "real proud" they haven't lost lives in a "real catastrophe" like Hurricane Katrina in 2015. He also jokingly mentions that the small U.S. territory's disaster threw the nation's budget "out of whack." **10/3/17**

▪ Donald Trump airs his displeasure with the news media by tweeting, "Why isn't the Senate Intel Committee looking into the Fake News Networks in OUR country to see why so much of our news is just made up-FAKE!" **10/4/17**

▪ NBC News reports that Secretary of State Rex Tillerson refers to Donald Trump as a "moron" during a White House staff meeting. Tillerson did not confirm nor deny the accusations, stating that he would not comment on such "trivial matters." **10/4/17**

▪ The president, during the annual dinner featuring top U.S. military commanders and personnel, tells the press during a group photo: "You guys know what this represents? Maybe it's the calm before the storm." When asked what he meant by the remark, Trump responds, "You'll find out." Speculation about the cryptic comment runs from an attack on North Korea, to military intervention in Venezuela. **10/5/17**

▪ After Senator Bob Corker (R-TN) announces that he will not seek re-election in 2018. Donald Trump lashes out at Corker in a series of blistering attacks, tweeting, "Senator Bob Corker "begged" me to endorse him for re-election in Tennessee. I said 'NO' and he dropped out (said he could not win without my endorsement). He also wanted to be Secretary of State. I said 'No Thanks.' He is also largely responsible for the horrendous Iran Deal! Hence, I would fully expect Corker to be a negative voice and stand in the way of our great agenda. Didn't have the guts to run." Corker fires back at the president, tweeting, "It's a shame the White House has become an adult day care center. Someone obviously missed their shift this morning." Corker then doubles down on his attack, telling a *New*

York Times reporter that Trump's reckless threats towards other countries could set the nation "on the path to World War III." **10/8/17**

∎ Vice President Pence flies to Indianapolis to watch an NFL football game between the Colts and 49ers. After several players kneel during the National Anthem, Pence, his wife, and staff exit the stadium. It was later revealed that Donald Trump planned the affair, which cost the American taxpayers over $250,000. **10/8/17**

∎ The president comments on how little praise he received for assisting Puerto Rico after Hurricane Maria by tweeting, "Nobody could have done what I've done for #PuertoRico with so little appreciation, So much work." **10/8/17**

∎ Donald Trump tweets an insult aimed at Senator Bob Corker, calling him "Liddle Bob Corker," and accusing him of being tricked by the *New York Times* because he had his interview with them recorded. **10/10/17**

∎ The president, in an interview with Forbes Magazine, responds to the charges that Secretary of State Rex Tillerson called him a "moron," by stating, "If he did that, I guess we'll have to have to compare IQ tests. And I can tell you who is going to win." A White House spokesperson says later that day that Trump was "joking," during the interview. **10/10/17**

∎ Donald Trump threatens NBC's broadcast licenses because he is miffed at the way he is being treated by the network. Trump tweets, "With all of the Fake News coming out of NBC and the Networks, at what point is it appropriate to challenge their License? Bad for country!" **10/11/17**

∎ The president serves notice that he may curtail federal relief workers from Puerto Rico, effectively ending assistance from the recovery of Hurricane Maria. Trump tweets, "We cannot keep FEMA, The Military & The First Responders, who have been amazing (under the most difficult circumstances) in P.R. forever!" **10/12/17**

■ The president's administration announces that he will immediately halt health care cost-sharing reductions related to the Affordable Care Act (Obamacare), ending $7 billion dollars in federal subsidies for low-income Americans to purchase health insurance. **10/12/17**

■ The president makes comments about his reaching out to the families of fallen U.S. soldiers, and accuses other presidents of not doing so. At a press conference in the Rose Garden, Trump states, "If you look at President Obama and other presidents, most of them didn't make calls. I like to call when it's appropriate, when I think I am able to do it." His comments are immediately criticized by staff and supporters of former presidents George W. Bush, and Obama. **10/16/17**

■ Donald Trump, in a personal phone call to a grieving military father who lost his son in battle, states that he would write him a $25,000 check and that his staff would establish an online fundraiser, but neither promise is kept. The White House reports that the check was mailed after a long delay. Trump also reportedly insults the wife of a fallen U.S. soldier, recently killed in an ambush in Niger, by saying that her husband, "knew what he was signing up for, but I guess it hurts anyway." Trump denies making the statement, and says that he had "proof" he did not say what was reported. However, Rep. Frederica S. Wilson (D-FL), who was traveling in the limousine of the bereaved family, claimed that she overheard the conversation over the limo's speakerphone. **10/18/17**

■ Chief of Staff John F. Kelly holds a press conference criticizing Rep. Frederica Wilson for revealing the details of Donald Trump's conversation with the family of fallen soldier LaDavid Johnson, by calling her an "empty barrel." Kelly also accuses Wilson of taking credit for acquiring the funds to open a federal building in Miami. Video of Rep. Wilson's speech at the dedication of the building however, showed that she spoke solely about her efforts to get the building named after two fallen FBI agents, not about funding. Donald Trump adds to the controversy by tweeting, "The fake news is going crazy with wacky Congresswoman

Wilson (D), who was SECRETLY on a very personal call, and gave a total lie on content." **10/19/17**

▮ The Associated Press finds that Donald Trump's claims that he had made calls to "virtually everybody" who lost a loved one in the military during his administration are false. He reportedly only reached out to 10 of the 20 families affected during his tenure. **10/20/17**

▮ Billionaire progressive donor Tom Steyer launches a $10 million campaign, calling for the impeachment of Donald Trump. Steyer purchases commercial airtime on various cable networks, including CNN, and FOX (which later suspends the campaign on its network), which states that Trump, "brought us to the brink of nuclear war, obstructed justice at the FBI, and in direct violation of the Constitution, he's taken money from foreign governments and threatened to shut down news organizations that report the truth." **10/20/17**

▮ Senator Jeff Flake (R-AZ), announces that he will not run for re-election. In an emotional speech on the Senate floor, Flake criticizes Donald Trump, claiming that his behavior is "dangerous to our Democracy." He also states that, "We must never regard as normal the regular and casual undermining of our democratic norms and ideals. We must never meekly accept the daily surrendering of our country-the personal attacks; the threats against principles, freedoms and institutions; the flagrant disregard for truth and decency." Flake continues, "We must stop pretending that the degradation of our politics and the conduct of some executive branch are normal. They are not normal. Reckless, outrageous, and undignified behavior has become excused and countenanced as 'telling it like it is' when it is actually just reckless, outrageous, and undignified." Response from the White House to Flake's remarks come from press secretary Sarah Huckabee Sanders, saying that Flake's comments were "petty," and she suggests that he chose not to run (as did Sen. Bob Corker R-TN) for re-election because he could not win. **10/24/17**

■ Donald Trump goes on a Twitter-fueled rampage as the Mueller investigation indictments draw near. Trump posts four times in a 24 minute span, all of which attack Hillary Clinton or the DNC, and charges that they colluded with the Russian government during the 2016 U.S. presidential elections. Trump tweets, "Instead they look at phony Trump/Russia, 'collusion' which doesn't exist. The Dems are using this terrible (and bad for our country) Witch Hunt for evil politics, but the R's are now fighting back like never before"......."There is so much GUILT by Democrats/Clinton and now the facts are pouring out. DO SOMETHING!" Later that morning, Trump tweets, "All of this 'Russia' talk right when the Republicans are making their big push for historic tax cuts & Reform. Is this Coincidental? NOT!" Trump follows up his tweetstorm the following day with one post which reads, "Report out that Obama Campaign paid $972,000 to Fusion GPS. The firm also got $12,400,000 (really) from DNC. Nobody knows who OK'd it." Trump did not list any sources that would justify his allegations or the dollar figures he cited. **10/30/17**

■ Special prosecutor Robert S. Mueller III reveals charges against three former members of the Trump administration, including former campaign chairman Paul Manafort. The indictments include allegations that the three men (including former Trump policy adviser George Papadopoulos and Manafort business partner Richard Gates), made false statements to FBI investigators about contacts with Russian officials, conspiracy to launder money, and other related charges. Donald Trump begins a tweet stream shortly after the charges are filed, by posting, "Sorry, but this is years ago, before Paul Manafort was part of the Trump campaign. But why aren't Crooked Hillary & the Dems the focus????" Trump later added, "Also, there is NO COLLUSION." **10/30/17**

CHAPTER 11

THE MONTH OF NOVEMBER begins with Donald Trump having his Twitter account temporarily deleted by a rogue employee of the company on their last day at work. The interruption lasts all of 11 minutes, but wouldn't you like to be a fly on the wall of the Oval Office when it happened? "Hillary! Podesta! Pelosi! It's all their fault!"

Trump's attacks in November include: Sen. Elizabeth Warren (D-MA), who he once again slurs by referring to her as "Pocahontas" (in a ceremony to honor World War II Navajo Code Talkers, (let the irony of that one roll around in your noggin for a bit), and former-Senator Al Franken (D-MN), (referring to him as "Al Frankenstein" to mock the beleaguered representative from Minnesota). Trump remains silent however on alleged child molester Roy Moore, who runs for the Senate in a special election in Alabama. When it comes to judging character, Trump's criteria is paper-thin. Bow to the king, or get Twitter bombed.

Donald Trump becomes the first person to refuse *Time Magazine's* prestigious "Person of the Year" award without actually winning it. Apparently Trump now has the ability to turn down major honors even if they aren't offered (Time never gave him the award). Besides, the photo shoot would take away too much time at the links!

Let's see…wrapping up November we have Trump's dustup with UCLA basketball's dad-from-hell LaVar Ball, being called an "old lunatic" by Kim-Jong un, and ah yes, a lovely snit with British Prime Minister Theresa May who thumps Trump's re-tweeting of inflammatory anti-Muslim videos. Good stuff to discuss at Thanksgiving family dinners, right?

- A rogue employee of Twitter deletes Donald Trump's account, during his/her last day working for the social network. When visitors to Trump's personal account check his activity (@realDonaldTrump), they are greeted with a message stating that it did not exist. The deletion (which lasted for 11 minutes), is originally called an "employee error" by Twitter, but later turns out to be intentionally done. **11/3/17**

- The president pressures the Department of Justice and FBI to begin investigating defeated presidential candidate Hillary Clinton for a number of questionable activities during the 2016 U.S. presidential campaign. In his remarks, he urges law enforcement to "do what is right and proper" regarding Clinton. Trump, who has often criticized Attorney General Jeff Sessions for not taking on Clinton or protecting him from special prosecutor Robert S. Mueller III's Russia probe, tells reporters: "A lot of people are disappointed in the Justice Department, including me." **11/3/17**

- The White House issues its National Climate Change Assessment report stating that climate change is being caused almost entirely by human activity, which is in stark contrast to previous statements on climate change delivered by the Trump administration. **11/4/17**

- Donald Trump, during his diplomatic tour of Asia, reacts to a North Korean message, which refers to him as an "old lunatic," by writing on Twitter, "Why would Kim Jong un insult me by calling me old, when I would NEVER call him "short and fat?" **11/11/17**

- Also during his Asian swing, Trump declares that he believes Russian President Vladimir Putin was telling the truth when he said that his country did not meddle in the 2016 U.S. presidential election. This revelation flies in the face of information from American intelligence sources, which point conclusively to Russian interference. Trump later walks back his remarks by stating, "What I said is that I believe (Putin) believes that." **11/11/17**

∎ A new *Washington Post*-ABC News survey shows that Donald Trump has the lowest approval ratings for any sitting president in over 70 years of polling. Only 37% approve of Trump's handling of his job. Also, nearly 59% of Americans polled disapprove of his performance in office. **11/13/17**

∎ The president publicly criticizes Senator Al Franken, (D-MN.) who became embroiled in a controversy over sexually inappropriate behavior with a woman during a USO trip to Iraq in 2006. Trump takes aim at Franken by tweeting, "The Al Frankenstein (purposefully misspelling the Senator's name), picture is really bad. Speaks a thousand words. Where do his hands go in pictures 2, 3, 4, 5, & 6 while she sleeps?" This is a reference to pictures being taken of Franken while he pretends to squeeze the woman's breasts while she is asleep on a plane. Trump criticizes Franken, while staying uncharacteristically silent over the controversy surrounding Judge Roy Moore, who is running in a special Senate election to replace Jeff Sessions in Alabama. Moore has been accused of sexual misconduct and lewd behavior by numerous women, including a then-14 year old girl. **11/16/17**

∎ Donald Trump once again attacks failed 2016 U.S. presidential candidate Hillary Clinton, who had made some disparaging comments about him, by posting on Twitter, "Crooked Hillary Clinton is the worst (and biggest) loser of all time. She just can't stop, which is so good for the Republican Party. Hillary, get on with your life and give it another try in three years." **11/18/17**

∎ The president uses Twitter to scold three UCLA basketball players who were arrested in China for shoplifting, during a goodwill tour by the college team. Trump, apparently agitated that he was not being given credit for helping the players get released without going to jail, tweets, "Do you think the three UCLA Basketball players will say thank you President Trump? They were headed for 10 years in jail." Trump also tweets on the issue several days later, criticizing LaVar Ball, father of one of the UCLA players, by stating, "Now that the three basketball players are out of China and saved from years in jail, LaVar Ball, the father of LiAngelo, is unaccepting of what I did for his son and that shoplifting is no big deal. I should have left them in jail." He then continues his tirade on the subject by tweeting, "Shoplifting is a very big deal in China, as it should be (5-10 years in jail), but not to father LaVar. Should have gotten his son out during my next trip to China instead. China told them why they were released. Very ungrateful!" **11/19/17**

- The President, still steaming from a supposed slight from LaVar Ball, father of UCLA basketball player LiAngelo for not paying his respect to Trump for his actions granting release for his son in a shoplifting incident in China tweets, "It wasn't the White House, it wasn't the State Department, it wasn't father LaVar's so-called people on the ground in China that got his son out of a long term prison sentence-IT WAS ME. Too bad! LaVar is just a poor man's version of Don King, but without the hair." **11/19/17**

- The president reacts to another NFL pre-game protest. While playing in Mexico's Azteca Stadium against the New England Patriots, Seattle Seahawks running back Marshawn Lynch stands at attention during the playing of the Mexican National Anthem, while kneeling for the U.S. Anthem. Trump tweets the next day, "Great disrespect! Next time NFL should suspend him for remainder of season. Attendance and ratings way down." **11/20/17**

- Donald Trump tweets about Time Magazine's upcoming "Person of the Year" award, by stating, "Time Magazine called to say that I was PROBABLY going to be named 'man (person) of the year,' like last year, but I would have to agree to be interviewed and a major photo shoot. I said probably is no good and took a pass. Thanks anyway." Time later responds via Twitter that Trump's claim was incorrect, and that it doesn't comment on its own choice until publication. **11/25/17**

▌ Donald Trump, in his ongoing war with the press, tweets the following statement, "We should have a contest as to which of the networks, plus CNN and not including FOX, is the most dishonest, corrupt and/or distorted in its political coverage of your favorite president (me). They are all bad. Winner to receive the FAKE NEWS TROPHY!" **11/27/17**

▌ At a White House event intended to honor the World War II Navajo Code Talkers, the President mocks Sen. Elizabeth Warren (D-MA), by once again calling her "Pocahontas." The term is regarded as a racial slur to many Native-Americans, and to add insult to injury, the ceremony honoring the Code Talkers is held in front of a portrait of Andrew Jackson, who signed the Indian Removal Act into law in 1830. **11/28/17**

▌ Donald Trump weighs in on the firing of the Today Show's Matt Lauer for sexual harassment by firing off a tweet on the subject. Trump comments, "So now that Matt Lauer is gone when will the Fake News practitioners at NBC be terminating the contract of Phil Griffin? And will they terminate low ratings Joe Scarborough based on the 'unsolved mystery' that took place in Florida years ago. Investigate!" Trump's tweets were referencing the death of an intern in his Florida district office in 1999, while Scarborough served in Congress. Phil Griffin is the president of MSNBC. **11/29/17**

▌ A federal judge delivers another blow to the Trump Administration by issuing an injunction prohibiting the U.S. government from withholding funding to communities who declare themselves to be "Sanctuary Cities." District Judge William H. Orrick of San Francisco rules that the executive order issued by Trump violates the separation of powers doctrine, as well as the Fifth and Tenth Amendments. **11/30/17**

▌ The president shares three inflammatory anti-Muslim videos on Twitter, from the extremist group Britain First. The videos, which have not been verified as authentic, show supposed acts of Muslim violence against non-Muslims. Trump's re-tweets create widespread criticism from Britain, including a statement from Prime Minister Theresa May, who states that Trump was "wrong" to share the videos with his 44 million followers that came from a group that promotes "hateful narratives." Trump responds to May a day later, by tweeting, "@Theresa_May, don't focus on me, focus on the destructive Islamic Terrorism that is taking place within the United Kingdom. "We're doing just fine!" **11/30/17**

CHAPTER 12

AS THE MONTH OF December begins, Donald Trump gives America a wonderful holiday gift, wrapped in shiny paper and tied with a beautiful bow, as he tells the country that due to his efforts, people are once again allowed to say "Merry Christmas." Hallelujah, Donald!

But unfortunately, the season of good cheer doesn't extend to former National Security Adviser Michael Flynn, who fails to get a gift pardon from the president, and pleads guilty to lying to FBI investigators. Maybe you'll get that gift pardon next year, Mikey! But you can't say that Trump didn't completely forget to get Flynn something, as he DID ask then-FBI Director James Comey to "take it easy" on him.

December brings with it the beginnings of lawyerly shenanigans, as Trump's legal team begins to mount the "He can't obstruct justice because he's above the law" balderdash, which will eventually boil down to "He can't collude either…not that it's a crime, right?"

Trump complains that all immigrants from Haiti to the U.S. "have AIDS," and once Nigerian immigrants get to our hallowed shores; they'll "never go back to their huts." So much for Christmas spirit, eh? Ebenezer Scrooge would be so very proud.

And in keeping with the whole Christmas/Holy Land theme, Donald Trump infuriates Middle Eastern leaders by naming Jerusalem as Israel's capital city, which causes Muslims in the region to boot the U.S. out of the Israeli-Palestinian peace process. Oh, well, that's one less job for the Swiss army knife of a son-in-law Jared Kushner to labor over. Merry Christmas, everyone!

▪ Former national security adviser Michael Flynn pleads guilty to lying to the FBI about his contacts with Russian Ambassador Sergey Kislyak. This represents the first admission of guilt by a member of the Trump cabinet. Flynn served as national security adviser for less than one month, before being fired by Trump for lying about his Russian contacts to Vice President Mike Pence. **12/1/17**

▪ Donald Trump, during an early morning tweetstorm, states he knew Michael Flynn, former national security adviser, had lied to FBI investigators. Trump tweets, "I had to fire General Flynn because he lied to the Vice President, and the FBI." In previous statements by the White House, Flynn was only lightly chided for false statements made to Pence. Later that morning, Trump also denies that he told then-FBI Director James Comey to back off the investigation of Flynn, which Comey documented after a one-on-one meeting with Trump in the White House. Trump also states his displeasure with the FBI, tweeting, "After years of Comey, with the phony and dishonest Clinton investigation (and more) running the FBI, its reputation is in Tatters-worst in History! But fear not, we will bring it back to greatness." FBI Director Christopher Wray reacts to Trump's remarks, by staunchly defending the Bureau, stating, "There is no finer institution." He also rebuts Trump's accusations directly, by claiming, "My experience has been that our reputation is quite good." **12/3/17**

▪ A lawyer for Donald Trump, John Dowd, makes an audacious claim that the president cannot be found guilty of obstruction of justice. The controversial comment signals a new strategy in Trump's defense in the ever-expanding Russia probe. Dowd makes his claims in response to a recent Trump tweet that he was aware that then-National Security Adviser Michael Flynn lied to the FBI about his Russian contacts, before firing him in February. Trump's personal lawyer makes the claim, (which was first floated by constitutional scholar Alan Dershowitz) that Trump is protected under the U. S. Constitution's Article II, because he is the chief law enforcement officer in the country. **12/4/17**

▪ The president issues a statement that recognizes Jerusalem as Israel's capital, infuriating Palestinians and the Arab world, which recognize Jerusalem as the Palestinian capital and holy city. Protests begin after the announcement, with violent clashes between Israeli officers and Palestinian citizens, which result in several deaths. The Israeli air force also bombs Palestinian settlements in the Gaza Strip, in retaliation for missiles being fired at Israel. **12/6/17**

▪ Donald Trump holds a campaign-style rally in Pensacola, Florida, just miles from the Alabama border, in order to draw support for Roy Moore, who is running to replace Jeff Sessions in the U.S. Senate during a special election. (Moore has been accused of having improper relationships with several women in their teens while he was in his 30's). Trump takes the opportunity to criticize Moore's accusers, defense attorney Gloria Allred (who is representing one of the women), Democratic members of Congress Charles Schumer and Nancy Pelosi, and former presidential candidate Hillary Clinton. Trump's comments in the 80 minute free-wheeling speech also include jabs at the press, and against the "rigged system" in U.S. Government. **12/8/17**

▪ The president visits the opening of the Mississippi Civil Rights Museum in Jackson, Mississippi, amid controversy. The national president of the NAACP, the mayor of Jackson, and Rep. John Lewis (R-GA), all refuse to attend if Trump is present during the opening ceremony, with Rep. Lewis calling it "an insult." **12/9/17**

▪ Donald Trump fans the flames of the sexual harassment controversy by launching a Twitter attack against Senator Kirsten Gillibrand (D-NY). Trump fires back at Gillibrand after she had publicly called for him to resign the presidency amid claims that he had sexually assaulted women before he took office. Trump tweets, "Lightweight Senator Kirsten Gillibrand, a total flunky for Chuck Schumer and someone who would come to my office 'begging' for campaign contributions not so long ago (and would do anything for them), is now in the ring fighting against Trump. Very disloyal to Bill and Crooked-USED!" Gillibrand responds to Trump's tweet by firing back that she would not be silenced by a president whose comments she described as a "sexist smear." **12/12/17**

∎ Democrat Doug Jones wins a U.S. Senate seat against Republican Roy Moore in an Alabama special election. Moore, who was accused of sexual misconduct with several young women, (including a minor) is supported by Donald Trump. The president tweets about the race, records robocalls on his behalf, and also speaks at a rally just before the election. However, after Moore is defeated, Trump appears to walk back his support by posting on Twitter, "The reason I originally endorsed Luther Strange (and his numbers went up mightily), is that I said Roy Moore would not be able to win the General Election. I was right! Roy worked hard but the deck was stacked against him." **12/12/17**

∎ During a summit of Muslim leaders (the Organization of Muslim Cooperation) in Istanbul, Turkey, Palestinian president Mahmoud Abbas states that due to Donald Trump's announcement supporting Jerusalem as Israel's capital city, the U.S. was now unfit to mediate the Mideast conflict going forward. He is joined in his position by Turkish President Recep Tayyip Erdogan, who states that it is "out of the question" for Washington to continue to work on resolving the conflict between Israel and the Palestinians, and he also adds, "that process is over." **12/13/17**

∎ The Department of Health and Human Services is instructed to avoid the use of certain words when talking about issues of climate change, scientific evidence, and the disadvantaged. The words "vulnerable," "entitlement," and "diversity" are to be eliminated while preparing verbiage for the 2018 U.S. budget. The Centers for Disease Control employees are advised to avoid words such as: "fetus," "transgender," "evidence-based," and "science-based," while preparing their budget presentations. **12/21/17**

∎ Donald Trump promises to cut off U.S. funding to countries who oppose his decision to recognize Jerusalem as Israel's capital, ahead of a United

Nations vote that would potentially condemn the United States for its actions. U.S. Ambassador Nikki Haley goes as far as directly threatening opposing U.N. members, tweeting that the president would retaliate against them if they voted in favor of the resolution. Haley says that Trump asked her to report back to him on the countries "who voted against us," and that the U.S. will be "taking names." Several countries push back at the remarks, calling them "bullying tactics." **12/21/17**

▪ The U.S. Government shuts down after Senate Republicans fail to reach the 60 vote threshold which is necessary to pass a spending bill to continue paying for basic government services. Both Democrats and Republicans place blame on each other for the shutdown. It is the earliest shutdown of government during a president's first term in office. Trump postpones a $100,000 per couple fundraiser at Mar-a-Lago to stay in Washington until the impasse is broken. As a result of the shutdown, the White House places the following message on their phone answering system for incoming calls: "Thank you for calling the White House. Unfortunately we cannot answer your call today. Congressional Democrats are holding our government funding, including funding for our troops and other national security priorities, hostage due to an unrelated immigration debate. Due to this obstruction, the government is shut down." **12/22/17**

▪ Andrew McCabe, the FBI's deputy director, announces his retirement from the bureau, effective in March 2018, when he reaches full pension status. McCabe, who was targeted by Republicans for his role in both the Hillary Clinton email investigation and Russia probe, is criticized by Donald Trump in several tweets after his retirement is announced. Trump states that McCabe was "racing the clock" to retire with full benefits. **12/23/17**

▪ The *New York Times* reports that Donald Trump was involved in a contentious meeting with his cabinet over immigration. Trump allegedly complained that the reported 15,000 immigrants from Haiti to the U.S. "all have AIDS." He also reportedly cast ill will on 40,000 Nigerian immigrants by bellowing that "they would never go back to their huts" in Africa once they had seen the United States. **12/23/17**

■ Donald Trump posts several end-of-the-year tweets, complaining how unfairly he is being treated by the national media. Trump tweets, "The stock market is setting record after record & unemployment is at a 17 year low. So many things accomplished by the Trump Administration, perhaps more than any other President in first year. Sadly, will never be reported correctly by the Fake News Media." Trump doubles down on his comments the next day, tweeting, "The Fake News refuses to talk about how Big and how Strong our BASE is. They show Fake Polls just like they report Fake News. Despite only negative reporting, we are doing well, and nobody is going to beat us. MAKE AMERICA GREAT AGAIN." **12/24/17**

■ Donald Trump takes credit for using the term "Merry Christmas" in public by tweeting, "People are proud to be saying Merry Christmas again. I am proud to have led the charge against the assault of our cherished and beautiful phrase. MERRY CHRISTMAS!!!!!" **12/25/17**

■ The president once again lashes out at the Russia investigation with a Twitter post. "Wow, @fox and friends. Dossier is bogus Clinton Campaign, DNC funded dossier. FBI CANNOT (after all this time) VERIFY CLAIMS IN DOSSIER OF RUSSIA/TRUMP COLLUSION. FBI TAINTED. And they used this crooked Hillary pile of garbage as the basis for going after the Trump Campaign." **12/26/17**

■ Donald Trump claims that his administration has had more legislation passed than any other in history. However, the facts indicate that he has signed fewer laws than any president since Dwight Eisenhower. **12/27/17**

■ While golfing at Mar-a-Lago Resort, pictures surface on network news programs of Trump on the links, through hedges, using telephoto lenses. While the pictures and video are being taken, a white, unmarked panel truck parks in front of the resort, blocking the views of the photojournalists, who are shooting from across the street, on public property. **12/27/17**

▮ The president, addressing record end-of-year cold on the U.S. East Coast, tweets more flippant comments about global warming. Trump tweets, "In the East it could be the COLDEST New Year's Eve on record. Perhaps we could use a little bit of that good old Global Warming that our country, but not other countries, was going to pay TRILLIONS OF DOLLARS to protect us. Bundle up." **12/28/17**

▮ Donald Trump gives a wide-ranging, unscheduled interview to the *New York Times* while at his Mar-a-Lago resort. Among the president's comments are that no collusion occurred between his campaign and Russia (which he repeated 16 times during a 30 minute interview), and that the collusion was actually between Russia and the DNC (Democratic National Committee). Trump also states, "I have the absolute right to do what I want to do with the Justice Department," and he predicts that he will win re-election in 2020, because the press needs him to gather ratings and readership. He muses, "Six months before the election, they'll be loving me because they're saying, 'please, please don't lose Donald Trump.'" It is noteworthy to mention that Trump's impromptu interview occurs with no member of the White House staff or any advisers present. During the session, Trump reportedly makes 24 false or misleading statements. **12/28/17**

CHAPTER 13

JANUARY 2018 GETS OFF to a rather Trumpian start as the president creates his very own awards show for "Fake News" on Twitter. Categories include: "fakey fake fake" news stories that bothered the president, and "holy crap, that story was so true we've gotta' label it fake," and the ever-popular, CNN/*Washington Post*/*New York Times* "Death to America" fake news award.

Donald Trump wonders aloud in January why pearly-white folk from Norway don't immigrate to America. Uh, maybe healthcare, family-leave benefits, and the lack of him as their president make the Scandinavian Peninsula a bit more alluring than the good old US of A?

During January, Trump threatens Kim Jong un ("my nuclear button is bigger than yours"), Michael Wolff ("you better not publish *Fire and Fury*"), and poorer nations ("shithole countries"). Well, Kim still has his own button, Wolff made a small fortune off his book, and as far as we know, Trump isn't planning a visit to Haiti or Africa anytime soon.

And even though Donald Trump, and I quote, says "Right now, in a number of states, the laws allow a baby to be born from his or her mother's womb in the ninth month...It is wrong; it has to change," at the annual Right to Life march, he still wants us to know that he's "really smart," and a "very stable genius at that." Uh, no.

To put a "capper" (crapper?) on January, the prestigious Guggenheim Museum offers to send the White House a solid gold toilet to display instead of a Van Gough painting requested by Melania. Trump, who probably has numerous golden commodes in Trump Tower, refuses the offer.

- The president kicks off 2018 with a flurry of tweets about Pakistan (threatening to cut off foreign aid), Iran (siding with regime change protesters), and former Hillary Clinton aide, Huma Abedin (for supposedly disregarding safety protocols with passwords on a personal computer). **1/1/18**

- Donald Trump claims that he has overseen the "safest" year on record for aviation travel in the U.S. during 2017, with zero deaths occurring due to airline crashes. However, U.S. airline data shows that there have been no commercial airline crashes or deaths in this country since 2009. **1/2/18**

- The *Washington Post* reports that during the first year of his presidency, Donald Trump has made 1,950 false or misleading claims. This is an average of 5.6 per day. At his current pace, he will meet or exceed 2,000 such claims before he reaches a full year in office. **1/2/17**

- The president announces via Twitter, "I will be announcing THE MOST DISHONEST & CORRUPT MEDIA AWARDS OF THE YEAR on Monday at 5:00 o'clock. Subjects will cover Dishonesty and Bad Reporting in various categories from the Fake News Media. Stay Tuned." **1/2/18**

- Donald Trump, responding to a speech from North Korean leader Kim Jong un being in possession of a nuclear weapon that could strike the United States, from the push of a button that is, "always on my desk," responds via Twitter by stating, "North Korean Leader Kim Jong un just stated that the "Nuclear Button" is on his desk at all times. Will someone from his depleted and food starved regime please inform him that I too have a Nuclear Button, but it is much bigger & more powerful than his, and my Button works!" **1/3/18**

- Author Michael Wolff releases excerpts from a soon-to-be-published book he has written about the early days of the Trump presidency. *Fire and Fury: Inside the Trump White House,* uses interviews with current and former White House staff, including former presidential adviser Stephen K. Bannon, who claims in the book that Donald Trump Jr.'s meetings at

Trump Tower with Russian representatives were "treasonous" and "unpatriotic." Donald Trump immediately fires back at Bannon's remarks, stating, "Steve Bannon has nothing to do with me or my presidency." He also adds, "When he was fired, he not only lost his job, he lost his mind." **1/3/18**

■ The president disbands a controversial panel which was formed to study alleged voter fraud during the 2016 presidential election. The voting commission was established by Trump to prove that Democrats cast millions of illegal ballots for Hillary Clinton during the election. It was hindered by lawsuits and uncooperative state election boards, and was never able to prove that any voter fraud had been committed. **1/3/18**

■ Donald Trump, reacting to Michael Wolff's book *Fire and Fury,* takes to Twitter to bash the author's claims of Trump's diminished mental capacity. Trump tweets, "Now that Russian collusion, after one year of intense study, has proven to be a total hoax on the American public, the Democrats and their lapdogs, the Fake News Mainstream Media, are taking out the old Ronald Reagan playbook and screaming mental stability and intelligence....Actually, throughout my life, my two greatest assets have been mental stability and being, like, really smart. Crooked Hillary Clinton also played these cards very hard, and, as everyone knows, went down in flames. I went from VERY successful businessman to top TV star...To President of the United States (on my first try). I think that would qualify as not smart, but genius...and a very stable genius at that." Trump directly attacks Wolff by tweeting, "Michael Wolff is a total loser who made up stories in order to sell this really boring and untruthful book. He used Sloppy Steve Bannon, who cried when he got fired and begged for his job. Now Sloppy Steve has been dumped like a dog by almost anyone. Too bad." **1/3/18**

■ In a related story, a lawyer representing Donald Trump sends a cease and desist letter to Henry, Holt and Co., publishers of Wolff's book *Fire and Fury,* trying to prevent them from publishing the book. Lawyers for Trump also send a cease and desist letter to Stephen Bannon, charging him with violating a confidentiality agreement he had with the president while he was employed at the White House. **1/4/18**

▉ The *New York Times* reports that the president instructed White House lawyers to prevent Attorney General Jeff Sessions from recusing himself from the Russia Investigation. Sessions disregarded the president's request. **1/4/18**

▉ Donald Trump flip flops on supporting the Foreign Intelligence Surveillance Act (FISA) after watching Andrew Napolitano condemn the legislation on *Fox and Friends*. After a 30 minute phone conversation with House Speaker Paul Ryan (R-Wis.), Trump again reverses field by issuing a tweet that states, "Today's vote is about foreign surveillance of foreign bad guys on foreign land. We need it. Get smart." **1/11/18**

▉ According to various news reports, Donald Trump claims, "I have a good relationship with Kim Jong un (of North Korea). Based on the back and forth between the two world leaders, this would seem to be an egregious claim. Trump however, immediately responds to the report via Twitter by saying he was misquoted. Says Trump, "Obviously I didn't say that. I said '*I'd* have a good relationship with Kim Jong un.' Big difference." **1/11/18**

▉ According to a report from the *Wall Street Journal*, a lawyer for the president paid $130,000 in "hush money" to adult film star Stormy Daniels, (*nee* Stephanie Clifford) to avoid talking publically about a sexual relationship she had with Donald Trump. The encounter, which allegedly occurred in 2006, was initially denied by the lawyer who supposedly arranged the payment (Michael Cohen), the White House, and by Ms. Daniels herself. **1/12/18**

▉ The president, while at a bipartisan meeting on immigration in the White House Cabinet Room, demands to know why people from "shithole countries" are being accepted into the United States, rather than people from Norway. The remark stuns members of Congress who attended the meeting, and his words seem to build on comments he made in 2017 about Haitians all "having AIDS", and Nigerians" "living in huts." The White House did not deny the comments by Trump, but tried to downplay their significance by stating that he is "fighting for permanent solutions that make our country great by welcoming those who can contribute to our society." Reaction domestically and from around the globe is swift and extensive, with most condemning Donald Trump's words, and labeling him a racist. **1/12/18**

■ The president denies making comments about Haiti, El Salvador, and African nations, which include calling them "shithole countries" during an Oval Office meeting on immigration. On Twitter, Trump posts, "Never said anything derogatory about Haitians (sic) other than Haiti is, obviously a very poor and troubled country. Never said 'Take them out.' Made up by Dems. I have a wonderful relationship with Haitians. Probably should record future meetings-unfortunately, no trust." Trump also tweets, "That language used by me at the DACA meeting was tough, but that was not the language used. What was really tough was the outlandish proposal made-a big setback for DACA!" **1/12/18**

■ The president announces that he is cancelling a scheduled trip to London by stating, (that he is) "Not a big fan of the Obama Administration having sold the best located and finest embassy in London for 'peanuts' only to build a new one in an off location for 1.2 billion dollars. Bad deal. Wanted me to cut the ribbon-No!" Polls indicate that Trump is unpopular in London, and protests would most certainly arise if he were to take on a State visit. Reports also find that President Obama did not sell the London Embassy. All transactions surrounding the previous and current locations were authorized under President George W. Bush. **1/12/18**

■ Donald Trump launches into another Twitter attack on Michael Wolff, author of *Fire and Fury*, by posting, "So much Fake News is being reported. They don't even try to get it right, or correct it when they are wrong. They promote the Fake Book of a mentally deranged author, who knowingly writes false information. The Mainstream Media is crazed that WE won the election!" **1/13/18**

▪ Special Counsel Robert S. Mueller issues a subpoena to former White House strategist Stephen K. Bannon to appear in front of a grand jury involving the continuing Russia investigation. It is reported that Bannon is also subpoenaed by the House Intelligence Committee due to his refusal to answer questions from investigators. Bannon's attorney William Burck tells the committee that Bannon is willing to speak with investigators, but could not answer questions because the White House told him not to respond, effectively creating a "gag order" on Bannon. **1/16/18**

▪ White House Chief of Staff John F. Kelly speaks to Democratic lawmakers, and states that Donald Trump's comments about building a wall on the border with Mexico during the 2016 U. S. presidential campaign were "uninformed." Kelly says that the United States will never actually construct a wall across the entire 2,000 mile span, and that the Mexican government won't pay for it. Trump tweets a response claiming that "the wall will be paid for, directly or indirectly, or through longer term reimbursement from Mexico," He follows with another tweet which says, "the wall is the wall, it has never changed from the first day I conceived it." **1/17/18**

▪ The president's *Fake News Awards* appear on Twitter, with FOX News anchors announcing the "winners." The program goes largely unnoticed by the public, and creates no major media buzz. **1/17/18**

▪ Carl Higbie, a Trump appointee who runs the external affairs unit in the Corporation for National and Community Service, resigns after six months in office after CNN uncovers racist statements he made about African-Americans and Muslims in 2013. **1/19/18**

▪ Donald Trump misspeaks at the annual March for Life event in Washington, with the following quote, "Right now, in a number of states, the laws allow a baby to be born from his or her mother's womb in the ninth month.. It is wrong; It has to change." The White House issues a statement immediately afterwards, claiming that Trump meant to say "torn," not "born." **1/19/18**

■ The president, on the day of the annual Women's March (1/20), tweets, "Beautiful weather all over our great country, a perfect day for all women to march. Get out and celebrate the historic milestones and unprecedented economic success and wealth creation that have taken place over the last 12 months. Lowest female unemployment in 18 years." **1/20/18**

■ Donald Trump's re-election campaign releases a 30 second ad which is critical of Senate Democrats' role in the government shutdown issue. The ad promises to build a border wall with Mexico to increase security, and attacks Democrats who oppose the spending plan. The ad reads, "Democrats who stand in our way will be complicit in every murder committed by illegal immigrants." Senator Bernie Sanders (I-VT) calls the spot, "really unbelievable and so sad for our country." While House Speaker Paul Ryan states that he doesn't know if the ad is "productive." **1/22/18**

■ In a Politico interview, Family Research Council President Tony Perkins says that Donald Trump would get a "do-over" with regards to his alleged affair with porn actress Stormy Daniels. Perkins claims that evangelicals are willing to give Trump a "mulligan" because they were "tired of being kicked around by Barak Obama and his leftists." **1/23/18**

■ Some members of the U.S. Senate claim that there is a "secret society" involving those who are trying to undermine the presidency of Donald Trump, which includes members of the government and the FBI. Fueled by reports of lost emails between Peter Strzok and Lisa Page (romantically linked FBI agents who were removed from the Russia investigation by Robert S. Mueller, following the discovery of anti-Trump emails), Rep. Trey Gowdy (R-SC) seizes on a text exchange between the two agents that refers to a "secret society." To further fan the flames of controversy, Senator Ron Johnson (R-WI.) claims that "I have heard from somebody who has talked to our committee (Senate Homeland) that there is a group of individuals in the FBI who are holding secret off-site meetings." Johnson, who refuses to release his source, plans to ask the Department of Justice to aggressively investigate the situation. **1/24/18**

■ Donald Trump reverses field when asked if he would agree to be interviewed by special counsel Robert S. Mueller, stating, "We'll see what happens." When pressed by the media as to whether or not he would agree to such a meeting, Trump repeatedly defends his position by saying there was "no collusion" between his campaign and Russia during the 2016 U.S. presidential election. In June 2017, Trump told reporters that he's "100 percent" ready to testify for Mueller if asked to. **1/24/18**

■ The White House contacts the Guggenheim Museum to borrow a Vincent Van Gough painting for display in First Lady Melania Trump's private living quarters, and is rebuffed. Instead of the Van Gough painting *Landscape With Snow*, the Guggenheim's curator offers up an alternative piece of artwork, an 18-karat, fully functioning solid gold toilet, entitled *America*. The display has been described as a metaphor for U.S. wealth and waste. **1/25/18**

■ The *New York Times* reports that inside informants claim Donald Trump ordered White House counsel Don McGahn to fire special counsel Robert S. Mueller III in June of 2017, due to the Russia investigation. McGahn did not follow the president's order, and reportedly threatened to quit if he were made to comply. When questioned about the accusation, Trump called the report "fake news." **1/25/18**

■ After nearly a year of criticism from the president, FBI Deputy Director Andrew McCabe resigns his position from the bureau. McCabe had been attacked by Trump for supposed bias in favor of Hillary Clinton, which involved his wife taking $500,000 in campaign contributions from Clinton ally Terry McAuliffe (then-governor of Virginia), in a failed Democratic run for the Virginia legislature. **1/30/18**

■ In an unprecedented move, FBI Director Christopher A. Wray issues a public rebuke to the president, criticizing his intent to publish a House Intelligence Committee memorandum that calls into question surveillance of a former Trump campaign adviser. Wray privately warns the White House against releasing the memo, but when it becomes apparent that the FBI's warnings weren't being taken seriously, he issues a two-paragraph message to the press. "With regard to the House Intelligence Committee's memorandum, the FBI was provided a limited opportunity to review this memo the day before the Committee voted to release it. As expressed during our initial review, we have grave concerns about material omissions of fact that fundamentally impact the memo's accuracy," the statement reads. **1/31/18**

CHAPTER 14

MAYBE IT WAS THE blah weather, but February was a relatively quiet month in the Trump universe. The president starts out by claiming that his State of the Union speech had the highest television ratings ever, but once again, like his boasts of inaugural crowd size, Trump's pants remain perpetually on fire.

Donald Trump's designated protester, VP Mike Pence, more or less "takes a knee" while refusing to stand for the combined North/South Korea Winter Olympic team procession as they march by the presentation podium. Oddly enough, Pence caused quite the hullabaloo when he walked out of an NFL game last fall when players were kneeling in protest. Confused? So are we.

Donald Trump's alleged extra-marital affairs continue to surface, as a magazine article claims that a Trump surrogate paid 1998 Playmate of the year Karen McDougal $150,000 to keep her quiet about a supposed dalliance. If you're keeping score on Trump, that's two women (including Stormy Daniels), and $280,000 paid. Some *Art of the Deal*, huh?

Showing his "Rambo" side, the president weighs in on how he would have reacted if he had been at the scene of the horrific Parkland, Florida school shootings by saying "I believe I'd run in there," (to protect the students). Critics of "Cadet Bone Spurs" claim that he'd probably be running in the opposite direction; in a hurry.

And finally, poor, overworked First Son-in-Law Jared Kushner loses his "top secret" clearance at the White House. Now, WHO is going to plan that doggone military parade?

- Donald Trump claims that his State of the Union speech has the highest ratings ever for a presidential address. The Nielsen rating service however, reports this statement to be untrue, with speeches given by numerous preceding presidents (including Pres. Bush, Clinton, and Obama), having had larger audiences than Trump's. **2/1/18**

- The president orders release of the House Intelligence Committee's partisan memo on the Russia investigation. The declassified memo comes under immediate scrutiny for its lack of concrete findings that the FBI or Justice Department acted improperly in their inquiry surrounding the Trump campaign and Russian influence during the 2016 U.S. presidential election. Nevertheless, Donald Trump takes to Twitter to proclaim that the Republican memo, "Totally vindicates 'Trump' in probe." This follows earlier comments from the president regarding findings in the memo, who previously stated, "I think it's a disgrace what's happening to our country." Trump also opines, "A lot of people should be ashamed of themselves and much worse than that." **2/2/18**

- The president criticizes Democrats during his State of the Union address, calling them "un-American," and he agrees with a shouting member of the crowd that the Democrats were "treasonous." The White House issues a statement that Trump's comment was made in a "tongue- in-cheek" manner. **2/5/18**

- Donald Trump threatens to shut down the U.S. Government if Congress doesn't move to fix perceived faults in the nation's immigration policy regarding the deportation of criminal gang members. **2/6/18**

- The *Washington Post* reports that the president has ordered the Pentagon to plan a grand military parade in Washington, D.C. during the year, in order to showcase U.S. military might. Trump reportedly wants a parade, "like the one in France," (which he attended with French president Macron during a Bastille Day celebration in 2017). **2/6/18**

▌ Top White House aide Rob Porter resigns his position after reports surface that he had abused both of his ex-wives. Chief of Staff John F. Kelly, following public allegations, praises Porter as a "man of integrity and honor." After a picture is published of one of Porter's ex-wives (Colbie Holderness) with a black eye, supposedly from Porter, Kelly continues to praise him, and condemns domestic violence in the same statement. The president, commenting on Porter's resignation, says, "it's a, obviously tough time for him" Trump also acknowledges that he was "sad" to learn of the violence allegations, but continues to defend Porter by stating, "As you probably know, he says he's innocent. And I think you have to remember that." Following that remark, Trump follows up a few days later by tweeting, "Peoples (sic) lives are being shattered and destroyed by a mere allegation. Some are true, and some are false. Some are old, and some are new. There is no recovery for someone falsely accused-life and career are gone. Is there no such thing as due process?" Critics immediately seize on Trump's tweet, claiming that he did not include any condemnation of spousal abuse. **2/7/18**

▌ Vice President Mike Pence, while attending the Winter Olympics at Pyeongchang, South Korea, refuses to stand during the Opening Ceremonies when the combined athletes of North and South Korea pass in front of leaders from both nations, where Pence and his wife were seated. Critics are quick to point out the hypocrisy of Pence sitting to protest at a sporting event, while the White House condemns NFL players from taking a knee during the National Anthem at pro football games in the U.S. **2/9/18**

▌ Donald Trump announces that he will not de-classify a memo drafted by Democrats which responds to a memo released by Republicans, that addresses supposed government surveillance of Trump and his associates by the FBI during the Russia investigation. His reason for not releasing the memo is that it supposedly contains, "numerous properly classified and especially sensitive passages," but that he would re-address its release if the proper revisions are made. **2/10/18**

■ Longtime Trump attorney Michael Cohen admits that he personally paid $130,000 to adult film actress Stormy Daniels, in response to accusations that she was paid "hush money" directly from the Trump Organization or Trump presidential campaign, which could be considered an unreported campaign expense. Cohen does not say why he paid Daniels just before the 2016 U.S. presidential election, or whether Trump reimbursed him, or knew about the payment. **2/13/18**

■ After several days of conflicting statements from the White House as to what was known about Rob Porter's domestic violence episodes, The FBI reveals to the Senate Intelligence Committee that their investigation of Porter had been concluded by late summer, and that it was not "ongoing" as claimed by members of the Trump administration. FBI Director Christopher A. Wray, tells members of the committee that his bureau had concluded its investigation, and besides providing White House Council several bits of updated information on Porter, was no longer involved in an active probe of his past actions. **2/14/18**

■ The *New Yorker Magazine* publishes a story that claims Donald Trump had an extra-marital affair with a former playboy centerfold, who was paid $150,000 for her story from the tabloid *National Enquirer*, which then buried the story from being published. The alleged liaison with 1998 Playmate of the Year Karen McDougal, supposedly happened in July 2006, while Trump was attending a Lake Tahoe celebrity golf tournament. **2/16/18**

■ Special Counsel Robert S. Mueller III issues indictments against 13 Russian nationals who were involved in using U.S. social media to influence the 2016 U.S. presidential election. The 37 page indictment claims that Russian agents ran a highly coordinated attack against Democratic candidate Hillary Clinton, and that they sought to create discord among American voters beginning as far back as 2014. Donald Trump reacts to the indictments by tweeting, "Russia started their anti-U.S. campaign in 2014, long before I announced that I would run for president. The results of the election were not impacted. The Trump campaign did nothing wrong-no collusion!" **2/16/18**

▮ After a horrific school shooting in Parkland, Florida, in which 17 students and teachers were gunned down, Donald Trump backs a plan to arm between 20-40% of all U.S. teachers in classrooms, in order to deter further school shootings. Trump also proposes that these teachers be paid bonuses for being armed while in school. **2/22/18**

▮ The president, while speaking to dozens of U.S. governors at the White House about the Parkland, Florida school shootings, imagines the role he would have played to prevent armed assailant Nikolas Cruz from killing 17 students and educators by claiming, "You really don't know until you test it, but I think-I really believe I'd run in there, even if I didn't have a weapon." Trump makes the statement to governors while not clearly outlining a response to the most recent U.S. school shooting. Instead of proposing future policy, Trump instead states, "Don't worry about the NRA. They're on our side." **2/26/18**

▮ Jared Kushner, senior adviser and presidential son-in-law, has his national security clearance downgraded from the "top secret" to "secret" level, meaning that he would no longer have access to certain classified material that previously was made available to him while serving in the White House. The reasons given for the downgrade revolve around concerns that his lack of government experience and business debt could have left him vulnerable to foreign leverage during sensitive foreign negotiations. **2/27/18**

▮ One day after testifying before the House Intelligence Committee, Trump Communications Director Hope Hicks resigns her position with the White House. Hicks tells the committee that she had told several "white lies" for Trump while serving under the president. **2/28/18**

▮ Reports surface that after a series of meetings in the White House between Senior Adviser Jared Kushner and Joshua Harris, a founder of Apollo Global

Management in November, 2017. The private equity firm lent $184 million dollars to Kushner's real estate business, Kushner Companies, in order to help finance a mortgage on a Chicago skyscraper. Kushner Companies also accepted an even larger loan ($325 million) to help finance office buildings in Brooklyn, after Kushner had a White House meeting with Citigroup's chief executive, Michael L. Corbat in spring 2017. **2/28/18**

■ Embattled Attorney General Jeff Sessions pushes back against Donald Trump after the president complains about him on Twitter, saying that Sessions' response to Republican concerns about the FBI was "disgraceful." Sessions responds with a tweet of his own by stating that he will "continue to discharge my duties with integrity and honor." **2/28/18**

CHAPTER 15

ONE OF THE GREATEST pleasures for the anti-Trump crowd is watching Alec Baldwin's portrayal of Donald Trump on *Saturday Night Live.* But even though they say that imitation is the sincerest form of flattery, the president isn't amused. His tweet attack on "Alex" Baldwin goes nowhere, and one can only assume that "the Orange One" turns a bright shade of red each Saturday night when Baldwin appears on camera.

Donald Trump's month includes making up false statistics about the U.S.'s trade deficit with Canada, and later admits that he lied. Canadians just shrug and say "eh?" And, just to make sure that he's "large and in charge" of relations with foreign leaders, Trump congratulates Vladimir Putin for his Russian election "win," while ignoring briefing notes with the words "DO NOT CONGRATULATE" in rather large print in front of them. Maybe his aides should have used crayon?

The House Intelligence Committee shuts down their Russia investigation by stating that there was no collusion between Russia and the Trump campaign. Trump tweets the findings, and takes a victory lap. Mueller?..Mueller?..Mueller?

And, in a Trumpian "dead man walking" sequence, Secretary of State Rex Tillerson is given his exit papers in favor of CIA Director Mike Pompeo. Also, in magnanimous Trump fashion, public affairs staffer Steve Goldstein is canned for revealing that Tillerson learned he was fired by tweet, instead of during a face-to-face meeting. Wonder if Rex wants to double-down on that "moron" statement?

■ The president announces that he will impose tariffs of 25% on foreign-made steel, and 10% on foreign-made aluminum imported into the U.S. Trump makes the unexpected announcement, (which immediately rattled stock markets world-wide), and defends his decision via Twitter, by stating, "When a country (USA) is losing many billions of dollars on trade with virtually every country it does business with, trade wars are good, and easy to win." House Speaker Paul Ryan (R-WI), responds to Trump's decision by issuing a statement through a spokesperson which says, "We are extremely worried about the consequences of a trade war and we are urging the White House not to advance this plan." Ryan goes on to claim that the tariffs would "jeopardize" economic gains from the recently instituted GOP tax legislation. **3/1/18**

■ One day after Russian president Vladimir Putin announces to the world that his country now possesses a devastating nuclear missile designed to thwart U.S. missile intercept systems, Donald Trump engages in a Twitter war with actor Alec Baldwin, who portrays Trump in occasional sketches on NBC's *Saturday Night Live*. Trump tweets, "Alex (sic) Baldwin, whose dieng (sic) mediocre career was saved by his terrible impersonation of me on SNL, now says playing me was agony. Alex (sic), it was agony for those who were forced to watch. Bring back Darrell Hammond, funnier and a far greater talent!" The president's second version of the tweet corrects his misspellings and misidentification of Baldwin, whose name is spelled "Alec." Baldwin fires back with a response of his own by tweeting, "Agony though it may be, I'd like to hang in there for the impeachment hearings, the resignation speech, the farewell helicopter to Mara-A Lago. You know. The Good Stuff. That we've all been waiting for." **3/2/18**

■ Former Trump campaign staffer Sam Nunberg appears on CNN and MSNBC to claim that he will defy a grand jury subpoena from Special Counsel Robert S. Mueller III, stemming from the ongoing Russia investigation. Nunberg's interviews border on the bizarre, as he speculates that the president knew about the now-famous Russian Trump Tower meeting, and that Mueller was trying to prove that Nunberg's ally, lawyer Roger

Stone, was colluding with Julian Assange of WikiLeaks. The interviews are so unsettling that at one point CNN host Erin Burnett asks Nunberg if he had been drinking before he came on camera, because she smelled alcohol on his breath. **3/5/18**

■ Donald Trump's top economic adviser, Gary Cohn, resigns from his position in the White House due to a disagreement over Trump's proposed tariffs on imported steel and aluminum products. Cohn had strongly urged the president not to place the tariffs, arguing that it would negatively affect the U.S. economy, and result in a loss of jobs. **3/6/18**

■ The Stormy Daniels affair resurfaces in the news, as Daniels' lawyer Michael Avenatti argues that Donald Trump failed to sign the now-famous non-disclosure agreement stemming from an alleged affair between Daniels (whose real name is Stephanie Clifford) and Trump, which was brokered just weeks before the 2016 U.S. presidential election. Daniels threatens to publically reveal details about the affair, but Trump's lawyers file a temporary restraining order against her. Daniels then proceeds to sue Trump, and gives an interview to CBS's *60 Minutes* news program, which is not immediately aired. Michael Avenatti offers to have Daniels give back the $130,000 paid to her in order to eliminate the non-disclosure agreement. A deadline that is set for Trump to respond passes, and Avenatti tweets that it's time to "buckle up." **3/7/18**

■ The president accepts an invitation to meet with North Korean dictator Kim Jong un for nuclear disarmament talks. Reports indicate that the talks were most likely brokered by South Korean president Moon Jae-in. Trump teases an announcement of the upcoming meeting by appearing unannounced during a routine White House press briefing. Details of the planned meeting are fluid, without details of where the meeting would be held, who would participate, and what would be discussed. **3/9/18**

■ The president, in Pennsylvania to support GOP Congressional candidate Rick Saccone in a special election, gives a divisive, nearly 1 1/2 hour speech to a rabid crowd, while barely acknowledging the candidate. Trump instead uses the spotlight to advocate the death penalty for convicted drug dealers in the U.S. He also criticizes NBC News anchor Chuck Todd, (calling him a "sleeping son of a bitch"), CNN ("fake as hell"), and spews several falsehoods about the percentage of women who supported him in the 2016 U.S. presidential election (saying that 52% of all women voted for him when it was actually 52% of white women). Trump also calls out Sen. Elizabeth Warren (D-MA), by referring to her as "Pocahontas," and insults Rep. Maxine Waters (D-CA), by saying that she is a "low IQ individual." **3/11/18**

■ Donald Trump reverses field on gun control issues such as raising the age limit for purchasing assault rifles and universal background checks, and instead, promotes an NRA-backed proposal to arm teachers in the classroom. **3/12/18**

■ The House Intelligence Committee announces that they are shutting down their Russia investigation with findings that there was no collusion between Donald Trump's election campaign and Russia. The committee's report is issued by the Republican majority and had no input from Democratic members who were preparing their own response. Meanwhile, Donald Trump, giddy from the news, takes to Twitter to celebrate. Trump Tweets, "THE HOUSE INTELLIGENCE COMMITTEE HAS AFTER A 14 MONTH LONG IN-DEPTH INVESTIGATION, FOUND NO EVIDENCE OF COLLUSION OR COORDINATION BETWEEN THE TRUMP CAMPAIGN AND RUSSIA TO INFLUENCE THE 2016 PRESIDENTIAL ELECTION." **3/12/18**

■ The president, ending a stormy relationship with Rex Tillerson, fires his Secretary of State, and plans to replace him with CIA Director Mike Pompeo. Steve Goldstein, the undersecretary of state for public diplomacy and public affairs is also fired after informing the press that Tillerson learned about the firing from a Twitter post by Trump, and not by a phone call or face-to-face meeting. **3/13/18**

■ The president admits during a fundraising speech that he made up a fact that claimed the U.S. had a trade deficit with Canada, and tried to convince Canadian Prime Minister Justin Trudeau of the validity of his claim. Trudeau did not agree with Trump's assessment, and challenged him on it. **3/15/18**

■ Attorney General Jeff Sessions fires former FBI Deputy Director Andrew McCabe, only two days before he was to retire from the agency, setting up a possible loss of pension benefits. Sessions claims that the firing was necessary because both the Justice Department inspector general and a special disciplinary office of the FBI declared that McCabe made unauthorized disclosures to the press, and lacked "candor" during recent testimony. McCabe immediately issues a statement criticizing his termination, which said, in part, "This attack on my credibility is one part of a larger effort not just to slander me personally, but to taint the FBI, law enforcement, and intelligence professionals more generally. It is part of this Administration's ongoing war on the FBI and the efforts of the Special Counsel investigation which will continue to this day." McCabe also adds, "Their persistence in this campaign only highlights the importance of the Special Counsel's work." **3/16/18**

■ It is reported an analytics firm that played a key role in Donald Trump's 2016 presidential campaign, was suspended from Facebook for violating their terms of service agreement regarding personal data sharing. Cambridge Analytica used personal information from Facebook, and improperly shared it for use by clients. In response to the news, Massachusetts Attorney General, Maura Healy states that she will open up an official probe of the social media giant, and its ties to Cambridge Analytica. **3/17/18**

■ Donald Trump fires off an angry stream of tweets aimed at Robert S. Mueller III's Russia investigation. Trump tweets in one of his attacks, "Why does the Mueller team have 13 hardened Democrats, some big Crooked Hillary supporters, and zero Republicans? Another Dem. recently added... does anyone think this is fair? And yet, there is NO COLLUSION!"

Trump follows up with another tweet, stating, "The Mueller probe should have never been started in that there was no collusion and there was no crime. It was based on fraudulent activities and a Fake Dossier paid for by Crooked Hillary and the DNC, and improperly used in FISA COURT for surveillance of my campaign. WITCH HUNT!" Trump's personal attorney John Dowd calls for an end of the Mueller probe, but lawmakers on both sides of the aisle warn of serious consequences if the president were to interfere in the investigation. **3/17/18**

■ The president launches into new attacks on fired FBI Director James Comey and his former deputy, Andrew McCabe (also fired), claiming that memos the two men made during conversations with him are "Fake Memos." Both Comey and McCabe claim to have written memos based on meetings with Trump, mainly to protect themselves from blowback from the president and other White House staffers. **3/17/18**

■ Donald Trump's national security advisers urge him not to congratulate Vladimir Putin on his "victory" in the recently-held Russian presidential election. Reports surface that before Trump placed the call, he was given a note in his security briefing notes that stated, "DO NOT CONGRATULATE." Trump not only congratulates Putin, but fails to bring up several other issues with the Russian leader, including the recent gas poisoning of a former Russian agent and his daughter in Britain with a powerful nerve agent. **3/20/18**

■ John Dowd, one of Donald Trump's lead attorneys handling the Russian probe, resigns from his post in the West Wing. It is speculated that Dowd's legal philosophy of cooperation with the Mueller investigation led to him falling into disfavor with the president. **3/22/18**

■ In an ongoing succession of staff changes in the White House, Donald Trump removes H.R. McMaster from his post of national security adviser and replaces him with FOX News commentator and former U.N. Ambassador John Bolton. Bolton becomes Trump's third national security adviser in his first 14 months in office. The firing was made despite assurances by press secretary Sarah Huckabee Sanders that McMaster's position was safe. Sanders tweets, "Just spoke @POTUS and Gen. H.R. McMaster. Contrary to reports, they have a good working relationship and there are no changes at the NSC." **3/22/18**

■ Over one million U.S. citizens participate in the "March for Our Lives" protests, led primarily by students. The gun control demonstrations occur in hundreds of cities across America, but draw no statement from Donald Trump, who flies to Mar-a-Lago for a weekend getaway. **3/24/18**

■ The president announces that Joseph diGenova, a lawyer and FOX News contributor, will not join his legal team to help represent him in the Russia investigation, as was previously announced. Trump reportedly could not reach an agreement with diGenova and wife Victoria Toensing (a partner in her husband's law firm) after a formal White House interview. **3/25/18**

■ Stormy Daniels, the adult film actress who claims she had an extra-marital affair with Donald Trump in 2006, is interviewed by CBS's *60 Minutes*. During the segment with Anderson Cooper, Daniels definitively states that her one-time affair did occur, despite previous written claims to the contrary. The actress defends her denials, and claims they were due to threats by Trump lawyer Michael Cohen, and from an unknown man who physically threatened her in a parking lot in Las Vegas, in front of her then-infant daughter. Although the White House issues a statement denying Daniels' claims after the interview airs, the president makes no comments to the press, or on Twitter, about Daniels. **3/26/18**

■ David Shulkin, the embattled head of the Department of Veterans' Affairs, announces that he is leaving his cabinet post. He is replaced by Donald Trump's personal physician, Rear Admiral Ronny L. Jackson. The Shulkin departure marks the highest turnover rate in cabinet positions from a U.S. presidency, who was elected, and did not succeed another president. **3/28/18**

■ Donald Trump calls Roseanne Barr to congratulate her on the success of her ABC re-boot of the sitcom *Roseanne*, in which she plays a Trump supporter (as she is in real life). **3/29/18**

■ Donald Trump slams Amazon, which is owned by Jeff Bezos, (who also owns the *Washington Post*), over payment of taxes on Internet purchases by consumers. Trump tweets, "I have stated my concerns with Amazon long before the election. Unlike others, they pay little or no taxes to state and local governments, use our Postal System as their Delivery Boy (causing tremendous loss to the U.S.), and are putting many thousands of retailers out of business." According to Amazon's most recent tax filings, the company reportedly paid $100 million to $200 million in taxes at the state level in 2017. **3/29/18**

CHAPTER 16

APRIL, 2018

THE MONTH OF APRIL contains no "confusion" (when U.N. ambassador Nikki Haley smacks down the White House by accusing her of not being informed on certain issues), and an incredibly large "illusion" (Trump's false claims that the U.S. is being invaded by "large caravans" of people on the southern border).

Media becomes a centerpiece of Donald Trump's month, as word of Sinclair Communication's "must-run" news segments supporting the president and his agenda draw widespread condemnation from, uh, media professors across the nation. Trump's view? The fake media from Sinclair is real, and the real media from everyone else is….well, fake! Go figure.

After trashing James Comey's new book, *A Higher Loyalty*, his book sales skyrocket. Trump; the nation's nightmare, a publicist's dream.

April also brings the on again-off again DACA kerfluffle, a hasty withdrawal of White House "frat brother" Ronny L. Jackson's name from consideration to head the Department of Veterans' Affairs, the sunset of House Speaker and Trump apologist Paul Ryan, and the continual bubbling up of accusations from Stormy Daniels (one half of Trump's, uh, "close friends with nearly $300,000 of "benefits").

And this month, we also find out that the United States military has a new classification of weaponry, as Donald Trump tells both Syria and Russia that we will be sending missiles their way that will be "nice, new, and smart." This is apparently an attempt by the White House to justify increased military spending to replace missiles that were, "surly, aged, and intellectually-challenged."

■ The president uses the backdrop of Easter Sunday to tweet that he is ending any hope for millions of undocumented children in the U.S. (known as "Dreamers"), to stay in the country. Donald Trump tweets, "NO MORE DACA DEAL," and instructs Republicans in Congress to pass tough anti-immigration laws. Trump also threatens Mexico with an American withdrawal from NAFTA if they do not do more to secure their border with the U.S. The president goes on to tweet about FOX News reports of "large caravans of people" coming into the U.S. illegally. **4/1/18**

■ Sinclair Broadcasting, owners of 173 television stations in 81 U.S. markets, issues a "must-run" editorial piece for all of their affiliates, which echoes Donald Trump's attack on the media and "fake news." Trump seizes on the reports by tweeting, "So funny to watch Fake News Networks, among the most dishonest groups of people I have ever dealt with, criticize Sinclair Broadcasting for being biased." Trump follows up with another tweet the following day, stating, "The Fake News Networks, those that knowingly have a sick and biased AGENDA, are worried about the competition and quality of Sinclair Broadcast. The "Fakers" at CNN, NBC, ABC, and CBS have done so much dishonest reporting that they should only be allowed to get awards for fiction." **4/2/18**

■ During a roundtable discussion in West Virginia, Donald Trump tosses his prepared talking point notes into the air, and begins to wander off script. Trump rambles on about many topics that have drawn his ire in the past, and once again raises claims that millions of illegal immigrants voted during the 2016 U.S. presidential election. **4/5/18**

■ A fire at Trump Tower in Manhattan kills one man (a resident), and injures several firefighters fighting the blaze. Donald Trump responds to the news (ignoring any personal suffering), tweeting, "Fire at Trump Tower is out. Very confined (well-built building). Firemen (and women) did a great job. THANK YOU!" **4/8/18**

- Numerous college journalism schools sign and publish a letter condemning Sinclair Broadcasting's "must-run" corporate statement on the media, where local news anchors are instructed to read a script that echoes Donald Trump's frequent attacks on what he calls "fake news." **4/7/18**

- Michael Cohen, Donald Trump's longtime personal attorney, falls under federal investigation for possible bank and wire fraud, along with campaign finance violations. Agents from the FBI raid Cohen's residence, Manhattan office, and hotel room simultaneously, seizing records related to the Stormy Daniels payment, and other personal finance information. Donald Trump responds to the raid by commenting, "It's a disgrace, it's an attack on our country in a true sense. It's an attack on all we stand for." Trump also states, "Attorney-client privilege is dead." **4/9/18**

- White House homeland security adviser Tom Bossert resigns his position with the Trump administration, just one day after national security adviser John Bolton begins his job. Reports surface that Bolton had asked for Bossert's resignation. **4/10/18**

- House Speaker Paul Ryan announces that he will not seek re-election, and will leave Congress when his term ends. The move sends shockwaves through the GOP, which is facing difficult 2018 midterm elections, as Democrats, angry and frustrated with Donald Trump, mount serious challenges to incumbent Republicans in both the House and Senate. **4/11/18**

- After chemical weapons attacks on Syrian civilians by the regime of Bashar-al-Assad, the president promises military action against the Syrian government, and tweets a warning to Syrian ally, Russia, telling them to "get ready," because American missiles "will be coming, nice and new, and smart." White House press secretary Sarah Huckabee Sanders tries to walk back the president's comments, saying, "We're maintaining that we have a number of options, and all of those options are still on the table." She also says, "Final decisions haven't been made on that front." **4/11/18**

- Donald Trump lashes out at former FBI Director James Comey, in the wake of Comey's upcoming book, "A Higher Loyalty." Trump's tweets aim to discredit Comey, by calling him a "LEAKER & LIAR," and a "Weak and untruthful slime ball." Trump's Twitter attacks also claim that Comey botched the investigation of Hillary Clinton's emails, and that it was a "great honor" to have fired him. **4/13/18**

- James Comey, in an interview with ABC News says that Donald Trump is "morally unfit," to be president, and that it was "possible" that the Russians had materials that could be used to blackmail him. Trump tweets a response, claiming, "Slippery James Comey, a man who always ends up badly and out of whack (he is not smart!), will go down as the WORST FBI Director in history, by far!" After the interview airs on ABC, Trump fires off another Tweet, saying that "Comey and (former FBI Deputy Director) Andrew McCabe (and others) committed many crimes." **4/15/18**

- The Michael Cohen legal case takes an interesting turn as Cohen reveals that FOX's Sean Hannity is one of his three clients. Hannity denies that he is a client of Cohen's, but says that he had a "minor relationship" with him. **4/16/18**

- Stormy Daniels releases an artist's sketch of the man she said threatened her to remain silent about her alleged affair with Donald Trump. After airing the sketch on ABC's *The View*, the president responds with a tweet, "A sketch years later about a nonexistent man. A total con job, playing the Fake News Media for Fools (but they know it)." **4/17/18**

- U. S. ambassador to the United Nations, Nikki Haley, announces tough, new sanctions against Russia, only to have the White House walk them back within 24 hours. Chief White House economic adviser Larry Kudlow tells CNN that Haley, "got ahead of the curve," and that "there might have been some momentary confusion" by the ambassador. Haley responds a short time later in a statement saying, "With all due respect, I don't get confused." The war of words revolves around the White House's insistence that sanctions against Russia were not fully agreed to, verses reports that Donald Trump changed his mind about the sanctions. **4/17/18**

- The president once again lashes out at former FBI Director James Comey after the release of his book *A Higher Loyalty*. Trump states his displeasure by tweeting, "So General Michael Flynn's life can be totally destroyed while Shadey (sic) James Comey can Leak and Lie and make lots of money from a third rate book (that should have never been written). Is that really the way life in America is supposed to work? I don't think so." **4/20/18**

- The president lashes out at the *New York Times* for their article claiming that his personal lawyer Michael Cohen might "flip" against him if he is found guilty in the special counsel's investigation into the Trump campaign's connections to Russia. Trump tweets, "Sorry, I don't see Michael doing that, despite the horrible Witch Hunt and the dishonest media!.... non-existent 'sources' and a drunk/drugged up loser who hates Michael, a fine person with a wonderful family." **4/21/18**

- Donald Trump admits that lawyer Michael Cohen did indeed represent him in the ongoing Stormy Daniels accused affair. Trump says during a telephone interview with FOX News' *Fox and Friends* program, that "Michael represents me, like with this crazy Stormy Daniels deal, he represented me." Trump also tries to downplay Cohen's importance to his overall legal representation by stating, "As a percentage of my overall legal work, (he did) a tiny, tiny fraction." **4/26/18**

- As accusations against him mount, White House physician Ronny L. Jackson withdraws his name from consideration to head the Department of Veterans Affairs. Jackson, Trump's personal doctor, had been accused of professional misconduct, including several incidents of drunken behavior, improperly handling out medications without reviewing patient history, and contributing to a hostile work environment. **4/26/18**

■ The president greets U.S. Winter Olympians and members of the U.S. Paralympics team at the White House and demeans the paralympic athletes by stating that he watched their competitions uneasily. Trump's comment was, "and I watched- it's a little tough to watch too much, but I watched as much as I could." **4/27/18**

CHAPTER 17

MAY IN TRUMP-LAND BEGINS with a story about the sacking of Trump's longtime personal physician's office by the president's emissaries to uh, "retrieve" his medical records. One can only assume they were looking for things like bone spurs, and maladies related to The Donald's "adventurous" history with women.

Word leaks out about what questions Robert S. Mueller III would like to ask the president if he agrees to testify about his campaign's ties to Russia. Like his daily security briefings, Trump's lawyers show the questions to him in bullet-point fashion, with colorful pictures, so he won't get distracted and start tweeting.

Rudy Giuliani, America's favorite crazy uncle, says during an interview that the Founding Fathers created immunity for a sitting president. That rumbling sound you hear is the turbine-like speed at which Washington, Adams, Hamilton, Jefferson, and the other FF's are spinning in their graves over Rudy's balderdash.

Donald Trump cancels a meeting planned with Korea's Kim Jong un, beginning a pattern of breakups and make ups that would make a love-struck high school couple blush. "He loves me, he hates me."

And to wrap up May, the president shows his displeasure with the cancellation of ABC's re-boot of *Roseanne*, after the show's star engages in an Ambien-fired racist smackdown of Valerie Jarrett. Reports surface that the president wasn't as upset with the cancellation as he was with ABC's refusal to re-create *The Apprentice* with Trump reprising his famous role, featuring members of the White House cabinet as contestants.

▋ Donald Trump's longtime personal physician, Dr. Harold N. Bornstein, tells reporters that the president's bodyguard, lawyer, and another man entered his office and took all of Donald Trump's medical files. Dr. Bornstein, who did not file a police complaint, said that he felt "raped, frightened, and sad" during the incident which allegedly occurred in February, 2017, likening it to "a raid." The physician decided to come forward only after witnessing the treatment of Dr. Ronny L. Jackson, who recently withdrew his name as a nominee to run the Department of Veterans Affairs. **5/1/18**

▋ The *New York Times* releases a series of questions they say were crafted by special counsel Robert S. Mueller III's team to ask the president if they were to interview him in the ongoing Russia investigation. Although no one claims responsibility for the leaked questions, the *Times* states that their sources were not members of Trump's legal team. Trump reacts predictably, sending tweets that call the release "disgraceful," and that Mueller's investigation is a "witch hunt." **5/1/18**

▋ The Trump legal team has another shake-up, as White House lawyer Ty Cobb announces his retirement, and is replaced by Emmet Flood. Flood previously represented Bill Clinton during House impeachment proceedings while he was president. **5/2/18**

▋ Rudolph Giuliani, representing Donald Trump in the Russia investigation as part of his legal team, proclaims that the president is immune from being subpoenaed by Robert S. Mueller III's probe. Giuliani claims that the "Founding Founders" created immunity for a seated president, something the Supreme Court has never defended. In the same interview (with Fox News Channel's Sean Hannity), Giuliani states that Donald Trump has indeed made a series of payments reimbursing his attorney Michael Cohen for the $130,000 payment made to Stormy Daniels. Trump had previously disavowed any knowledge of money being paid to the adult film actress. **5/3/18**

▪ The president makes a decision to withdraw the U.S. from the Iran nuclear agreement, citing that the Obama-era pact was "defective to its core," and that the U.S. would immediately re-impose sanctions on Iran, which were lifted after the initial agreement was signed. None of the other original nations in the pact (China, Russia, Germany, the U.K., and France) join the U.S. in its actions. **5/8/18**

▪ Clearly frustrated that the news media is not airing favorable coverage of his administration, an angry Donald Trump lashes out on Twitter. Trump posts, "The Fake News is working overtime. Just reported that, despite the tremendous success, we are having with the economy and all things else, 91% of the Network News about me is negative (Fake). Why do we work so hard in working with the media when it is corrupt? Take away credentials?" **5/9/18**

▪ Homeland Security Secretary Kirstjen Nielsen nearly resigns her position after being berated by Donald Trump during a closed-door cabinet meeting in the White House. Trump, angry about the reported number of illegal aliens crossing the U.S. border with Mexico, reportedly lashes out at Nielsen, claiming that the solution is to, "shut it down," and also yelling, "We're closed." The back and forth argument lasts nearly 30 minutes, and results in Nielsen drafting a letter of resignation, according to inside sources. **5/10/18**

▪ Kelly Sadler, a press aide in the White House, dismisses Sen. John McCain's (R-AZ) opposition to Gina Haspel's confirmation as CIA Director, by saying, "he's dying anyway," during a meeting on the upcoming vote. The leaked remark draws sharp criticism from both sides of the political aisle. Sen. Lindsey O. Graham (R-SC) remarks, "It's (a) pretty disgusting thing to say. If it was a joke, it was a terrible joke." **5/11/18**

▪ During an immigration roundtable discussion in Fresno, California, the president makes several disparaging remarks regarding asylum seekers, and refers to certain immigrants as "animals." **5/16/18**

■ The *New York Times* reports that Donald Trump, Jr. met with princes from Saudi Arabia and the United Arab Emirates (UAE), along with an Israeli social media expert who were eager to help his father, Donald Trump Sr., win the 2016 U.S. presidential election. The meeting was arranged by Eric Prince, former head of Blackwater, a major private security contractor, and speaks to the possibility that other nations besides Russia were attempting to help elect Trump, which is illegal under U.S. law. **5/19/18**

■ The president, after continually tweeting about the now-year long Muller Russia investigation, calls on the Department of Justice to investigate whether an FBI agent infiltrated his presidential campaign, for political purposes. **5/20/18**

■ The president cancels a summit with North Korea's Kim Jong un, citing the "tremendous anger and open hostility" shown by the Korean leader. Trump says that meeting Kim at this time would be "inappropriate." North Korea's statements also include referring to Vice President Pence as a "political dummy," due to his comments about the North Korean government. **5/24/18**

■ In a series of tweets over Memorial Day weekend, the president attempts to blame Democrats for immigrant families being separated during detainment. Trump tweets for his followers to, "put pressure on the Democrats to end the horrible law that separates children from their parents." Trump's tweets are roundly debunked, as no such law exists. **5/26/18**

■ Roseanne Barr is fired from her re-booted ABC sitcom *Roseanne* following incendiary remarks and racist tweets she made about Valerie Jarrett, a former Clinton aide. Donald Trump responds to Barr's firing by tweeting that Disney Chief Bob Iger (which owns ABC) is displaying a double standard because Iger contacted Jarrett after the comments were made, but never contacted Trump when he was being treated "unfairly" by ABC. Trump tweets, "Iger, where is my call of apology? You and ABC have offended millions of people, and they demand a response. How is Brian Ross (ABC News reporter) doing? He tanked the market with an ABC lie, yet no apology. Double standard." **5/30/18**

CHAPTER 18

REMEMBER WHEN THE NFL Super Bowl champions used to stand in front of the White House as a team, holding a jersey with the president's name on the back of it? Well, it's now just a memory, because with Donald Trump as POTUS, It might be awhile before you see it again, as the NFL champion Philadelphia Eagles are "disinvited" because of their lack of commitment to attend the ceremony. Reports surface that a backup tackle, kicker, and "guy who hangs around the team a lot and smells like beer" are the only ones who say they'd show up.

The separation of children from the families of immigrants trying to enter the U.S. takes a nasty turn, as it is reported that nearly 2,000 children are being held in special facilities, like a shuttered Wal-Mart. Outrage across the nation is divided sharply between those who are shocked that children are being taken from their families, and those who can't believe that kids are actually being held in a Wal-Mart.

During the Group of Seven (G-7) meeting in Quebec City, the president demands that Russia and BFF Vladimir Putin be reinstated into the group, re-establishing the G-8. Only after members tell Trump that G-7 letterhead and business cards with his name on it have been ordered, and can't be cancelled, does he relent.

June finds Sarah Huckabee Sanders looking on Yelp for Trump-friendly restaurants in the D.C. area, as she is un-ceremoniously ousted from the Red Hen restaurant. Maybe she should have read the sign out front which read, "No shirt, No shoes, No admission that you speak for a morally-bankrupt administration, No service."

■ Rudy Giuliani, Donald Trump's lawyer, makes a claim that he (Trump) could shoot former FBI director James Comey in the Oval Office, and not be indicted for the crime while he was president. This follows a story from the *New York Times* in which Trump's lawyers claim in a memo to special counsel Robert S. Mueller III that the president had the legal powers to pardon anyone charged in the Russia probe. Additionally, the lawyers claim that as "chief law enforcement officer" of the country, Trump could terminate the probe, and that he does not have to submit to any subpoena from Mueller, if one were to be issued. **6/4/18**

■ Donald Trump "disinvites" the NFL champion Philadelphia Eagles from the traditional champions White House visit, because of low numbers of the team willing to commit to attending. Trump then uses Twitter to take a swipe at the NFL by posting, "Staying in the Locker Room for the playing of our National Anthem is as disrespectful to our country as kneeling, Sorry!" The White House also schedules an event in place of the Eagles' snub by arranging a "Celebration of America" rally on the White House lawn. Trump uses the hastily-arranged occasion to fan the flames of the NFL protest controversy, by once again deriding players who choose to kneel. **6/4/18**

■ During a phone call between Canadian Prime Minister Justin Trudeau and Donald Trump, the U.S. president states that the Canadians burned down the White House during the War of 1812, which is untrue. It is not clear whether Trump was joking, or did not actually know that it was British forces that burned down the White House to retaliate against a U.S. attack against the British colony of York, Ontario. **6/6/18**

■ In an extraordinary rebuke against the Group of Seven (G-7) leaders meeting in Quebec City, Donald Trump states that former member of the original Group of Eight (G-8), Russia, should be reinstated for membership. Russia was ousted from the then-G-8 due to its invasion of Ukraine, and annexation of Crimea. Most of the members of the G-7 (with the exception of Italy), remain strongly opposed to Trump's suggestion. **6/8/18**

■ Donald Trump engages in a verbal war with Canadian Prime Minister Justin Trudeau and the rest of the G-7 Summit, throwing the meeting into chaos. Trump refuses to sign the G-7's final communiqué after he tweets that Trudeau was "very dishonest and weak" where tariffs were concerned. **6/9/18**

■ After an historic summit meeting with North Korea leader Kim Jong un in Singapore, Donald Trump tells the American public that North Korea no longer poses a nuclear threat to the U.S. Trump tweets, "President (Barack) Obama said that North Korea was our biggest and dangerous problem. No longer-sleep well tonight." **6/13/18**

■ Donald Trump discovers that Kim Jong un's people are completely obedient to him, and points out that he'd like the same level of respect, by saying, "When he speaks, his people sit up in attention. I want my people to do the same." **6/15/18**

■ The battle on immigration heats up as the Trump administration's policy of separating immigrant children from their parents at the U.S. border continues. It is reported that children are transported to special holding facilities, including a shuttered Wal-Mart. Nearly 2,000 children are taken from their parents during a six-week period. Attorney General Jeff Sessions defends the administration's "Zero Tolerance" policy for illegal immigration by quoting Romans 13 from the Bible, stating that laws need to be followed "because God has ordained the government for his purposes." When questioned about the policy, White House press secretary Sarah Huckabee Sanders defends Sessions by saying, "It's the law, and that's what the law states." Donald Trump also enters the discussion, falsely claiming that it was "their (Democrats) law" that was causing family separations. Trump also says, "We have to break up families. The Democrats gave us that law, and they don't want us to do anything about it." **6/16/18**

■ Bowing to intense political and media pressure, the president abandons his administration's policy of separating migrant children from their parents when they are apprehended at the U.S. border with Mexico. **6/20/18**

■ First Lady Melania Trump boards an airplane bound for Texas to visit shelters holding migrant children, wearing a jacket proclaiming, "I REALLY DON'T CARE, DO U?" Mrs. Trump's spokesperson, Stephanie Grisham speaks in defense of the coat, by stating, "It's just a jacket. There was no hidden message." Donald Trump also weighs in on his wife's apparel by claiming that she wore the jacket to attack the "Fake News" media. **6/21/18**

■ Backlash against White House employees surfaces, as press secretary Sarah Huckabee Sanders is asked to leave a Lexington, Virginia restaurant after she sat down to order dinner with friends. Stephanie Wilkinson, owner of the Red Hen restaurant, states that the reason for asking Huckabee Sanders to leave has to do with her opposition to the Trump administration. Characteristically, the president weighs in on the affair on Twitter, posting, "The Red Hen Restaurant should focus more on cleaning its filthy canopies, doors, and windows (badly needs a paint job) rather than refusing to serve a fine person like Sarah Huckabee Sanders." **6/23/18**

■ Donald Trump, in a series of tweets, advocates taking away the legal rights of undocumented immigrants by denying them basic due-process rights when they cross the U.S. border. Trump tweets, "We cannot allow all of these people to invade our Country. When somebody comes in, we must immediately, with no Judges or Court Cases, bring them back from where they came." **6/25/18**

■ The president threatens the Harley-Davidson motorcycle company with massive taxes if they follow through with plans to move some manufacturing out of the country, in response to heavy European Union (E.U.) tariffs against their products. Trump accuses the company of using tariffs as an excuse for the company's long-planned relocation move. **6/26/18**

■ Donald Trump criticizes longtime NY Congressman Joe Crowley, who lost a Democratic primary to a political newcomer (Alexandria Ocasio-Cortez), by tweeting, "Wow! Big Trump Hater Congressman Joe Crowley, who many expected was going to take Nancy Pelosi's place, just LOST his primary election. In other words, he's out! That is a big one that nobody saw happening. Perhaps he should have been nicer and more respectful, to his president!" **6/27/18**

▌ A compromise House bill on immigration fails to pass by a vote of 301-121. The bill, which was negotiated by both the hardline Freedom caucus and GOP moderates, was first criticized, then supported by Donald Trump, who flip-flopped on his position, causing confusion with House members who sought guidance from the White House on the issue. **6/27/18**

▌ Protestors from across the U.S. demonstrate against the harsh immigration policies of the Trump administration during "Families Belong Together" rallies. More than 600 marches occur in cities in all 50 states, which protest Trump's policy of separating children of immigrants from their parents who enter the country illegally. **6/29/18**

CHAPTER 19

JULY WILL LONG BE remembered for Trump's meeting with Russia's Vladimir Putin, and whether the American people would/wouldn't believe he was siding with the dictator, and if he would/wouldn't be able to confuse everyone by saying that he would/wouldn't have said what he would/wouldn't have meant in the first place. Capisce?

Members of the Trump team continue to be bothered by "the great unwashed," who badger them in grocery stores, book shops, restaurants, and parking lots. Kellyanne Conway is told to "look in a mirror," by one heckler, and she supposedly replies, "I would, but I can't see my own reflection."

July also reportedly is the month when Donald Trump tells the public not to believe anything the media reports about him. And since they often report that he claims to be harder on Russia than any other president, we'll follow him on that one.

The "Trump Baby" balloon makes an appearance in London, and many people who see it claim that it is a stunning likeness of the president, an over-blown bag of wind that has to be tied down, lest is sail off in random directions.

Dribs and drabs for the month; Scott Pruitt, under fire, resigns his position with the EPA. Pruitt never actually understood what he was supposed to be doing, because he thought EPA means for "Every Pollutant Available." And July will long be remembered for Donald Trump claiming that U.S. citizens need to have ID with them in order to buy a box of Ho-Ho's at the grocery store.

▪ Donald Trump visits the U.K. on a stopover visit after the NATO summit, and faces massive protests from tens of thousands of Londoners who march in their city with a giant "Trump Baby" balloon at the center of the crowd. The inflatable, is a 20 foot tall depiction of a snarling Donald Trump in a diaper, with a cell phone in his right hand. **7/4/18**

▪ Scott Pruitt, head of the Environmental Protection Agency, resigns his post after being dogged by numerous controversies, based on ethical lapses, unbridled spending, and questionable management decisions. **7/5/18**

▪ Donald Trump mocks the #MeToo movement while speaking at a campaign rally in Montana, by stating that he'd need to toss the female Elizabeth Warren (D-MA) (who he again derided by referring to her as "Pocahontas") a DNA kit "gently" if he were to ask her to take such a test of supposed Native-American roots, because he is a male. Trump also uses the rally to attack Rep. Maxine Waters' (D-CA) IQ, by stating, "I mean honestly, she's somewhere in the mid-60's I believe." Trump also mocks former President George H.W. Bush during the rally, making fun of the "1000 points of light" speech from his presidency. **7/5/18**

▪ Reports surface that members of Donald Trump's inner circle are being heckled in and around Washington, when they appear in public. Kellyanne Conway is told to "look in a mirror" by a shopper in a D.C. supermarket. Senior Trump adviser Stephen Miller is "flipped off" by a bartender in a restaurant where he had ordered takeout sushi, causing him to throw away the food, fearing it had been tampered with by restaurant employees. Former member of Trump's White House, Stephen K. Bannon is called "a piece of trash" in a downtown bookstore. Members of Congress are also verbally assailed, as protesters call out, "Where are the babies, Mitch?" to Senate Majority Leader Mitch McConnell (R-KY) as he walks through a restaurant parking lot. **7/9/18**

▪ U.S. officials attempt to weaken an international resolution that promotes breast-feeding by mothers, in an effort to boost the sale of commercially produced infant-formula products. Trade consequences are threatened against Ecuador, a supporter of the breast-feeding policy, if they were to bring the resolution to the World Health Assembly floor. **7/8/18**

∎ Donald Trump meets with members of NATO, and immediately criticizes member nations for failing to reach the agreed-upon 2% of their GDP on defense spending, by demanding that all members hit the financial target as soon as possible, even though NATO agreements call for all members to be at 2% by 2024. Trump then ups the ante by suggesting the group of nations pledge to push their defense spending to 4% of GDP, which is higher than current U.S. contributions. The president also shocks NATO representatives by claiming that Germany is being held "captive to Russia" because of natural gas purchases they are making from them. **7/11/18**

∎ Special counsel Robert S. Mueller III indicts 12 Russians who are accused of hacking computers belonging to the Democratic National Committee (DNC). The incitements are issued against members of the Russian military agency, also known as the GRU, and reflect the first time that Mueller has directly linked a member of the Russian government as being involved in hacking U.S. interests. The indictments show that Russians were involved in compromising information from Hillary Clinton's campaign, in an attempt to influence the outcome of the 2016 U.S. presidential election. Muller's indictments also indicate that Russian hacking began in earnest the day after Donald Trump publically urged Russia to search for missing emails from the Clinton campaign. Trump's comment was, "Russia, if you're listening, I hope you're able to find the 30,000 emails that are missing," **7/13/18**

∎ In an almost unbelievable fashion, Donald Trump sides with Russian president Vladimir Putin against the findings of American intelligence agencies, by refusing to press Putin on Russian hacking of Democrats in order to interfere with the 2016 U.S. presidential election. After meeting with the Russian president in Helsinki, Finland, Trump, during a post-meeting press conference, instead accepts Putin's "extremely strong and powerful" denial that Russia had no involvement in hacking U.S. interests. Trump then proceeds to attack the ongoing Russia investigation, claiming that the Mueller probe is a "disaster for our country," and a "total witch hunt." Trump's actions are swiftly and widely criticized by politicians on both sides of the aisle, with numerous Democrats and Republicans banding together to condemn the president's remarks. **7/16/18**

■ One day after his tumultuous press conference with Russian president Vladimir Putin, the president tries to walk back several comments he made while on the podium about Russian election meddling. His first reversal is a statement that he meant to say, "I don't see any reason it *wouldn't* be Russia, instead of saying, "I don't see any reason why it *would* be Russia." Shortly thereafter, Trump also reverses field on Vladimir Putin's suggestion that the two nations exchange investigative teams to assist with the Mueller probe, and that he now believes Russia did interfere with the 2016 U.S. presidential election. **7/17/18**

■ Donald Trump sends a threatening message to Iranian president Hassan Rouhani via Twitter, in response to Rouhani's earlier tweet, warning nations that they would resist any outside attempts to destabilize their nation. Trump angrily tweets, "NEVER, EVER THREATEN THE UNITED STATES AGAIN OR YOU WILL SUFFER CONSEQUENCES THE LIKES OF WHICH FEW THROUGHOUT HISTORY HAVE EVER SUFFERED BEFORE. BE CAUTIOUS!" In response to Trump's all-caps tweet, House Speaker Paul Ryan responds that he thought the president was just "trolling" people. **7/22/18**

■ Shortly after claiming that he believes Russia interfered in an American election, the president changes his course and now states that Russian intervention in the 2016 U.S. presidential election is a "big hoax," **7/23/18**

■ The White House announces that the president is considering revoking security clearances for several members of U.S. security agencies who have been critical of his handling of the issue regarding Russian intervention in the 2016 U.S. presidential election. Targeted for clearance revocation are former FBI Director Michael Hayden, former FBI Director James Comey, former National Security Adviser Susan Rice, former FBI Deputy Director Andrew McCabe, former CIA Director John O. Brennan, and former Director of National Intelligence James R, Clapper, Jr. **7/23/18**

■ In an attempt to play down his remarks over Russian intervention during the 2016 U.S. presidential election, Donald Trump tries to change the narrative by tweeting, "I'm very concerned that Russia will be fighting very hard to have an impact on the upcoming Election. Based on the fact that no President has been tougher on Russia than me, they will be pushing very hard for the Democrats, They definitely don't want Trump." **7/24/18**

■ During a speech at the annual convention of the Veterans of Foreign Wars, Donald Trump tells the crowd to ignore what is being reported in the mainstream media, and only believe in what he says. Trump remarks, "Stick with us, don't believe the crap you see from these people." Trump's comments draw immediate comparisons to the dystopian novel *1984*, by George Orwell, when he wrote, "the party told you to reject the evidence of your eyes and ears. It was their final, most essential command." *7/24/18*

■ The president announces a $12 billion dollar emergency aid plan for farmers who are being adversely affected by Trump's new tariffs, during an ever-escalating trade war with other nations. The bailout is met with widespread derision by Republican senators Rand Paul (R-KY), and Ben Sasse (R-NE), among others, who criticize the president's tariffs, despite his insistence that his plan will work, and that the people need to "be a little patient." **7/24/18**

■ The attorney for embattled former Trump personal lawyer, Michael Cohen, releases a taped conversation between Trump and Cohen that sheds new light on the alleged Trump affair/payoff involving former Playboy model Karen McDougal, and American Media, Inc. (*National Enquirer*). The somewhat garbled tape recording confirms that Trump was aware of

AMI's payout of $150,000 to "catch and kill" McDougal's story of the affair with Trump, and Cohen's suggestion that Trump pay AMI for the rights to that story. **7/25/18**

■ Former Trump lawyer Michael Cohen drops a bombshell allegation that then-candidate Donald Trump knew in advance about a meeting between Donald Trump, Jr., Paul Manafort, Jared Kushner, and several Russians claiming to have compromising information on Hillary Clinton's campaign, which took place in Trump Tower in June, 2016. Cohen makes the accusation but has no additional information to back it up. **7/27/17**

■ In a stunning Twitter announcement, the president vows to shut down the U.S. government over immigration policy. Trump tweets, "I would be willing to 'shut down' government if the Democrats do not give us the votes for Border Security, which includes The Wall!" **7/29/18**

■ The trial of former Trump campaign chairman Paul Manafort begins. Manafort is charged with bank and tax fraud, revolving around his work with a Russia-friendly Ukrainian political party. The case is being prosecuted by the special counsel investigating Russian interference in the 2016 U.S. presidential election. **7/29/18**

■ Donald Trump engages in a Twitter war with leading conservative backer Charles Koch. After Koch, head of Koch Industries (and also a major financial contributor to GOP candidates) criticizes Trump's policy of tariffs, the president responds on social media, "The globalist Koch Brothers, who have become a total joke in real Republican circles are against Strong Borders and Powerful Trade. I never sought their support because I don't need their money or bad ideas." Trump also goes on to post, "I have beaten them at every turn." **7/31/18**

■ In another attempt to change the narrative on the Russia investigation, Donald Trump takes to Twitter to proclaim, "Collusion is not a crime, but that doesn't matter because there was No Collusion (except by Crooked

Hillary and Democrats!)." Trump had repeatedly stated in speeches and on Twitter that there was "no collusion" between his campaign and Russia leading up to the 2016 U.S. presidential election. **7/31/18**

▪ During a campaign rally speech in Tampa, Florida, Donald Trump states that citizens need personal ID to purchase groceries. The president was making a case that stricter voter identification was needed in the U.S., and used this false example to back up his claim. **7/31/18**

CHAPTER 20

"I LOVE A PARADE..." except when it costs around $22 million to host it. Due to a rather high price tag, Donald Trump is forced to postpone his wonderful military exhibition scheduled for November in Washington, D.C. As Trump grouses about the high costs of having the parade, thousands of tenants in various high-rent Trump properties around the country are screaming, "Karma, bitch!"

August 21st was a double-barreled shotgun blast for Donald Trump-due to the admissions of guilt from one close Trump surrogate, (personal lawyer Michael Cohen) and the conviction of another, (campaign chairman Paul Manafort) of federal crimes. The two men have a wealth of knowledge about Trump and his operation, both personal and political, and the possibility of "flipping" (exchanging evidence for a lighter sentence) remains a possibility, Trump suggests that this practice should be outlawed (snitches get stitches?).

The ever-beleaguered president rounds out the month by playing "flag-footsie" with recently departed Senator John McCain (R-AZ), by raising and lowering the American flag over the White House so much, the pole needed re-greasing. And if the McCain controversy wasn't enough for the "dog" days of summer, Donald Trump does his best impression of Humphrey Bogart in the *Caine Mutiny* by claiming that Google and other search engines were out to get him, with bad stories ("I would have produced that algorithm, but they fought me at every turn"). Hope your August was better than 45's!

■ Feeling increased pressure from Robert S. Mueller III's Russia investigation, Donald Trump opines that Attorney General Jeff Sessions should shut down the probe. Trump tweets, "This is a terrible situation and Attorney General Jeff Sessions should stop this Rigged Witch Hunt now, before it continues to stain our country any further. Bob Mueller is totally conflicted, and his 17 Angry Democrats that are doing his dirty work are a disgrace to the USA!" **8/1/18**

■ After hearing that NBA superstar LeBron James said in an interview with CNN's Don Lemon, that he found Trump to be divisive for the country, the president lashes out on Twitter, criticizing the intelligence of both men. Trump states on Twitter, "LeBron James was just interviewed by the dumbest man on Television, Don Lemon. He made LeBron look smart, which isn't easy to do." Shortly thereafter, First Lady Melania Trump praises James's creation of his "I Promise School" for at-risk children in his hometown of Akron, Ohio, which flies in the face of her husband's criticism. **8/4/18**

■ During another Trump tweetstorm, the president once again viciously attacks the press by posting, "The Fake News hates me saying that they are the Enemy of the People only because they know it's TRUE. I am providing a great service by explaining this to the American People. They purposely cause great division & distrust. They can also cause War! They are very dangerous & sick." **8/5/18**

■ Donald Trump admits that his son Donald Jr. met with a Kremlin-aligned lawyer during the 2016 U.S. presidential campaign in order to obtain damaging information about Hillary Clinton. In a tweet, Trump states, "Fake News reporting a complete fabrication, that I am concerned about the meeting my wonderful son, Donald, had in Trump Tower. This was a meeting to get information on an opponent, totally legal, and done all the time in politics-and it went nowhere." He also took the opportunity to remove himself from the controversy about the meeting by posting, "I did not know about it." It is illegal for U.S. political campaigns to receive items of value (including information) from foreign governments, or its agents. **8/5/18**

■ FBI agent Peter Strzok is fired by the bureau. It is rumored that the firing was related to leaked negative email comments he made about then-presidential candidate Donald Trump, which became the subject of numerous presidential tweets. The FBI's Office of Professional Responsibility previously determined that Strzok should be punished by a 60-day suspension, but that was overruled by FBI Deputy Director David Bowdich. **8/6/18**

■ The *New York Times* reports that Senior U.S. National security officials pushed NATO to secure a formal agreement before the actual July, 2018 meeting began, in order to prevent Donald Trump from upending the communiqué. **8/9/18**

■ After players once again kneel during the playing of the National Anthem during pre-season NFL football games, the president responds via Twitter. Trump condemns the protesting players as showing disrespect to the country. This time however, he takes a deeper swipe at the protesters (who are predominately African-American), by stating, "Numerous players from different teams, wanted to show their 'outrage' at something that most of them are unable to define." **8/10/18**

■ The president authorizes the doubling the rate of tariffs on steel and aluminum from Turkey, partly due to Turkey's failure to release American pastor Andrew Brunson, who was jailed after a failed coup in Turkey. The tariffs increase pressure on a deeply troubled Turkish economy. **8/10/18**

■ Donald Trump issues a broadside attack against Attorney General Jeff Sessions once again, for not actively taking action to end the Russia investigation. Trump describes Sessions as being "scared stiff," and "missing in action," because he had recused himself from the investigation before it began. **8/11/18**

■ The president travels to a northern New York military base to sign the $716 billion defense policy bill, named after critically ill U.S. senator John McCain (R-AZ). Trump signs the bill after making his remarks, but does not mention the senator's name. In fact, Trump takes the opportunity to criticize McCain for casting the vote that doomed his attempt to repeal the Affordable Care Act. **8/13/18**

■ A war on words breaks out between the president and former White House staffer Omarosa Manigault-Newman, after she releases a tell-all book of her time working for Donald Trump. Manigault-Newman's book, entitled *Unhinged*, paints a bleak picture of the Trump presidency, in which she suggests that the president is "not fit" to serve as POTUS. Predictably, the president fires back at Manigault-Newman, claiming that his former *Apprentice* partner was "vicious, but not smart," and calls her "a lowlife." The next day, Trump follows up on his attacks on his former employee, by calling her "a dog" on Twitter. **8/14/18**

■ Former CIA Director John Brennan has his national security clearance revoked by the president. The White House's official statement claims that Brennan's clearance was revoked for making "a series of unfounded and outrageous allegations- wild outbursts on the internet and television-about this Administration." However, many members of the media, along with political and military figures see Trump's action as the beginning of the creation of a Nixon-like "enemies list." **8/15/18**

■ Over 300 newspapers across the U.S. run opinion columns striking back at Donald Trump's attack on the press. The effort, led by the editors of the *Boston Globe*, denounces the president's claims of the press publishing "fake news" and becoming "enemies of the people." Trump responds via Twitter, stating, "There is nothing I would want more for our country than true FREEDOM OF THE PRESS. The fact is that the press is FAKE NEWS, pushing a political agenda or just plain trying to hurt people." **8/16/18**

▮ The president cancels his controversial U.S. military parade scheduled for November, 2018 citing high costs being charged by the city of Washington, D.C., estimated to be $21.6 million dollars. Trump responds on Twitter, posting, "The local politicians who run Washington D.C. (poorly) know a windfall when they see it." The mayor of the city responds to Trump with her own Twitter post, claiming, "Yup, I'm Muriel Bowser, mayor of Washington, D.C., the local politician who finally got thru to the reality star in the White House with the realities ($21.6 M) of parades/events/demonstrations in Trump America (sad)." **8/17/18**

▮ On NBC's *Meet the Press*, Donald Trump's personal lawyer Rudy Giuliani states that he fears the president is being lured into an interview with Robert S. Mueller III in the ongoing Russia probe, in order to set up a "perjury trap." In trying to defend his position, Giuliani tells host Chuck Todd that "truth isn't truth," in regards to testimony the president might give. **8/20/18**

▮ In simultaneous, stunning fashion, two former members of Donald Trump's inner-circle (lawyer Michael Cohen and presidential campaign chairman Paul Manafort) are either found guilty, or plead guilty to federal crimes which were a result of the Mueller Russia investigation. Cohen, facing up to 12 years in prison, pleads guilty to eight crimes in a Manhattan courtroom. The charges include tax evasion and making false statements to a bank to obtain financing. Stunningly, Cohen also admits that he violated campaign finance laws by arranging to pay two women (Karen McDougal and Stormy Daniels), in order to buy their silence about alleged affairs with Donald Trump. Cohen also admits that the payments were made "in coordination with and at the direction of a candidate for federal office," which directly implicates the president. Predictably, Donald Trump issues several denials of any wrongdoing via Twitter, and turns the focus to former Pres. Obama's campaign funding violations. And, in a final jab at his former lawyer, Trump tweets, "If anyone is looking for a good lawyer, I would strongly suggest that you don't retain the services of Michael Cohen." In the other legal proceeding, Paul Manafort is found guilty of eight counts (out of 18 charged) of tax evasion and bank fraud, and faces a possibility of 80 years in prison for his crimes. Once again, Donald Trump takes to social media for damage control, calling Manafort "a good man," and that his former campaign chairman's conviction "doesn't involve me." **8/21/18**

■ Donald Trump, during an interview on cable's *Fox and Friends*, declares that the stock market in the U.S. would crash if Democrats claim the House of Representatives during the 2018 mid-term elections, and bring impeachment proceedings against him. Trump tells the interviewer, "I don't know how you can impeach someone who's done a great job." Later in the interview, Trump states that individuals under indictment who give evidence against others who are "higher up" in an investigation in exchange for a lighter sentence ("flipping") should not be allowed to do so. Trump states, "It almost ought to be outlawed. It's not fair." Trump was referring to his former lawyer, Michael Cohen, who pled guilty to tax evasion and other crimes earlier in the week, and is rumored to be ready to exchange information with investigators about Trump, in exchange for a lighter sentence. **8/23/18**

■ The president, trying to turn attention away from the ongoing Russia probe, encourages Attorney General Jeff Sessions to investigate the supposed wrongdoings of his political rivals. Sessions, defends the Department of Justice, by tweeting, "Department of Justice will not be improperly influenced by political considerations." Trump responds, "Jeff, this is GREAT, what everyone wants, So look into all of the corruption on the 'other side' including deleted emails, Comey lies and leaks, Mueller conflicts, McCabe, Strzok, Page, Ohr." **8/24/18**

■ The federal investigation into alleged campaign finance violations involving Donald Trump, take a serious turn as Allen Weisselberg, chief financial officer for the Trump Organization is granted immunity by federal prosecutors. Weisselberg, a long-time Trump employee, has knowledge of all financial dealings of Trump's businesses, foundations, and personal accounts. At the same time, David Pecker, CEO of American Media, Inc. (publisher of the *National Enquirer*), is also granted immunity by federal prosecutors, who will delve into allegations involving AMI's participation in paying "hush money" to women allegedly involved in extra-marital affairs with Donald Trump. **8/24/18**

■ Senator John McCain (R-AZ) succumbs to brain cancer and dies at his home in Arizona at the age of 81. It is reported that staffers within the White House advocated for the release of an official statement praising the late senator for his military and political service to the country, and this idea was nixed by Donald Trump, who issues his own Twitter post, (featuring a picture of the himself on it) which does not praise McCain in any way, but instead delivers sympathy to his family. After Trump's post, the flag over the White House is lowered for a brief amount of time over the weekend, and then raised back to full-staff in the early hours of Monday morning. Trump issues no proclamation to keep flags at half-staff, and many government flags in Washington (including the Capitol and Washington Monument), remain lowered. Trump and McCain were frequently at odds during the senator's life, and it is reported that McCain's family requested Donald Trump not be invited to his funeral. Instead of Trump, former presidents Barack Obama and George W. Bush are asked to deliver eulogies. **8/25/18**

■ Donald Trump misreads his approval rating in a *Wall Street Journal/* NBC News poll, and tweets the following, "Over 90% approval rating for your all-time favorite (I hope) President within the Republican Party, and 52% overall." The poll numbers actually show that his approval rating is 44%, and 52% of those polled *disapprove* his performance. **8/26/18**

■ The president, while coloring pictures with children during a stop in Ohio to address the opioid crisis, uses a blue marker to color in stripes on an American flag. The flag only has red and white stripes, with white stars on a blue background. **8/26/18**

▪ After intense pressure from both parties, and members of the White House staff, the president relents, and issues a proclamation to honor John McCain, and his service to the nation. The American flag over the White House is once again lowered to half-staff, until his internment service. **8/27/18**

▪ Donald Trump's top economic adviser Larry Kudlow announces that the Trump administration will be "taking a look" at the search engine Google based on the president's feeling that the company is biased against him. Trump tweets that search engine returns for "Trump News" were "RIGGED for me and others so that almost all stories & news is BAD." Kudlow says that the government is looking at whether and how Google could be could be regulated by the government. **8/28/18**

▪ Donald Trump tweets that China was behind a hack of Hillary Clinton's emails, based on an article he read on the right-wing *Daily Caller*. Trump tweets, "Hillary Clinton's emails, many of which are classified Information, got hacked by China. Next move better be by the FBI or DOJ or, after all of their other missteps (Comey, McCabe, Strzok, Page, Ohr, FISA, Dirty Dossier, etc.) their credibility will be forever gone." The FBI responds to Trump's claims by issuing a statement which reads, "The FBI has not found any evidence the servers were compromised." **8/28/18**

▪ According to a Donald Trump tweet, White House counsel Don McGahn is resigning from his position in the fall. McGahn, who assisted the president in reshaping the federal judiciary, is the most recent attorney connected with the Trump administration to resign, or be forced out. **8/29/18**

▪ Donald Trump courts the evangelical vote by stating the importance of getting out the vote in the upcoming mid-term elections, warning of "violence" from opponents if Republicans lose control of Congress. Trump tells the gathering of Christian ministers, pastors, and other religious supporters that if Democrats win, they "will overturn everything that we've done and they'll do it quickly and violently." Trump also alludes that the "violence" will come at the hands of anti-fascist groups like Antifa. **8/29/18**

■ A *Washington Post*/ABC News poll shows Donald Trump with a 60% disapproval rating with American voters. The same poll shows that 63% of Americans support Robert Mueller's Russian investigation. **8/31/18**

■ The president accuses NBC and news anchor Lester Holt of altering a tape during an interview in which he cited the Russia investigation as his reason for firing FBI Director James Comey. Trump tweets, "What's going on at @CNN is happening to different degrees at other networks-with @ NBCNews being the worst. The good news is that Andy Lack(y) is about to be fired(?) for incompetence and much worse. When Lester Holt got caught fudging my tape on Russia, they were hurt badly!" **8/31/18**

CHAPTER 21

AS IF THE BOOK *Fire and Fury* by Michael Wolff wasn't enough to send #45 over the edge, the new Trump tell-all, *Fear*, by Robert Woodward, must have made him apoplectic. The compelling inside- the-White House reveal claims that Trump staffers pulled papers off the president's desk so he wouldn't be able to sign them, and that his lawyers were mortified at his rambling responses to mock interviews done to prepare him to be questioned by Robert Mueller in the Russia investigation. Predictably, the White House calls Woodward's book "fiction," but many Americans remember that he (along with Carl Bernstein), were the gentlemen who took down Richard Nixon. "I am not a crook," and "this is a witch hunt," seem fairly synonymous, eh?

And if one bad journalistic bashing this month isn't enough, the *New York Times* reports that there is a secret "resistance" in the White House aimed at keeping Donald Trump from spiraling down the rabbit hole they see him headed towards. The article claims that some in the White House sought to use the 25th Amendment to the U.S. Constitution to remove Trump from office. Although the Trump administration vehemently denies this claim, the term "25th amendment" becomes Google's most sought-out term, edging "Khloe Kardashian's baby" from the top spot.

And to wrap things up for the month, Donald Trump accuses China (not Russia, mind you), of interfering with U.S. elections, because they are upset that Trump's policies on trade are hurting their economy, and don't want him to win more support at the polls. He later mentions that China has respect for him and his "very, very large brain." And so it goes...........

▮ On Labor Day, the president attacks the head of America's largest union, the AFL-CIO. Trump tweets, "Richard Trumka, the head of the AFL-CIO, represented his union poorly on television this weekend. Some of the things he said were so against the workingmen and women of our country and the success of the U.S. itself, and it is easy to see why unions are doing so poorly. A Dem!" **9/3/18**

▮ Noted author Bob Woodward releases portions of a new book detailing the dysfunction and chaos inside Donald Trump's White House. Among the stories told in the book *Fear,* are that his most loyal aides tried repeatedly to get him to control his impulses, and in some cases, they removed sensitive paperwork from his desk so he would be unable to act on certain pending issues. The book also gives details of a supposed mock interview with Trump that would most likely mimic questions which he would be asked to answer from Special Counsel Robert S. Mueller III, if he agreed to be interviewed about his business or personal connections to Russia. Trump's performance in the practice session is so disheveled and contradictory; his attorneys began a defensive stance to prevent him from being personally interviewed by Mueller. Predictably, the White House fires back at Woodward with Defense Secretary Jim Mattes calling the book "fiction" and Press Secretary Sarah Huckabee Sanders stating that it is "nothing more than fabricated stories, many by former disgruntled employees." **9/4/18**

▮ The *New York Times* publishes an explosive anonymous opinion column written by a senior White House staffer, claiming that there is a secret "resistance" movement within Trump's inner-circle aimed at keeping the president's actions in check. The article paints a picture of a president becoming more and more erratic and paranoid about who he can and cannot trust in the White House, as the author of the op-ed claims that removing the president under the 25th Amendment to the U.S. Constitution was discussed among some staffers. Trump reportedly explodes in anger upon learning of the column, and begins tweeting that the source is "phony," and if the person who wrote it does exist, "he/she must be turned over to the government for 'national security' purposes." Trump later tweets a single word sign of frustration, "TREASON?" **9/5/18**

■ In the wake of the furor of the anonymous *New York Times* op-ed article about the "resistance" against Donald Trump from inside the White House, numerous members of his administration release public statements declaring that they are not the author of the article. And, in a related story, Sen. Rand Paul (R-KY) suggests that White House staffers with direct access to the president should undergo a lie detector test to prove their innocence. **9/6/18**

■ An exasperated Donald Trump says that Attorney Jeff Sessions should have the Department of Justice launch an investigation into the source of the *New York Times* op-ed article which is highly critical of him. Trump claims that the DOJ needs to get involved for "national security" reasons. **9/7/18**

■ The president makes a false statement about the U.S. economy on Twitter, by claiming that "The GDP Rate (4.2%) is higher than the Unemployment Rate (3.9%) for the first time in over 100 years!" Research shows that the GDP rate has been higher than the unemployment rate for 185 individual months since 1946. **9/10/18**

■ Results from a *Washington Post*-ABC News national poll show that only 38% of U.S. voters approve of the job that Donald Trump is doing as president, and 60% disapprove. The approval rating reflects a six point drop from April's 44% rating. **9/10/18**

■ Donald Trump uses the backdrop of the anniversary of the 9/11 attacks to launch a new offensive against the FBI and Department of Justice. Trump, reacting to a claim by Rep. Mark Meadows (R-NC), tweets, "New Strzok-Page texts reveal 'Media Leak Strategy,' @FoxNews. So terrible and NOTHING is being done at DOJ or FBI-but the world is watching, and they get it completely." Trump also delivers several other tweets addressing the Russia investigation before changing his tone to honor the victims of the 9/11 terrorist attacks. **9/11/18**

▪ The president, still struggling from criticism of the handling of Puerto Rico's recovery efforts following 2017's Hurricane Maria, tells reporters, "I think we did a fantastic job in Puerto Rico." Critics of the cleanup and recovery efforts on the island point out nearly 3,000 residents died from the hurricane and its aftermath, with power finally being completely restored after one full year. Trump lashes out at a George Washington University study that confirms the 3,000 deaths by tweeting, "This was done by the Democrats in order to make me look as bad as possible when I was successfully raising Billions of Dollars to help rebuild Puerto Rico. If a person died for any reason, like old age, just add them onto the list. Bad Politics, I love Puerto Rico." **9/11/18**

▪ According to the *Washington Post's* Fact Checker column, Donald Trump reportedly has made over 5,000 false or misleading statements during his term in office, which averages out to be 8.3 per day. **9/13/18**

▪ Former Trump campaign chairman Paul Manafort pleads guilty to corruption charges and agrees to cooperate with federal prosecutors in the ongoing Russia probe. **9/14/18**

▪ In a stunning move, the president orders the Department of Justice to de-classify and release materials related to the investigation of Russian meddling during the 2016 U.S. presidential elections. Most of the materials Trump wants released concern themselves with former campaign adviser Carter Page, former FBI Director James Comey, Deputy Director Andrew McCabe, Justice Department official Bruce Ohr, and FBI agents Peter Strzok and Lisa Page, all of whom are political targets of the president. **9/17/18**

▪ Donald Trump, still fuming over Jeff Sessions's recusal from the Russia investigation, says, "I don't have an Attorney General." Trump's comment is made during an interview with Hill.TV, where he also claims that sessions was, "mixed up and confused" during his Senate confirmation hearings, and that his performance leading the Department of Justice was, "sad." **9/19/18**

▪ After an accusation of sexual assault by Supreme Court nominee Brett Kavanaugh from Christine Blasey Ford (which allegedly occurred while both were teenagers), Donald Trump remains uncharacteristically silent on social media for several days. However, with his nominee's appointment apparently in danger of failing, Trump launches into a Twitter attack against Ford. Trump tweets, "I have no doubt that, if the attack on Dr. Ford was as bad as she says, charges would have been immediately filed with local Law Enforcement Authorities by either her or her parents." **9/21/18**

▪ Reports of written memos by then-acting FBI Director Andrew McCabe suggest that Deputy Attorney General Rod J. Rosenstein advised McCabe record his conversations with the president, and that the two discussed use of the 25th Amendment to the U.S. Constitution to have him removed from office. **9/21/18**

▪ Donald Trump repeats a claim in front of the U.N. General Assembly that his administration has accomplished more in two years than "almost any administration." The statement is met with widespread laughter in the chamber. Trump tries to shrug off the response to his comments, but appears to be taken aback by it. **9/25/18**

▪ A third woman accuses Supreme Court nominee Brett Kavanaugh of improper sexual behavior during drunken high school parties, and makes her statement through attorney Michael Avenatti (who also represented Trump accuser Stormy Daniels), on the eve of a Senate vote to confirm Kavanaugh to the Court. Donald Trump, increasingly frustrated by the number of women accusing the judge of sexual misconduct (now three), lashes out on Twitter, stating, "Avenatti is a third-rate lawyer who is good at making false accusations, like he did on me and he is now doing on Judge Brett Kavanaugh. He is looking for attention and doesn't want people to look at his past record and relationships-a total low-life!" **9/26/18**

▪ The president accuses China of interfering with U.S. elections, but provides no concrete proof to back his claim. Trump makes his allegation to the U.N. Security Council, stating that China, "has been attempting to interfere in our upcoming 2018 election, coming up in November against my administration. They do not want me to win because I am the first president to ever challenge China on Trade, and we are winning on Trade-we are winning on every level. We don't want them to meddle or interfere in our upcoming election." Trump's comments are not backed up by any of his national security advisers. **9/26/18**

■ Donald Trump holds a rambling 83 minute news conference during a break in the U.N. General Assembly meeting. The conference, displays a combative, belligerent, and sometimes humorous Trump, and covers a full spectrum of grievances about his treatment by the press, the economy, and the lack of federal judges he has been able to appoint versus the number of judges appointed under former president Obama. Among the gems that Trump reveals is that China has total respect for him, and his, "very, very large brain." **9/26/18**

■ Under intense pressure from negative public opinion of Brett Kavanaugh's scheduled vote by the U.S. Senate, outgoing senator Jeff Flake (R-AZ), tells the Senate Judicial Committee that he will not support Kavanaugh's appointment in a full Senate vote, unless a week-long FBI investigation of the judge's behavior while in high school and college is held. Donald Trump reluctantly approves the investigation, claiming that the FBI can, "interview whoever they deem appropriate, at their discretion." However, reports surface that the White House is tightly scripting the scope of the investigation, and is consulting only with Republicans on the Judiciary Committee. **9/28/18**

CHAPTER 22

OCTOBER BRINGS NEW REPORTS of the misdeeds of Donald Trump's father, Fred C. Trump, who sought to avoid paying taxes the way a politician seeks to avoid giving a straight answer to an interview question on *60 Minutes*. Trump, Sr. hid millions of dollars from his companies, according to a story in the *New York Times*, and funneled that money to his children. We know that Donald Trump's claim of being a "self-made" success with only a $1 million dollar loan from his father was only off by a mere $400 million or so due to his daddy's illegal largess.

As the month meandered on, Trump spends some time in a persnickety tiff with Democratic presidential candidate Elizabeth Warren ("Pocahontas"), takes potshots at porn star Stormy Daniels ("Horseface"), and her lawyer Michael Avenatti ("3rd rate lawyer"), but had nice things to say regarding WWE star-turned politician Rep. Greg Gianforte ("Any guy who can do a body slam-he's my kind of guy"), along with Mad-About-Trump rapper Kanye West, who says that Trump was "the flyest man on the planet," whatever that means.

The decrepitly unfunny episodes during this month include the gunning down of 11 Jewish worshipers at a synagogue in Pittsburgh, PA, and the brutal killing and dismembering of *Washington Post* reporter and Saudi Arabian national Jamal Khashoggi by a covert Saudi hit squad in Turkey. And who could forget the capture of Cesar Sayoc Jr., who mailed dozens of explosive devices to supposed Trump enemies, and the president's complaints that the reporting of "this Bomb stuff" was getting in the way of his campaign efforts?

▮ Donald Trump mocks Brett Kavanaugh's accuser, Christine Blasey Ford, while speaking at a campaign rally, calling into question Ford's account of the alleged sexual assault by the Supreme Court nominee. Trump tells an enthusiastic crowd, as Blasey Ford, "I don't know. Upstairs? Downstairs? Where was it? But I had one beer. That's the only thing I remember." Trump goes on to claim that Kavanaugh's life was "in tatters" from Blasey Ford's accusations, and that men were going to be fired from their jobs after being falsely accused of inappropriate sexual behavior. **10/2/18**

▮ A bombshell story released by the *New York Times* reveals that Donald Trump's father may have been engaged in fraudulent tax schemes and shell companies which illegally funneled money to his five children, including Trump himself, in order to avoid paying millions of dollars in taxes to the U.S. government. The story also casts doubt on Trump's claim that he was a "self-made millionaire" who built his empire entirely from a $1 million dollar loan from his father, Fred C. Trump, and shows that the family patriarch gave his son Donald nearly $413 million dollars (in today's value) over the years. **10/2/18**

▮ Protestors march in Washington, D.C. and other cities across the U.S. ahead of a second scheduled vote to confirm Brett Kavanaugh to the U.S. Supreme Court. The protestors are angry that the Republican-ordered FBI probe of the judicial nominee, occurred too close to the Senate vote to confirm Kavanaugh, and was incomplete and partisan. In a related story, retired Supreme Court Justice John Paul Stevens comments that Kavanaugh should not be seated on the nation's highest court, based on his combative, heated testimony before the Senate Judicial Committee. **10/4/18**

▮ Donald Trump, attacking Democrats who fought the appointment of Brett Kavanaugh to the Supreme Court, tweets, "You don't hand matches to an arsonist, and you don't give power to an angry, left-wing mob. Democrats have become too EXTREME and TOO DANGEROUS to govern. Republicans believe in the rule of law-not the rule of the mob. VOTE REPUBLICAN!" **10/9/18**

■ Rapper Kanye West makes an appearance at the White House to have lunch with the president, and proceeds to engage in a profanity-laced rant about various issues on his mind, including a helium-filled plane, and that the president needs to be the "flyest man on the planet." **10/11/18**

■ During a *60 Minutes* interview, with Leslie Stahl on CBS, a painting of a svelte Donald Trump sitting around a table with past Republican presidents (Bush, Lincoln, Nixon, etc.), is visible on the screen. The painting was hung in a White House dining room, and is widely mocked by late-night television talk show hosts. **10/15/18**

■ Sen. Elizabeth Warren (D-MA), reveals that a DNA test she has taken shows some Native-American ancestry; an issue which the president has mocked repeatedly at his rallies. The test reveals that Warren had Native ancestors between 6-10 generations ago. White House spokesperson Kellyanne Conway dismisses the test as "junk science," but others claim that the findings leave Donald Trump on the hook for a $1 million dollar charitable donation he said he would make if Warren could prove Native-American heritage. Trump also attacks Warren on Twitter with a post stating, "Pocahontas (the bad version), sometimes referred to as Elizabeth Warren, is getting slammed. She took a bogus DNA test and it showed that she may be 1/1024, far less than the average American. Now Cherokee Nation denies her. DNA test is useless. Even they don't want her. Phony!" **10/15/18**

■ The White House announces that the federal deficit stands at $779 billion dollars, (which represents a 17% increase from the previous year) and will balloon to nearly $1 trillion dollars by 2020. Republican leaders, including the president, continue to claim that their tax cut law would generate enough increased revenue to shrink the deficit, but the new figures released show that this is not the case. **10/15/18**

■ Donald Trump, reveling in a federal judge's dismissal of a defamation lawsuit against him by Stormy Daniels, goes on Twitter to attack the physical appearance of the adult film actress and the qualifications of her attorney. Trump tweets, "Great, now I can go after Horseface and her 3rd rate lawyer" (Michael Avenatti). **10/16/18**

▌ At a campaign rally in Montana, Donald Trump praises Rep. Greg Gianforte (R-MT) for his special election victory in May, 2017. Gianforte pled guilty to punching journalist Ben Jacobs of the *Guardian*, and received a six-month deferred sentence, Trump tells his supporters, "Any guy that can do a body slam, he's my kind of-he's my guy." **10/19/18**

▌ U.S. resident, and Saudi national, Jamal Khashoggi, a contributing columnist for the *Washington Post*, is allegedly killed at the Saudi Arabian embassy in Turkey, Khashoggi was apparently lured to the embassy to gather paperwork for a planned wedding, but was apprehended, beaten, tortured, and his body was dismembered by a 15 man "hit team" of Saudi officials, who immediately left Turkey after killing the journalist. The Saudi government comes up with a story that Khashoggi got into a "fistfight" that turned deadly, and that they have arrested 18 Saudis who were involved in the murder. Donald Trump calls the move by the Saudi government a "great first step," but indicates that he believes the Saudi cover story to be credible. **10/20/18**

▌ The president makes dubious claims during several press conferences which are proven false by fact-checking media outlets. One of Trump's claims is that Americans would receive a 10% income tax reduction, which would begin before the November mid-term elections. This claim proves to be false, since Congress would have to approve such an action, and at that time, Congress was out of session until after the elections. Trump also tells reporters that a migrant caravan from Central America through Mexico towards the U.S. southern border contains "unknown Middle Easterners," who are "funded by Democrats." Neither Trump nor White House officials provide proof to support either of the assertions. **10/22/18**

- Twelve explosive devices are mailed to former presidents Barack Obama and Bill Clinton, former CIA director John Brennan, Rep. Maxine Waters (D-CA), Democratic patron George Soros, former Vice President Joe Biden, Sen. Corey Booker (D-NJ), former Director of National Intelligence James Clapper, actor Robert De Niro, and to the offices of CNN. The bombs are crude in design, and have a return address of Debbie Wasserman Schultz, former chair of the Democratic National Committee. Although the president and White House both issue strongly-worded criticisms of the mailings, many in politics and the news media question if the attempted attacks, aimed at perceived enemies of Donald Trump, have caused certain unstable supporters of the president to take violent action against them. **10/24/18**

- The president, after initially calling for the rhetoric of anger in the U.S. to be toned down with the recent discovery of explosive devices being mailed to prominent Democrats, and his critics, blows up on Twitter, stating, "Funny how lowly-rated CNN and others can criticize me at will, even blaming me for the current state of Bombs and ridiculously comparing this to September 11th and the Oklahoma City bombing, yet when I criticize them they go wild and scream, 'it's not presidential!'" **10/25/18**

- The president, frustrated that the story of an alleged bomber is taking precedence over his campaign rhetoric, tweets, "Republicans are doing so well in early voting, and at the Polls, and now this 'Bomb' stuff happens and the momentum greatly shows-news not talking politics. Very unfortunate, what is going on. Republicans, go out and vote!" **10/26/18**

- A suspect in the mass bomb mailing is apprehended in Florida. Cesar Sayoc Jr. is taken into custody, along with his white van, which is covered with pro-Trump and GOP stickers, and lined with signs attacking those who are the president's adversaries. When questioned about Sayoc, Trump denies seeing his (Trump's) face on stickers affixed to the white van, and states, "I heard he was a person who preferred me over others," but disavows any link between the bombing attempts, and his often inflammatory comments on Twitter and at campaign rallies, "There's no blame. There's no anything," claims Trump. **10/27/18**

■ A gunman shoots and kills 11 Jewish worshipers at the Tree of Life Synagogue in a suburb of Pittsburgh, PA. The lone gunman, Robert Bowers, is wounded and captured by police. Shortly after the incident, Donald Trump claims that the shooting could have been prevented if there were armed guards at the synagogue. Pittsburgh mayor Bill Peduto issues a statement that denounces Trump's claim, and instead focuses on the availability of guns in the U.S., which often fall into the wrong hands. **10/27/18**

■ In the aftermath of the Pittsburgh synagogue attack, the president attempts visit to meet with families of the shooting victims. One family declines the meeting, and more than one thousand people sign up to demonstrate against Trump during his visit. House and Senate leaders from both parties, including Senate Majority Leader Mitch McConnell (R-KY), House Speaker Paul Ryan (R-WI), Senate Minority Leader Charles Schumer (D-NY), and House Minority Leader Nancy Pelosi (D-CA), decline invites from the White House to appear with Trump during the visit. **10/29/18**

■ The president visits the Tree of Life Synagogue near Pittsburgh, PA to pay his respects for the 11 members who were shot dead by a deranged gunman, and is met by over 2,000 demonstrators, who oppose his being there so soon after the tragedy. Numerous mourners blame the president for his insensitive comments immediately after the shooting, about how it could have been prevented if armed security guards were in place during the services. **10/30/18**

■ Donald Trump seeks to end birthright citizenship in the U.S. through an executive order. In an interview with *Axios*, Trump wrongly proclaims that, "We're the only country in the world where a person comes in and has a baby, and the baby is essentially a citizen of the United States." More than 30 countries offer birthright citizenship. Critics of Trump's plan cite the U.S. Constitution's 14th Amendment as a barrier to Trump's intentions. **10/30/18**

CHAPTER 23

NOVEMBER IS A MONTH of Thanksgiving and turkey. However, the month brings some truly "foul" as opposed to "fowl" goings on at 1600 Pennsylvania Avenue. We begin out odyssey with the president telling U.S. troops stationed at the southern border with Mexico that they should consider rocks thrown at them by migrants to be "a rifle." The National Rifle Association, sensing an opportunity, immediately declares that rocks should now be protected under the Second Amendment, and begins a lobbying effort to prevent laws infringing on the rights of citizens to carry sedimentary protection.

There is a media kerfluffle in the White House as CNN's Jim Acosta and a female intern jostle for a microphone during a press conference. The event includes wrestling, name calling, a doctored videotape, and assorted shenanigans worthy of a WWE main event. No word was mentioned about the possibility of Jim McMahon sponsoring a rematch.

And November also brings us the president who has "very high levels of intelligence" claiming the following: Finland rakes their forest floors to prevent fires (they don't), voters need voter ID to buy cereal at a grocery store (they don't), people cast multiple votes at voting locations by changing hats (they don't), and that the U.S. border with Mexico was closed (it wasn't). And we're still not clear on whether or not Trump knows/doesn't know Matt Whitacre.

So sit back, enjoy the tryptophan-induced coma on Thanksgiving and revel in the Trumpian-induced tomfoolery of November.

■ The president continues his campaign against the migrant "caravan" which is continuing its journey to the U.S. through Mexico, by threatening to have up to 15,000 troops sent to the southern border in an attempt to stop the immigrants from entering the country. Trump, who is accused of using the migrant issue to whip up his base before the upcoming November midterm elections, says that any violence by members of the caravan will be met with force. Trump states, "They want to throw rocks at our military, our military fights back. We're going to consider-and I told them, consider it a rifle." **11/1/18**

■ In the wake of the president's warnings about a caravan of migrants set to invade the United States from the southern border, gun-toting paramilitary groups head to the area in anticipation of violence, and to "defend" their American turf. U.S. Customs and Border Protection officials are alerted about the groups, along with army commanders. **11/3/18**

■ After a testy exchange with CNN's reporter Jim Acosta during a White House press briefing, Donald Trump berates the anchor and his network, and tries to have a microphone pulled away from him after he tells Acosta to stop asking follow up questions, and sit down. Acosta refuses, which results in Trump ordering his press credentials to be suspended, preventing him from attending future White House briefings. The White House also accuses Acosta of "placing his hands on a young woman," as he tried to shield his microphone from a female intern who was trying to take it from him. The White House tweets a doctored video of the Acosta moving his arm toward the intern as she attempts to take it from him, which speeds up the footage, making it appear that Acosta acted in an aggressive manner. CNN files suit in U.S. District Court in Washington, D.C., claiming that the White House's actions against Acosta violated the reporter's First Amendment rights, as well as the right to continue doing his job, without possessing a "hard pass," which would enable him to have full access to the White House. **11/7/18**

■ The president forces Attorney General Jeff Sessions to resign the day following the 2018 midterm elections, and replaces him with Matthew G. Whitacre, who is currently Sessions' chief of staff. The appointment of Whitacre raises eyebrows as Trump bypasses Rod J. Rosenstein, who is deputy attorney general, in favor of an underling. It also creates fears that the president might seek to take action or move to control the Russia investigation, under Robert S. Mueller III. Whitacre has made statements in the past that indicate he is not in favor of the investigation. The president tries to quell the dissention by claiming, "I don't know Matt Whitacre," during a press briefing following the appointment. However, Trump stated something totally different one month earlier in a *Fox and Friends* interview, claiming, "I can tell you Matt Whitacre's a great guy. I mean I know Matt Whitacre." **11/7/18**

■ A report from the *Wall Street Journal* suggests that Donald Trump knew about hush money payments made to Karen McDougal and Stormy Daniels to cover up alleged affairs with both women, preceding the 2016 U.S. presidential election. The report shows that both women were paid in excess of $100,000 (Daniels was paid $150,000, and McDougal was paid $130,000), which would have been in violation of campaign finance rules. It also details that Trump requested that AMI (parent company of the *National Enquirer*) take the lead in arranging payment. The report alleges that information surrounding the illegal payments was obtained from Donald Trump's personal attorney Michael Cohen, Trump Organization CFO Allen Weisselberg, and David Pecker, AMI Chief Executive. **11/9/18**

■ The president takes a swipe at the hotly contested Florida Senate race between Republican governor Rick Scott, and current Democratic Senator Bill Nelson, and the Florida governor's race between Democrat Andrew Gillum and Republican Ron DeSantis, claiming that the elections have been "tainted." Trump tweets, "The Florida Election should be called in favor of Rick Scott and Ron DeSantis in that large numbers of new ballots showed up out of nowhere, and many ballots are missing or forged. An honest vote count is no longer possible-ballots massively infected. Must go with Election Night!" The White House is contacted for clarification of Trump's remarks, but offers no further explanation. **11/9/18**

■ The president takes a trip to Paris, France to honor the events commemorating the end of World War I, and immediately becomes embroiled in controversy. First, Trump draws scorn from world leaders because he does not attend a ceremony at a military cemetery for Americans, due to inclement weather (Trump tweets that it was the Secret Service's decision, not his). Other world leaders brave the driving rain to attend the ceremony. Next, he becomes involved in a Twitter war with French president Emmanuel Macron, attacking Macron's approval ratings, France's unemployment numbers, trade policies, and past military performance in World Wars I and II. Trump's attacks follow Macron's comments about Trump's claim of "nationalism," and how the European Union needed to create a "true European army" to protect the European Union's interests in the future. **11/10/18**

■ Donald Trump criticizes the state of California for the deadly wildfires that claim numerous lives and destroy thousands of homes and businesses by tweeting, "There is no reason for these massive, deadly and costly forest fires in California except that the forest management is so poor. Billions of dollars are given each year, with so many lives lost, all because of gross mismanagement of the forests. Remedy now, or no more Fed. Payments." News reports show that the U.S. Government has only given California $1.4 billion dollars in the past two years, to help with the aftermath of forest fires in the state, and that Trump's claim of "gross mismanagement" has no substance. **11/11/18**

■ The president continues to claim that voter fraud is occurring in the Florida Senate and Gubernatorial races. Trump states in an interview with the *Daily Caller*, "When people get in line that have absolutely no right to vote and they go around in circles. Sometimes they go to their car, put on a different hat, put on a different shirt, come in and vote again. Nobody takes anything. It's really a disgrace what's going on." Trump goes on to suggest voter fraud based on a lack of voter verification by claiming, "If you buy a box of cereal-you have a voter ID." Trump's assertion is not supported by fact, and is largely ignored by most government officials. **11/12/18**

∎ The president does not visit Arlington National Cemetery on Veteran's Day. Later, Trump admits, "I probably, you know, in retrospect, I should have, and I did last year, but we came in very late last night." **11/12/18**

∎ A federal judge, who is a Trump appointee, orders the White House to restore the press badge of CNN reporter Jim Acosta, citing that his Fifth Amendment rights (due process) were being violated. The ruling is met with support from numerous media and press outlets. Donald Trump calls the ruling "no big deal," and tells *Fox News Sunday* that the White House is drafting new rules covering press decorum for future briefings. **11/16/18**

∎ During another interview with *Fox News Sunday*, the president tells Chris Wallace that he deserves high marks for his presidency so far. Trump tells Wallace," I hate to do it, but I will do it. I would give myself an A-plus. Is that enough? Can I go higher than that?" **11/18/18**

∎ The president fires off a tweet mocking Rep. Adam Schiff (D-CA), who had earlier criticized Trump's appointment of Matthew Whitaker as the acting attorney general, by posting, "So funny to see little Adam Schitt (D-CA) talking about the fact that acting Attorney General Matt Whitaker was not appointed by the Senate, but not mentioning the fact that Bob Mueller (who is highly conflicted) was not confirmed by the Senate." It is quickly pointed out by Trump's critics that the error of the tweet (aside from the intentional slur of Rep. Schiff's name), is that a special counsel does not have to be approved by the Senate, but an attorney general must be. **11/18/18**

∎ While touring communities ravaged by wildfires in California, Donald Trump bizarrely tells reporters that raking the forest floors of leaves and twigs could have possibly prevented the state's devastating fires. Trump bases his claim from a meeting he had with Finland's president Sauli Niinisto. In his time with the Finnish leader, Trump says that Finland, which is a "forest nation," does not have wildfires because, "They spend a lot of time on raking and cleaning and doing things, and they don't have any problem." To make matters even worse, Trump twice mistakenly refers to Paradise, California, site of the devastating wildfires, as "Pleasure," during a news conference. **11/19/18**

∎ Reports surface that Ivanka Trump used a personal email server to send 100's of messages which dealt with governmental issues while serving in the White House. Lawyers for Ivanka Trump admit that the president's daughter did use a personal server, but stopped doing so when she received "guidance" on the proper procedures of government correspondence. **11/19/18**

∎ Retired Admiral William McRaven, makes a public statement that Donald Trump's words were, "The greatest threat to Democracy" in his lifetime. Trump responds by claiming that McRaven was a supporter of Hillary Clinton and former president Obama, and that al-Qaida leader Osama bin Laden should have been captured "sooner" under McRaven's watch, when he served as commander of the U.S. Special Operations Command under Obama. **11/19/18**

∎ A federal judge from the U.S. District Court in San Francisco issues a temporary nationwide restraining order to block the Trump administration from denying asylum to immigrants who cross the U.S. border illegally from Mexico. The Judge, Jon S. Tigar, states in his order that the Trump administration's actions violate federal law concerning asylum eligibility. He also states, "Whatever the scope of the president's authority, he may not rewrite the immigration laws to impose a condition that Congress has expressly forbidden." **11/20/18**

∎ The president issues a statement defending Saudi Arabia and Crown Prince Mohammed bin Salman, with regards to the killing of journalist

Jamal Khashoggi. Donald Trump claims that Saudi leaders have denied all charges that they were behind Khashoggi's death at the Saudi embassy in Turkey. He also downplays a CIA assessment that there was "high confidence" the Saudi prince ordered the killing. Trump says that Crown Prince bin Salman might have had knowledge of the crime, ("maybe he did, and maybe he didn't") but he refuses to call for any further action against the Saudi government. The president even defiantly tweets praise to the Saudis by posting, "Oil prices getting lower. Great! Like a big Tax Cut for America and the World. Enjoy $54, was just $82. Thank you Saudi Arabia, but let's go lower." **11/20/18**

▌ Reports surface from the *New York Times* that the president raised the possibility of investigating Hillary Clinton and former FBI Director James Comey for crimes they may have committed, but was discouraged from perusing any potential prosecution by White House Counsel Don McGahn, who told Trump that such action could lead to his impeachment. **11/20/18**

▌ Still holding a grudge from a year ago, Donald Trump tweets the following, "So-called comedian Michelle Wolf bombed so badly last year at the White House Correspondents' Dinner that this year for the first time in decades, they will have an author instead of a comedian. Good first step in a comeback of a dying evening and tradition! Maybe I will go?" **11/21/18**

▌ Chief Justice John Roberts issues a rare political statement aimed at Donald Trump, for accusing a federal judge of partisanship because he ruled against his administration's attempt to deny asylum for migrants who cross the U.S. border. Trump calls Jon S. Tigar an "Obama judge," drawing a response from Roberts who writes, "We do not have Obama judges or Trump judges, Bush judges, or Clinton judges. What we have is an extraordinary group of dedicated judges doing their level best to do equal right to those appearing before them." The president, stinging from Roberts' comments, tweets a response, "Sorry Chief Justice John

Roberts, but you do indeed have "Obama judges," and they have a much different point of view than the people who are charged with the safety of our country." **11/21/18**

■ On Thanksgiving Day, Donald Trump tells reporters that he is grateful for his "great family," and also for himself. Trump muses, "I made a tremendous difference in this country." Later that day, the president calls U.S. troops deployed to bases overseas from his Mar-a Lago resort, and while spending some time praising them for their service, uses his phone time to vent about judges who have blocked his immigration efforts, the economy, and oddly enough, trade (which has nothing to do with the military). Trump also goes on to claim that he ordered the U.S./Mexico border to be closed, stating, "Two days ago. We closed the border. We actually just closed it." The claim is disputed, as only one point of entry (San Ysidro, CA), was temporarily closed and re-opened the same day. The president also tries to put the Jamal Khashoggi assignation behind him, as he is asked who is responsible for the killing by stating, "Maybe the world should be held accountable, 'cause the world is a vicious place." **11/22/18**

■ The Trump administration releases a stunning climate change report the day after Thanksgiving, presumably to limit media exposure. The detailed findings of the 1,656 page National Climate Assessment, which is required by Congress, details the effects of global warming and the possible consequences to the U.S. economy, public health, infrastructure, and other areas. Unfortunately for the Trump administration, which has downplayed the effects of climate change and global warming, the report outlines dire outcomes for the country, which could result in the loss of billions of dollars of revenue due to labor-related declines in productivity and property damage. Donald Trump weighs in on the report (which was generated through the cooperation of 13 federal agencies) saying, that he is not among the "believers" who see climate change as a major issue. He follows up on his statement by claiming that, "One of the problems that a lot of people like myself, we have very high levels of intelligence but we're not necessarily such believers." **11/23/18**

▮ U.S. authorities fire tear gas at the Mexican border, as migrants from the Central American "caravan" attempt to cross into the country. Some angry migrants throw rocks and bottles at U.S. Border Patrol agents, but no injuries are reported. The president immediately weighs in on the situation, tweeting, "Mexico should move the flag waving Migrants, many of whom are stone cold criminals, back to their countries." He continues, "They are not coming into the USA." **11/25/18**

▮ General Motors announces the slashing of over 14,000 jobs and that five of their manufacturing plants will close in North America, in an effort to shore up the company's bottom line. Donald Trump angrily reacts to the news by threatening to cut off all federal subsidies to the car manufacturer. **11/26/18**

▮ Longtime Trump attorney Michael Cohen pleads guilty of lying to Congress about his knowledge of Donald Trump's plans to build a Trump Tower in Moscow after January 2016. This contradicts the president's claim that the building project was abandoned before his entry into the Republican presidential primary, leading up to the 2106 U.S. presidential election. Trump had repeatedly stated that he had no business interests in Russia, but Cohen's confession gives Robert Mueller's Russia investigation more proof of links between the Trump organization and Russia itself. The president, in response to the Cohen plea, says that his former attorney was a "weak person," and "not very smart," while denying the accusations. **11/29/18**

CHAPTER 24

DECEMBER OFTEN BRINGS HOLIDAY cheer to one and all, and the spirit of "giving" is taken full advantage of by Donald Trump who takes the opportunity to show how generous he can to be to his underlings. He gives Chief-of Staff John Kelly his freedom by announcing that the "adult in the room" is being gifted the heave-ho, and can hang his stocking somewhere other than the West Wing. He also gives America the gift of closing down his foundation, which is slightly less criminal than a crime cabal, just in time to revel in holiday cheer. And if this isn't enough, the president threatens to shut down the U.S. government just in time to assure that the holidays will be as un-pleasant as possible for over 800,000 Americans. "No, Johnny, you can't have that bike for Christmas this year. Our president needs money for the wall. But here's a nice MAGA hat for you." Ugh, even Ebenezer Scrooge would be appalled.

In keeping with the holiday theme, the president uses a lump of coal metaphor to describe former Secretary of State Rex Tillerson (dumb as a rock), and even tries to accuse NBC's *Saturday Night Live* of "collusion" with Democrats after an airing of a re-creation of *It's a Wonderful Life*, that depicts a world without an elected Trump. Oh, if only...........

So, enjoy the musings of December, and always remember how Donald Trump spent the holidays away from Mar-a-Lago tweeting, "I am all alone (poor me)." I'm sure the furloughed government workers he created were sympathetic.

▪ The president, showing increasing frustration over the Mueller probe, fires off two tweets directed at his former personal attorney Michael Cohen and longtime Trump supporter Roger Stone, which some legal experts say may cross the line of obstructing a federal investigation. Trump tweets, "Michael Cohen asks judge for no Prison Time! You mean he can do all of the TERRIBLE, unrelated to Trump, things having to do with fraud, big loans, Taxis, etc. and not serve a long prison term? He makes up stories to get a GREAT & ALREADY reduced deal for himself and get…his wife and father-in-law (who has the money?) off SCOTT FREE. He lied for this outcome and should, in my opinion, serve a full and complete sentence." Trump then turns his sights on Stone, who is being pressured to divulge what he knows about to WikiLeaks to federal investigators, by tweeting, "I will never testify against Trump! This statement was recently made by Roger Stone, essentially stating that he will not be forced by a rogue and out of control prosecutor to make up lies and stories about 'President Trump.' Nice to know that some people still have 'guts.'" Both tweets potentially cross the line of witness tampering and obstruction of justice, but no initial determination is made by federal investigators. **12/3/18**

▪ The Trump administration refuses to sign off on an agreement for a global warming report which was issued by the U.N. Intergovernmental Panel on Climate Change. Instead of voting in favor of the report, the U.S. delegation in Poland agrees to "note" the findings, but not support them. **12/3/18**

▪ Attorneys General from the District of Columbia and the state of Maryland issue subpoenas for Donald Trump's private business interests, seeking financial documents, in an investigation of the president's companies illegally profiting from gifts or payments bestowed by foreign governments. The subpoenas mainly focus on Trump's hotel in Washington, D.C., which has seen substantial increases in business from foreign entities, who may be staying at the president's hotel in order to curry favor with him. Payments to a president in any form from a foreign government are in direct violation of the emoluments clause in the U.S. Constitution. **12/4/18**

▪ According to a report in the *New York Times*, Donald Trump's golf resort in Bedminster, N.J. employs undocumented illegal immigrants as housekeepers. The Trump Organization denies the claim, and states that any employee found to be working at any of their properties illegally, would be terminated immediately. **12/6/18**

▪ During an appearance at a charity event in Texas, former Secretary of State Rex. Tillerson says that the president often asked him to take actions that violated the law. Tillerson said that he offered to help the president get certain laws changed in order to achieve his goals, but that Trump would not respond positively to those suggestions. The former secretary also says that Donald Trump did not read briefing papers, and was "undisciplined." Trump fires back at Tillerson by tweeting, "Rex Tillerson didn't have the mental capacity needed (to serve as Secretary of State). He was dumb as a rock and I couldn't get rid of him fast enough. He was lazy as hell." **12/7/18**

▪ Robert S. Mueller III releases information from his Russia investigation involving former Trump campaign chairman Paul Manafort and Michael Cohen, Trump's former personal attorney that potentially link the president to campaign finance violations during the 2016 U.S. presidential election. Information from Cohen seems to indicate that hush money payments made to Stormy Daniels and Karen McDougal were made at the direction of "Individual 1," which seems to indicate Donald Trump, and also that there were attempts by Russian operatives to reach out to the Trump campaign, in order to lend support and "political synergy" to his election effort. There also is information presented by Mueller's team that Trump's company continued to seek a business opportunity to build a Trump Tower in Moscow long into the 2016 U.S. presidential campaign, a fact that Trump's circle vehemently denies. **12/7/18**

▪ Soon after Robert Mueller's release of potentially damning information on the Trump campaign, the president tweets that the special counsel's findings totally clear him of wrongdoing by posting, "Totally clears the President. Thank you." Trump's tweet faces immediate backlash, as George

Conway (husband of Trump spokesperson Kellyanne Conway) responds via Twitter by stating, "Except for that little part where the U.S. Attorney's Office says that you directed and coordinated with Cohen to commit two felonies. Other than that, scot-free." **12/7/18**

■ The White House announces that Chief of Staff John F. Kelly will end his tenure at the end of 2018. Kelly, who was thought of as someone who was a "check" on the president's reckless urges, often clashed with him on policy, but lasted in the position longer than the man he replaced, Reince Priebus. **12/9/18**

■ Donald Trump comments on the ongoing investigation of illegal campaign contributions in the form of hush money payouts to women he allegedly had extramarital affairs with by tweeting, "Democrats can't find a Smocking (sic) Gun tying the Trump campaign to Russia after James Comey's testimony. No Smocking (sic) Gun…No Collusion." **12/10/18**

■ In a 17 minute televised White House meeting between the president and House Minority Leader Nancy Pelosi (D-CA) and Senate Minority Leader Chuck Schumer (D-NY), Trump promises to shut down the U.S. Government if the Democrats do not vote to give him the $5 billion dollars he wants to build a wall on the U.S. southern border with Mexico. The president tells Pelosi and Schumer, "I am proud to shut down the government for border security. I will take the mantle. I will shut it down." **12/11/18**

■ The president weighs in on his potential impeachment during an interview with Reuters, claiming that, "It's hard to impeach somebody who hasn't done anything wrong and who's created the greatest economy in the history of our country." Trump then goes on to say that if he were to be impeached, "the people would revolt," **12/12/18**

■ The president, after initially agreeing on a spending plan to prevent a government shutdown, changes his mind and threatens to allow a closure to occur if his demands for the funds to build a wall on the U.S. southern border are not met. Trump tweets, "The Democrats, whose votes we need in the Senate, will probably vote against Border Security and the Wall even though they know it is DESPERATELY NEEDED. If the Dems vote no, there will be a shutdown that will last for a very long time. People don't want Open Borders and Crime!" Senate Minority Leader Chuck Schumer (D-NY) responds to the president by tweeting, "You own the shutdown-your own words, @realDonaldTrump. The Senate UNANIMOUSLY passed a bi-partisan solution to avoid a shutdown, then you threw another temper tantrum and convinced the House to ignore that compromise. #Trumpshutdown." **12/12/18**

■ The president denies ordering Michael Cohen, his former personal attorney to pay hush money to women he allegedly had extramarital affairs with to prevent news of the liaisons becoming public during the 2016 U.S. presidential campaign. Trump claims that the payments were Cohen's responsibility, and that he should have known if the payments violated campaign finance law. Trump tells Fox News, "I never directed him to do anything wrong. Whatever he did he did on his own. I never directed him to do anything incorrect or wrong." Trump uses the rest of the interview to minimize his relationship with Cohen, who was recently sentenced to a three year prison term for various criminal conduct. The president says that the attorney did "more public relations than law," and that he was tasked with "low-level work" for Trump and his organization. **12/14/18**

■ Donald Trump, furious at NBC's *Saturday Night Live's* skit which lampoons him with a re-creation of the Christmas classic *It's a Wonderful Life*, featuring a world where Trump was never elected president, fires off an angry tweet aimed at the show. Trump tweets, "A REAL scandal is the one sided coverage, hour by hour, of networks like NBC & Democrat spin machines like Saturday Night Live. It is all nothing less than unfair news coverage and Dem. Commercials. Should be tested in courts. Can't be legal. Only defame & belittle! Collusion?" **12/16/18**

■ Donald Trump agrees to shutter his foundation as lawmakers allege that he used funds from it for personal and political benefit. New York Attorney General Barbara Underwood announces that the Donald J. Trump Foundation will dissolve, while her office continues to investigate Trump, and three of his eldest children, who are officers of the foundation. The AG also announces that she is seeking more than $28 million dollars in restitution, and is asking a judge to ban Trump family members, (including the president himself) from serving on the boards of any other New York nonprofit organization. **12/18/18**

■ Donald Trump announces that the U.S. will be withdrawing its troops from Syria and Afghanistan, which flies in the face of his military advisers, the Pentagon, and the U.S. State Department. Soon after the president's announcement, Secretary of Defense Jim Mattis announces his resignation. Mattis, who was often seen as a sobering voice of reason in the White House, pens an angry letter of resignation, which leaves no praise for Trump, but instead suggests that the president place someone in his (Mattis's) position that is better aligned with his vision. Mattis also says in the letter that the nation must be clear-eyed about threats from around the globe, including groups like ISIS. At the time of Mattis's resignation, a top U.S. envoy for Syria also submits his resignation letter, in protest of Trump's actions. The president, stung by Mattis's resignation, forces him to leave his position two months earlier than the scheduled departure date, and names Deputy Secretary of Defense Patrick Shanahan, a former executive at Boeing, to immediately replace him. **12/20/18**

■ The president, facing a Dow Jones Market index in freefall, inquires if he can legally fire Federal Reserve Chairman Jerome Powell, who he blames for raising interest rates, and market fluctuation. Although Trump takes no action on Powell, the assertion that he sought to fire him sends shock waves through an already jittery financial sector. **12/23/18**

■ Facing Democratic pushback on funding for his southern border wall with Mexico, Donald Trump refuses to approve funding to keep the U.S.

Government running, effectively shutting down one quarter of government workers, leaving nearly 800,000 employees with no paychecks, on the eve of Christmas. Trump cancels his scheduled holiday trip to his Mar-a-Lago resort in Florida and spends Christmas in the White House, volleying numerous tweets at his detractors on the border wall issue by posting, "I am all alone (poor me) in the White House waiting for the Democrats to come back and make a deal on desperately needed Border Security. At some point the Democrats not wanting to make a deal will cost our Country more money than the Border Wall we are talking about, Crazy!" Trump later tweets that he gave out a 115 mile long contract to build a border wall in Texas, which could not happen without funding approval from Congress. **12/23/18**

■ The Dow Jones Industrial Average drops dramatically in the days before Christmas, spooked by rising interest rates, and conflicting messages from the White House aimed at the Federal Reserve. The Dow closes at 21,792 on December 24th, which represents the worst December for U.S. stocks since 1931. **12/24/18**

■ Donald Trump visits a war zone for the first time during his presidency, as he travels to a U.S. military base in Iraq. Trump, who stays for just three hours, makes a political speech to the troops stationed there, raging about the Democrats' failure to support border wall funding. Trump also tells the troops that his efforts have given them their first pay raise in ten years, which was untrue, and that he "held out" for a 10% pay increase for them, which was also patently false. **12/24/18**

■ The president, upon returning from his trip to Iraq begins to attack House and Senate Democrats for not acting on his demand for funds to pay for the border wall with Mexico, by posting on Twitter. Among his many tweets, the president addresses the partial government shutdown by stating, "Do the Dems realize that most of the people not getting paid are Democrats?" **12/26/18**

- A second immigrant child dies at a U.S. border facility on Christmas Eve, prompting calls for better treatment and medical care for those apprehended while entering the U.S., and criticism of how children are being treated while awaiting immigration proceedings. **12/26/18**

- Donald Trump announces via Twitter that he intends to close the U.S. southern border with Mexico if he cannot gain cooperation from "obstructionist Democrats" who haven't agreed to provide the funds necessary to construct the wall. **12/28/18**

- The U.S. Office of Personnel Management reaches out to the 800,000 members of the civilian workforce furloughed by the government shutdown, suggesting that they arrange barter services with their landlords in exchange for a reduced rent payment, since they are not receiving paychecks from the federal government. Tony Reardon, president of the National Treasury Employees' Union calls the suggestion "laughable and unfortunate." **12/28/18**

- The president, in the middle of a government shutdown, signs an executive order to freeze federal employee pay raises, further complicating the financial plight of government employees not receiving pay due to the shutdown. **12/29/18**

- Donald Trump responds to criticism about the deaths of two immigrant children held at the U.S. border with Mexico by tweeting, "Any deaths of children or others at the Border are strictly the fault of the Democrats and their pathetic immigration policies that allow people to make the long trek thinking they can enter our country illegally. They can't. If we had a Wall, they wouldn't even try!" Trump adds, "The two children in question were very sick before they were given over to Border Patrol. The father of the young girl said it was not their fault, he hadn't given her water in days. Border Patrol needs the Wall and it will end. They are working so hard & getting so little credit! Not a word of sympathy here-much less remorse on the part of the government over the deaths of a 7-year old girl and an 8-year old boy while in its custody." **12/29/18**

▮ Former U.S. Army general Stanley McChrystal, who once worked in the Obama administration, claims in an interview with ABC's Martha Raddatz that he would never work for Donald Trump, claiming that the president does not tell the truth and that he was "immoral." Trump fires back on Twitter, attacking the former general by posting, "'General' McChrystal got fired like a dog by Obama. Last assignment a total bust. Known for big dumb mouth. Hillary lover!" **12/30/18**

▮ In an apparent swipe at Senator Elizabeth Warren (D-MA), who recently announced her intention to run for the U.S. presidency in 2020, Donald Trump answers a Fox News reporter's question on whether or not Warren could win, by responding, "Well, I don't know. You'd have to ask her psychiatrist." **12/31/18**

▮ Donald Trump falsely claims that former president Obama and his wife Michelle's home in Washington D.C. is surrounded by a ten foot high wall. Trump tweets, "President and Mrs. Obama built/has a ten foot Wall around their DC mansion/compound. I agree, totally necessary for their safety and security. The U.S. needs the same thing, slightly larger version." Upon fact checking Trump's claim, it is revealed that the Obamas have a security fence around portions of their home for the needs of Secret Service agents assigned to them, but no ten foot "Wall" exists. Says one of Obama's neighbors referring to Trump's claim, "He has a very large imagination." **12/31/18**

CHAPTER 25

IF DONALD TRUMP THOUGHT being president was fraught with the slings and arrows of political bickering and contempt during his first two years in office, January 2019 provides a whole new kettle of fish for him. Enter Nancy Pelosi…. Speaker of the House of Representatives and back in the saddle again. The lifelong political dynamo from California will present Trump with a female rival whom he can't intimidate, slap with a non-disclosure, or pay off (see: McDougal, Karen or Daniels, Stormy). This presents a unique dilemma for 45, as the Speaker becomes a perpetual slew of pins in his voodoo doll.

"The Wall" becomes trendy during the New Year, as the president A) falsely claims that other presidents told him that they should have had a wall built at the U.S. southern border with Mexico (denied by representatives of presidents Regan, Carter, Bush, and Obama) and B) even more falsely claims that he never said that Mexico would pay for it (except for the over 200 times he said it on the 2016 presidential trail). The president even goes on live TV to pressure Congress for a wall but all he gets are complaints that his remarks delayed a much-anticipated showing of *Dancing With the Stars*.

January is the month that the White House serves Happy Meals, including something called "hamberders" to a very perplexed Clemson national champion football team, the billionaire president tells furloughed government workers that he can "relate" to their not receiving paychecks. Also in this month of months, chief press secretary Sarah Huckabee Sanders tells a reporter that God "wanted Donald Trump to become president." So sit back, kick off your shoes, and enjoy the beginning to a rollicking 2019. Happy New Year!

■ The president rings in the New Year with a tweetstorm, by mocking his detractors. Trump tweets, "HAPPY NEW YEAR TO EVERYONE, INCLUDING THE HATERS AND THE FAKE NEWS MEDIA!" He adds, "2019 WILL BE A FANTASTIC YEAR FOR THOSE NOT SUFFERING FROM TRUMP DERANGEMENT SYNDROME. JUST CALM DOWN AND ENJOY THE RIDE, GREAT THINGS ARE HAPPENING FOR OUR COUNTRY!" **1/1/19**

■ U.S. Senator-elect Mitt Romney (R-UT) publishes an op-ed column in the *Washington Post* which is highly critical of Donald Trump's character, and for having, "Not risen to the mantle of office." Predictably, the president fires back on Twitter that Romney should be a "team player" and not a "Flake," (a reference to outgoing Senator Jeff Flake, who was highly critical of Trump while serving in the Senate). Trump also points out that, "I won big, and he didn't," which refers back to Romney's unsuccessful bid to win the 2012 U.S. presidential election. Romney's remarks also draw a strong rebuke from his niece, Ronna "Romney" McDaniel, who is chairwoman of the Republican National Committee, calling her uncle's remarks "disappointing and unproductive." In a related story, Donald Trump previously asked McDaniel to drop her family name "Romney" when she took her position with the GOP, and she complied with his request. **1/2/19**

■ Showing increasing frustration that government shutdown talks with Democrats are providing no solutions, the president uses a 95 minute long meeting of his cabinet to present a rambling dissertation on all things he is offended by, while seated behind a mock *Game of Thrones*- style poster of him with the caption "Sanctions are Coming." Donald Trump lashes out at former defense secretary James Mattis, calling him a "failure," and falsely states that the four-star general was "essentially fired," because Trump pushed up Mattis's exit date to remove him from his post. Trump also says about Mattis, "What's he done for me?" And for good measure, the president, who has never served in the U.S. military due to numerous questionable attacks of "bone spurs," suggests that he himself would have been a "good general." Trump also points out that his proposed border wall with Mexico is somehow comparable to a medieval-era wall surrounding the Vatican. And for good measure, Trump tells everyone present that, "They say I am the most popular president in the history of the Republican Party." The president then goes on to falsely claim that Russia fought in Afghanistan during the late 70's to "fight terrorism," and the war in that Middle Eastern country caused the collapse of the then-Soviet Union, by draining their finances. The bizarre claims are immediately lampooned by numerous political historians, and by the *Wall Street Journal*, which publishes an editorial taking aim at Trump's "reprehensible" retelling of history, and the "slander" of U.S. allies. **1/2/19**

- On the day that a new Congress is sworn in, and Nancy Pelosi is elected Speaker of the House of Representatives, which shifts the balance of the government away from total Republican control, Donald Trump gives an impromptu press conference to air grievances about the failure of an agreement to finance his sought after border wall with Mexico. The hastily-called press conference (only a five minute warning is given) features Trump and several Homeland Security and Border Patrol officials, lasts for 16 minutes, and ends without the president taking any questions from the press. **1/3/19**

- The president, feeling the heat of impeachment rhetoric from some in the Democratic Party, tweets his defense. "How do you impeach a president who has won perhaps the greatest election of all time, done nothing wrong (no Collusion with Russia, it was the Dems that colluded), had the most successful first two years of any president, and is the most popular Republican president in party history 93%?" Trump also blames recent declines in the U.S. financial markets on Democrats, tweeting that Democratic victories in the November 2018 midterm elections were responsible for the recent downturn. **1/4/19**

- Newly-elected member of the House of Representatives, Rep. Rashida Tlaib (D-MI), uses a profane reference about the president in front of her supporters by claiming, "We're going to go in and impeach the mother-fucker." Donald Trump, who is no stranger to using profane language against his detractors states that Tlaib, "dishonored her family," and that, "Her comments were disgraceful," and "Highly disrespectful to the United States of America." **1/4/19**

■ Donald Trump announces that he might declare a national emergency to build his long sought after border wall with Mexico, if he chooses to do so. "We can do it. I haven't done it. I may do it," declares the president during a press conference in the White House Rose Garden. Trump also doubles down on his demand that the wall be built of steel or concrete, and must be funded by at least $5 billion dollars. **1/5/19**

■ Donald Trump goes on an unprovoked rant on the media, launching into a tweetstorm about how he believes he's treated unfairly by the media. Trump posts, "With all of the success that our Country is having, including the just released jobs numbers which are off the charts, the Fake News & totally dishonest Media Concerning me and my presidency has never been worse. Many have become crazed lunatics who have given up on the TRUTH!" Trump continues, "The Fake News will knowingly lie and demean in order (to) make the tremendous success of the Trump Administration, and make me look as bad as possible. They use non-existent sources & write stories that are total fiction. Our Country is doing so well, yet this is a sad day in America!" Trump, still venting, continues. "The Fake News Media in our Country is the real Opposition Party. It is truly the Enemy of the People! We must bring honesty back to journalism and reporting." **1/7/19**

■ The president delivers a nine-minute national network address to America in order to build support for congressional funding for his long-promised southern border wall with Mexico. Trump uses the airtime to deliver a message that the wall is needed for border security, and that there is a "growing humanitarian and security crisis" at the border, and that Democrats are responsible for the current government shutdown. Trump paints a horrific picture of murders and rapes by undocumented immigrants, who are also smuggling drugs across the border. Even though Trump's speech is relatively sedate and mostly straightforward, fact checking of the address finds numerous false and misleading statements, which are quickly pounced upon by Democrats, and major news outlets. **1/7/19**

▮ In a stunning CNN interview, Donald Trump's personal attorney, Rudy Giuliani tells anchor Chris Cuomo that he never said that there wasn't collusion between the Trump presidential campaign and Russia, and that he only said that the president wasn't involved. Giuliani's remarks directly contradict earlier statements he made on Fox News and other media outlets, when he explicitly said that the entire Trump campaign had no involvement with Russia at all. **1/7/19**

▮ Donald Trump claims that some previous U.S. presidents told him that they should have ordered a wall built to protect the U.S. southern border with Mexico. Representatives from former presidents Reagan, Carter, Bush, and Obama all deny that such discussions with Trump had ever taken place. **1/8/19**

▮ The president tells reporters that he believes that "many (of the 800,000 furloughed U.S. government workers) of those people agree with what I am doing," referring to shutting the government down to secure funding for the border wall. The billionaire businessman turned president also says about the workers not receiving paychecks, "I can relate, and I'm sure the people on the receiving end will make adjustments. They always do." **1/9/19**

▮ Donald Trump abruptly walks out of a meeting with congressional Democrats after they do not agree to fund his southern border wall with Mexico. Trump allegedly asks House Speaker Nancy Pelosi (D-CA), "Will you agree to my wall?" Pelosi responds, "No," and Trump leaves the meeting. Trump later tweets that he said, "bye-bye" as he left because, "nothing else works." **1/9/19**

▮ Donald Trump, during an impromptu press conference at the White House, tells reporters that his oft-mentioned promise to have the Mexican government pay for the U.S. southern border wall is not what he said. Trump said that he never promised Mexico would pay, stating, "Obviously, I never said this, and I never meant they're going to write out a check." A fact check shows that Trump made the claim about Mexico funding the wall over 200 times during the 2016 U.S. presidential campaign, and it was featured on his website. Trump now claims that Mexico will indirectly pay for the wall through a revised NAFTA trade agreement, even though that legislation has not been ratified by Congress. **1/10/19**

■ The *New York Times* releases a story that the FBI launched an investigation to see if Donald Trump was acting to assist Russia while serving as U.S. president. The probe was initiated after Trump fired then-FBI Director James Comey, and was under the direction of then-acting Director Andrew McCabe. Trump, upon hearing the news, launches into a Twitter-fueled rage, posting, "The corrupt former leaders of the FBI, almost all fired or forced to leave the agency for some very bad reasons, opened up an investigation on me for no reason & with no proof, after I fired Lyin' James Comey, a total sleeze." He also adds, "My firing of James B. Comey was a great day for America. He was a Crooked Cop." **1/11/19**

■ Reports surface that show Donald Trump concealed details of lengthy private conversations he had with Russian President Vladimir Putin. In at least one instance, Trump ordered the seizure of his own interpreter's notes, and ordered the linguist not to discuss the conversation between the two world leaders with other administration officials. **1/13/19**

■ Donald Trump continues to insult and belittle his political rivals by mocking an Elizabeth Warren (D-MA) campaign video, tweeting, "If Elizabeth Warren, often referred to by me as Pocahontas, did this commercial from Bighorn or Wounded Knee instead of her kitchen, with her husband dressed in full Indian garb, it would have been a smash!" Trump's message draws immediate criticism from both sides of the political aisle, and from Native American groups. **1/14/19**

▮ Due to the government shutdown, the White House honors the national college football champion Clemson University by serving them fast food hamburgers, pizza, and chicken nuggets during their celebratory visit. The fast food was necessary because a majority of the White House food serving and preparation staff is furloughed during the shutdown. Trump then tweets about the event. "Great being with the National Champion Clemson Tigers last night at the White House. Because of the Shutdown I served them massive amounts of food (I paid), over 1000 hamberders (sic), etc. Within one hour, it was gone. Great guys and big eaters. Trump's misspelling of "hamburgers" draws mocking responses from late night talk show hosts, and a tweet from fast food chain Burger King, who posts, "Due to a large order placed yesterday, we're all out of hamberders. Just serving hamburgers today." Several weeks after the White House event, it is revealed that a majority of Clemson's African-American players did not attend the ceremony due to the president's "divisive politics" and "instances of racism." **1/15/19**

▮ Two unions representing government workers furloughed by the shutdown (National Treasury Employees and American Federation of Government Employees Unions), file suit against the Trump administration for requiring their employees to continue working without receiving pay. **1/15/19**

▮ House Speaker Nancy Pelosi (D-CA) calls for the president to postpone his scheduled State of the Union address, scheduled for the end of January, due to the government shutdown. Pelosi also offers Donald Trump an option to present the speech in writing, which he declines. The president, stinging from Pelosi's actions, cancels her congressional trip to Afghanistan. Trump sends a letter to Pelosi, informing her that the military airliner her team was scheduled to use would not be available, and also says that her "public relations event" could be re-scheduled after the government shutdown ends. **1/16/19**

▮ Reports surface that Donald Trump told personal attorney Michael Cohen to lie to Congress about the president's push to secure a lucrative condo project in Moscow during the months before the 2016 U.S. presidential election. The report, from *BuzzFeed News*, suggests that Cohen admitted lying to the office of Special Counsel Robert S. Mueller III under the direct orders of the president. The report draws a rare rebuttal from Mueller's office, saying that the report's "description of specific statements to the special counsel's office, and characterization of documents and testimony obtained by this office, regarding Michael Cohen's congressional testimony are not accurate." **1/17/19**

■ Vice President Pence claims in an interview with CBS News' *Face the Nation* that Donald Trump is like the late Dr. Martin Luther King Jr. because of his "inspiring" the country with the U.S. southern border wall with Mexico. Pence also uses a quote from Dr. King's "I Have a Dream" speech, stating, "Now is the time to make real promises of Democracy," in an attempt to link Trump to the slain civil rights leader. King's son, Martin Luther King III blasts Pence by saying that his father was a "bridge builder," not a "wall builder." **1/20/19**

■ The president posts a bizarre tweet suggesting that the 800,000 U.S. federal workers furloughed by the government shutdown are "honoring" the country in some way. Trump tweets, "To all of the great people who are working so hard for your Country and are not getting paid I say, THANK YOU-YOU ARE GREAT PATRIOTS! We must now work together, after decades of abuse, to finally fix the Humanitarian, Criminal & Drug Crisis at our Border. WE WILL WIN BIG!" **1/21/19**

■ Donald Trump informs House Speaker Nancy Pelosi (D-CA) that he intends to deliver his State of the Union address in the House chamber as scheduled. In a letter to Pelosi, Trump writes, "I will be honoring your invitation, and fulfilling my constitutional duty to deliver important information to the People and Congress of the United States of America regarding the state of our Union. I look forward to seeing you on the evening of January 29th in the chamber of the House of Representatives." Pelosi answers Trump almost immediately, denying him the right to speak in the House. Pelosi's response: "I am writing to inform you that the House of Representatives will not consider a concurrent resolution authorizing the president's State of the Union in the House chamber until government has opened." Trump then fires back at Pelosi, claiming, "The State of the Union has been cancelled by Nancy Pelosi because she doesn't want to hear the truth." One day after the letter exchange, Pelosi "disinvites" the president from delivering his speech, and Trump announces that he will postpone the speech until the government has reopened. **1/23/19**

■ Former Trump lawyer Michael Cohen postpones his scheduled February testimony before the House Oversight and Government Reform Committee, due to "ongoing threats against his family from President Trump and Mr. Rudolph W. Giuliani." Cohen claims through his attorney Lanny J. Davis that he has to, "put his family and their safety first." The "threats" against Cohen and his family are not identified. **1/23/19**

■ Federal agents arrest longtime Trump advisor Roger Stone, charging him with lying to investigators about the Trump Campaign's efforts to access emails stolen by the Russian government which would have contained information detrimental to Hillary Clinton and the Democratic Party during the 2016 U.S. presidential election. Special Counsel Robert S. Mueller III's investigation charges Stone with counts of obstruction and witness tampering, and points to his efforts to obtain damaging emails from WikiLeaks. The White House quickly issues a statement after Stone's arrest, stating, "This has nothing to do with the president." Donald Trump also weighs in on Twitter by posting that his arrest was the, "Greatest Witch Hunt in the History of our Country! NO COLLUSION!" **1/25/19**

■ While visiting the U.S. southern border in support of building a wall, Donald Trump says that border security is necessary to stop vans full of women who were, "Tied up with tape over their mouths. Electrical tape. Usually blue tape…Powerful stuff." ICE and U.S. Border Patrol personnel cannot verify claims that women are being assaulted in this manner at the border. **1/25/19**

■ Congress reaches an agreement to reopen the federal government, ending a 35-day shutdown, affecting 800,000 workers, by passing a bill to keep the government funded for a three-week period, while a solution for U.S. border security is worked out between Congress and the president. The impasse is broken as thousands of flights were being delayed in major U.S. airports due to a lack of air traffic controllers and TSA agents showing up for work. Trump tries to claim victory for breaking the stalemate, but is quickly criticized by conservative news outlets and members of his own party for his handling of the negotiations. **1/25/19**

■ A dozen undocumented workers at Donald Trump's National Golf Club in Westchester, NY are fired, just as Trump is embroiled in an immigration battle with Congress and fresh off a prolonged shutdown of the federal government over funding for his long-promised wall at the U.S. southern border with Mexico. The Trump organization reports that the workers were dismissed due to a routine audit which showed their immigration documents were found to be fraudulent. Some of the employees had worked for Trump for as long as 15 years, and had access to his family and living quarters. **1/26/19**

■ Donald Trump attacks Howard Schultz, former CEO of Starbucks, who is considering a run for president in 2020 U.S. as an independent by tweeting, "Howard Schultz doesn't have the 'guts' to run for President! I watched him on @60Minutes last night and I agree with him that he is not the 'smartest person.' Besides, America already has that! I only hope that Starbucks is still paying me their rent in Trump Tower!" **1/28/19**

■ The president embraces a proposal being touted in several U.S. states to allow public schools to offer Bible literacy classes. Trump tweets his support by posting, "Numerous states introducing Bible Literacy classes, giving students the option of studying the Bible. Starting to make a turn back? Great?" **1/28/19**

▪ According to reports, the 35-day government shutdown allegedly cost the United States $11 billion dollars, and that over $3 billion of those funds will never be recovered. **1/28/19**

▪ In a stunning rebuke to the president's foreign policy views, FBI Director Christopher Wray, CIA Director Gina Haspel, and Dan Coats, Director of National Intelligence, testify before the U.S. Senate that they disagree with many of Donald Trump's positions. At question is North Korea's willingness to denuclearize, Russian interference with U.S. elections, the Iran nuclear agreement, and the potency of the Islamic State (ISIS) in Syria. The three intelligence chiefs however, make no mention of an emergency at the U.S. southern border with Mexico in their testimony. The president fires back on Twitter, criticizing his senior officials by tweeting, "The Intelligence people seem to be extremely passive and naïve when it comes to the dangers of Iran. They are wrong! When I became President, Iran was making trouble all over the Middle East and beyond. Since ending the terrible Iran Nuclear Deal, they are MUCH different, but a source of potential danger and conflict. They are testing Rockets (last week) and more, and are coming very close to the edge." Trump goes on to say, "There (sic) economy is now crashing, which is the only thing holding them back. Be careful of Iran. Perhaps Intelligence should go back to school!" The day after the Senate testimony, Donald Trump holds a meeting with his top intelligence personnel, and tweets after the gathering that everyone was on the "same page" with regards to numerous world flash points (North Korea, Iran, ISIS and Russia), and that their remarks at the Senate hearing were "mischaracterized" by the media, even though the proceedings were televised live to the nation. **1/29/19**

▪ White House press secretary Sarah Huckabee Sanders tells a Christian television station that she believes that God "wanted Donald Trump to become president," in order to support a "lot of things that people of faith really care about." **1/30/19**

CHAPTER 26

FEBRUARY, BEING THE SHORTEST month of the year, allows the president a chance to "chill out" a bit, especially after a particularly rambunctious January. So it is reported that Mr. Trump engages in a large chunk of "Executive Time," which includes tweeting, yelling at the TV, and searching for reruns of *the Apprentice*.

Donald Trump actually delivers one of his better lines during the delayed State of the Union address, when he laments, "If there is going to be peace and legislation, there cannot be war and investigation." Betcha' Nancy P. wanted to bounce back with, "Since we can't reach you, we'll soon impeach you."

February brings with it a revelation from attorney Michael Cohen that the president did not want to win the 2016 U. S. presidential election. 64,000,000 million Americans tweet simultaneously that they were in total agreement. Cohen also testifies in front of the House Oversight Committee that the president green-lighted hush payments for women with whom he had affairs (shocking!), lied about having bone spurs that kept him out of the Vietnam War (disturbing!), and even had his lawyers threaten to sue his high school and college if they released his grades to the public (WTF?)

Finally, the month brings with it a denial from North Korea's Kim Jong un about knowing why American citizen Otto Warmbier left the U.S. strong and healthy, and departed North Korea wretched and broken, that Trump buys into. Kim also tells the U.S. president that North Korea no longer has nuclear weapons, Elvis is still alive, and asks if Trump could get Dennis Rodman to stop calling him.

▮ According to *Axios*, a leak of internal White House schedules shows that Donald Trump has spent approximately 60% of his time in office engaged in "Executive Time." This reportedly is the time in which the president watches television, tweets, holds impromptu meetings, and engages in other activities not directly related to formal governance. The White House responds to the released information with a tweet from Director of Oval Office Operations Madeleine Westerhout, who posts, "What a disgraceful breach of trust to leak schedules. What these don't show are the hundreds of calls and meetings @RealDonaldTrump takes every day. This POTUS is working harder for the American people than anyone in recent history. **2/3/19**

▮ The U.S. attorney's office in Manhattan orders Donald Trump's inaugural committee to turn over documents related to all financial transactions and other activities tied to the January, 2017 presidential inauguration in Washington, D.C. This follows a slew of questions about irregular fundraising attributed to the inauguration, which reached a record $107 million dollars, and spent lavishly. **2/5/19**

▮ During an informal luncheon with television news anchors before his scheduled State of the Union Address, Donald Trump launches into off-the-cuff insults against select Democrats, calling Sen. Charles Schumer (D-NY) a, "nasty son of a bitch," former vice president Joe Biden, "dumb," and claims that embattled Virginia governor Ralph Northam (D) "choked like a dog," at the press conference he had to defend himself against charges stemming from a racist photo of him in a medical school yearbook. Trump balances his partisan attacks by also dumping on the late Senator John McCain of Nevada, stating that his *New York Times* best-selling book, *The Restless Wave: Good Times, Just Causes, Great Fights and Other Appreciations,* "bombed." **2/5/19**

▮ The president delivers his delayed State of the Union address before Congress, and lashes out at Democrats for backing investigations of his campaign, business, and other endeavors by stating, "If there is going to be peace and legislation, there cannot be war and investigation. It just doesn't work that way." House Speaker Nancy Pelosi (D-CA) responds forcefully to Trump's remarks by reacting, "Presidents should not bring threats to the floor of the House. It's not investigation; it's oversight. It's our congressional responsibility, and if we didn't do it, we would be delinquent in our duties." After the House of Representatives launches a new investigation of Trump through their Intelligence Committee into the president's foreign business activities, he responds by calling the committee's chairman, Rep. Adam Schiff (D-CA), "a political hack." Trump also goes on to lament, "No other politician has to go through that. It's called presidential harassment. And it's unfortunate. And it really does hurt our country." **2/6/19**

■ As Elizabeth Warren (D-MA), officially announces her 2020 U.S. presidential campaign, Donald Trump launches into a mocking attack of the senator. Using a reference to a Native-American tragedy during the 19th century, Trump tweets, "Will she run as our first Native American presidential candidate, or has she decided that after 32 years, this is not playing so well anymore? See you on the TRAIL, Liz!" Trump's reference to the forced relocation of Native Americans which resulted in thousands of deaths, (Trail of Tears) creates immediate blowback from Native groups and others on social media. **2/9/19**

■ Donald Trump, frustrated with Congress's inability to provide financing for a border wall with Mexico, declares a national state of emergency, seeking to appropriate nearly $8 billion dollars to complete the barrier. Trump states, "I didn't need to do this, but I'd rather do it much faster. I just want it to get it done faster, that's all." House Speaker Nancy Pelosi (D-CA) calls the declaration a "power grab by a disappointed president, and numerous legal challenges are considered by Democrats to stop the process. **2/15/19**

■ Vice President Mike Pence is met with complete silence as he addresses attendees of the Munich Security Conference in Germany when he states,

"I bring greetings from the 45th president of the United States of America, President Donald Trump." Pence waits five full seconds for a response, but not one member of the conference applauds his announcement. A copy of Pence's speech provided by the White House notes "applause" after the Vice President's greeting. **2/16/19**

■ Sixteen states, including New York and California, enter into a lawsuit challenging the president's declaration of a national emergency in order to obtain funding for his sought after border wall with Mexico. The suit is filed in the 9th District Circuit Court in California, and contends that the president does not have the constitutional authority to divert U.S. funds to the wall project. **2/18/19**

■ The *New York Times* reports that Donald Trump tried to have acting Attorney General Matthew Whitaker place a judge who was favorable to the president, on the case of hush money paid to women for their silence during the 2016 U.S. presidential election. **2/19/19**

■ Donald Trump angrily reacts to a comment from director Spike Lee during his acceptance speech for best adapted screenplay during the 2019 Academy Awards presentation, after Lee stated, "The 2020 presidential election is around the corner. Let's all mobilize. Let's be on the right side of history." Trump responds on Twitter by posting, "Be nice if Spike Lee could read his notes, or better yet not have to use notes at all, when doing his racist hit on your President, who has done more for African Americans (criminal Justice Reform, Lowest Unemployment numbers in History, Tax Cuts, etc.) than almost any other Pres." **2/25/19**

■ Former Trump personal lawyer Michael Cohen delivers public testimony in front of the House Oversight Committee and paints a negative picture about the personal and professional life of the president. Among the revelations are that Trump never wanted to win the 2016 U.S. presidential election, but rather wanted the campaign to enhance the Trump Companies' brand, calling it the "greatest infomercial in political history."

Cohen also testifies that Donald Trump continued to pursue building a hotel in Moscow during the campaign, even after he claimed the project had ended when he became the Republican nominee. Cohen then details how he lied for Trump by making hush payments to women with whom Trump had affairs, about his false claims of bone spurs keeping from serving in Vietnam, and how Trump's company threatened legal action against his former high school and college if they were ever to release his grades to the public. Trump's former personal attorney accuses Trump of knowing about Roger Stone's contact with WikiLeaks, and the release of thousands of emails intended to hurt Democratic presidential nominee Hillary Clinton. When asked how many times he had lied or carried out nefarious actions on behalf of Donald Trump, Cohen responds that was "over 500 times." **2/27/19**

■ Reports surface that Donald Trump pressured then-Chief of Staff John F. Kelly to get his son-in law Jared Kushner top secret security clearance, a move not supported by top U.S. intelligence officials. **2/28/19**

■ The president, after a second failed summit with North Korea leader Kim Jong un, tells reporters that the Korean dictator insured him that he had no knowledge of the torture and subsequent death of 22 year old college student Otto Warmbier, and that the president took him at his word. The statement was met with a blistering rebuke from Warmbier's parents, who accuse Trump of using their son to cozy up to Kim. **2/28/19**

CHAPTER **27**

MARCH BEGINS WITH THE president delivering a rambling 2 ½ hour speech to the dazed members of the Conservative Political Action Committee (CPAC) in Maryland, where he rails about the under-reporting of crowd size at his inauguration, calls efforts by his political adversaries "bullshit," hugs an American flag, and speaks in a southern drawl. In a normal gathering, an ambulance would be called, and paramedics would examine the speaker for signs of a stroke. In this case, it's just another "get off my lawn" moment for Donald Trump.

The president flexes his muscles a bit as the snowy winter starts to fade in Washington, by reminding his detractors that not only does he control the military, but that he also has considerable sway with "Bikers for Trump." Thousands of Americans tremble of the thought of bearded, middle-aged men wearing too-tight leather jackets from their youth terrorizing them with late-night drive bys and loud mufflers.

March brings with it the usual airing of grievances from the president. He attacks George Conway (who is married to fan favorite, Kellyanne) by calling him "the husband from hell" (Melania Trump reportedly chuckled over that one), along with numerous spit wads thrown at the late Senator John McCain, (who gets far more publicity than any dead guy I can remember). Oh yah, that Mueller report came out this month, too. That allows Donald Trump to tweet the out the two longest words he knows repeatedly; (no) COLLUSION and (no) OBSTRUCTION. The Madness of March awaits.........

■ The president potentially violates ethics rules when he tweets about a Trump golf property being valuable to U.S. and U.K. relations. Trump tweets, "Very proud of perhaps the greatest golf course anywhere in the World. Also furthers U.K. relationship." The promotion of the Trump Scottish golf course (Turnberry) violates the emoluments clause of the U.S. Constitution. **3/2/19**

■ Donald Trump delivers a rambling 2 ½ hour speech to members of the Conservative Political Action Committee (CPAC) in Maryland. During his address, he denounces Democrats, rehashes the debate over his inaugural crowd size in Washington, hugs an American flag, and otherwise airs grievances of every kind. At one point during the speech, Trump calls efforts to hurt him politically "bullshit," and also attacks former Attorney General Jeff Sessions, by mocking his Southern drawl. **3/3/19**

■ The president makes a claim that the Cohen hearings being held by the House Oversight and Reform Committee, may have contributed to his termination of peace talks with Kim Jong un of North Korea. Trump tweets, "For the Democrats to interview in open hearings a convicted liar and fraudster, at the same time as the very important Nuclear Summit with North Korea, is perhaps a new low in American politics and may have contributed to the 'walk.' Never done when a president is overseas. Shame!" **3/3/19**

■ Reports surface that a Chinese business offered to provide clients with access to Donald Trump, which includes mingling, and photo opportunities. The company, GY Investments LLC, run by former massage parlor owner Li Lang, posted opportunities to access the president during "VIP" activities. **3/9/19**

■ Donald Trump makes a gaffe by referring to Apple CEO Tim Cook as "Tim Apple" during a White House event in which Cook was present. What should have been a simple slip of the tongue becomes viral, as Trump staunchly defends himself on Twitter by posting, "At a recent round table meeting of business executives, and long after formally introducing Tim Cook of Apple, I quickly referred to Tim + Apple as Tim/Apple as an easy way to save time and words. The Fake News was disparagingly all over this, & it became yet another bad Trump story." **3/11/19**

▪ During an interview with *Breitbart*, Donald Trump issues a thinly-veiled attack on his enemies. Trump states, "I actually think that the people on the right are tougher, but they don't have to play it tougher. Okay? I can tell you I have the support of the police, the support of the military, the support of Bikers for Trump-I have the tough people, but they don't play it tough-until they go to a certain point, and then it would be very bad, very bad." **3/14/19**

▪ The president uses the backdrop of the St, Patrick's Day weekend to air grievances against his detractors, by taking aim at the late senator John McCain (R-AZ), the television show *Saturday Night Live*, and even at a usual Trump favorite, *FOX News*. Trump's beef with SNL stems from actor Alec Baldwin's portrayal of him, which began during the 2016 U.S. presidential campaign, and has continued through his term in office. Trump was angry about the comedy show's parody of the classic movie *It's a Wonderful Life* shows the president as George Bailey, in an unflattering light. Trump explodes on Twitter by posting, "Should Federal Election Commission and/or FCC look into this? There must be Collusion with the Democrats and, of course, Russia! Such one sided media coverage, most of it Fake News. Hard to believe I won and am winning. Approval Rating 93% with Republicans. Sorry! #MAGA." Trump later proceeds to launch an attack on the late senator by tweeting, "So it was indeed (just proven in court papers) 'last in his class' (Annapolis John McCain that sent the Fake Dossier to the FBI and Media hoping to have it printed BEFORE the Election. He & the Dems, working together, failed (as usual). Even the Fake News refused this garbage!" Not to be outdone, the president lobs a volley at FOX News, his favorite news network, after they suspend host (and Trump mouthpiece) Jeanine Pirro over comments she made about Rep, Ilhan Omar (D-MN) not supporting the U.S. Constitution because she is Muslim and wears a hijab. Trump posts, "Bring back Judge Jeanine Pirro. The Radical Left Democrats, working closely with their beloved partner, the Fake News Media, is using every trick in the book to SILENCE a majority of our Country. They have all out campaigns against Fox News hosts who are doing too well." **3/17/19**

■ A report is issued by the *New Yorker* which shows the increasing dependency of Donald Trump has on the FOX News Network. The column points out that the president acts in concert with the right-leaning network, and that reporters at FOX have as much influence on him as his close advisers and members of his cabinet. **3/19/19**

■ The president engages in a highly public spat with George Conway, husband of White House adviser Kellyanne Conway. Trump fires off a Twitter attack on Conway after the conservative lawyer tweeted about Trump's mental state, by reposting a tweet from his 2020 campaign manager Brad Parscale, which states, "We all know that @realDonaldTrump turned down Mr. Kellyanne Conway for a job he desperately wanted. He barely worked @TheJusticeDepartment, and he was either fired/quit, didn't want the scrutiny? Now he hurts his wife because he is jealous of her success. POTUS doesn't even know him." Trump later tweets that Conway is a "stone cold LOSER & husband from hell!" **3/19/19**

■ Donald Trump once again attacks the late Senator John McCain (R-AZ) during an appearance at a General Dynamics tank factory in Lima, Ohio, Trump lashes out at McCain, saying that he "didn't get the job done" for veterans, and groused that he (the president) did not receive a proper thank you for assisting with arrangements for the late senator's funeral. **3/20/17**

■ The long-awaited release of the Muller report becomes a reality, as the special counsel submits his findings to Attorney General William P. Barr and the Justice Department. Barr then issues a four page summary of the report to Congress, which concludes that Donald Trump and his campaign did not conspire with Russians to interfere with the 2016 U.S. presidential election. Although the report vindicates Trump on the collusion charges, it leaves open the possibility of obstruction of justice, as the Mueller probe finds the question of interference with the investigation as "inconclusive." The president tweets in celebration after the summary is released, "No Collusion, No Obstruction, complete and Total EXONERATION. KEEP AMERICA GREAT!" **3/22/19**

■ The Trump administration takes aim at the Affordable Care Act once again, by moving to eliminate the national healthcare program through the Department of Justice. In a court filing, DOJ officials argue that the ACA, also known as "Obamacare," should be scrapped entirely, including legislation that protects millions of Americans with preexisting conditions, and allows young adults to stay on their parents' plan until age 26. Donald Trump tells reporters, "The Republican Party will soon be known as the party of health care. You watch." **3/26/19**

CHAPTER 28

APRIL BRINGS US THE release of the long-awaited Mueller report, a document that raises a lot of eyebrows, as well as the blood pressure of everyone in Washington. The document reads like the script of a bad Mexican Telenovela, and demonstrates among other things, that the Trump Administration did everything possible to collude with Russia on the 2016 U.S. presidential election, but didn't have the necessary skill set or competence to do so. As a result of the findings, we were treated to a Hosanna-like chorus of "No collusion. No conspiracy" from the president, even when a reporter asked him how his golf game was coming along.

We also find out this month from the current Scientist-in-Chief that seemingly innocent power producing windmills are killing machines, the likes of which rival the power of WMDs. The "very stable genius" declares that the turbines cause cancer, massacre innocent birdies by the truckload, and as an added consequence, destroy property values. Someone inform the Dutch!

Other assorted funzies in April include the president advising the French on how to fight the Notre Dame Cathedral fire (they told him his advice was bogus), claiming that *138 million* Sri Lanka citizens were killed in a terrorist attack (despite their population only being 21 million), misrepresenting where his father, Fred Trump was born (he says Germany, birth records say New York), and suing his own accounting firm (excessive litigation is a Trump cottage industry). And to wrap up our month of April, the president hits another milestone...10,000 lies told to the American public!

▮ Donald Trump, during a Republican fundraiser, claims that the noise of windmills "causes cancer." He also claims that a windmill placed near anyone's home causes their property value to decline by 75%. Not to be outdone, Trump goes on to state that windmills are a "graveyard for birds," indicating that many birds are killed each year during collisions with wind turbines. His statements may very well have been drawn from past experiences with trying to ban construction of wind turbines on the Aberdeenshire, Scotland golf property that Trump owns. **4/3/19**

▮ The president falsely claims that his father, Fred Trump, was born in Germany. Trump states to reporters, "My father is German-was German. Born in a very wonderful place in Germany, so I have a great feeling for Germany." The statement is quickly debunked, as public birth records show that Fred Trump, who is of German decent, was actually born in New York City. **4/3/19**

▮ Donald Trump's administration is dealt a blow by a circuit court barring the U.S. from returning asylum seekers attempting to enter the country through the southern border with Mexico while they wait to be processed by the U.S. immigration system. District judge Richard Seeborg of the U.S. 9th Circuit Court issues a preliminary injunction, temporarily halting the forced retention of asylum seekers in Mexico, drawing a sharp rebuke from the president, who tweets, "A 9th Circuit Judge just ruled that Mexico is too dangerous for migrants. So unfair to the U.S. OUT OF CONTROL!" **4/8/19**

▮ Attorney General William Barr states that he believes "spying did occur" against Donald Trump during the 2016 U.S. presidential campaign, but stops short of directly implicating any individuals or government bureaus of violating the law. When pressed on the issue, Barr replies, "I am not saying improper surveillance occurred. I am saying I am concerned about it, and I am looking into it." **4/10/19**

▮ The U.S. Treasury Department misses a deadline to deliver Donald Trump's tax returns to the House Ways and Means Committee. Treasury Secretary

Steven Mnuchin claims that his department hasn't decided to comply with committee chairman Rep. Richard Neal's (D-MA) request. Mnuchin writes a letter to the lawmaker, stating, "The legal implications of this request could affect protections for all Americans against politically-motivated disclosures of personal tax information, regardless of which party is in power." House Democrats claim that Mnuchin's refusal to hand over Trump's tax returns violates a 1924 statute that mandates the IRS provide any taxpayer's returns when requested by certain lawmakers. **4/13/19**

■ Julian Assange, the exiled founder of WikiLeaks, is evicted from the Ecuadorian embassy in London and is immediately held by British police as he awaits extradition to the U.S. to face charges he leaked classified diplomatic and military documents. Donald Trump, who previously praised WikiLeaks repeatedly during his presidential campaign, for releasing documents which were damaging to Hillary Clinton's campaign, tells reporters, "I know nothing about WikiLeaks. It's not my thing." **4/11/19**

■ In a related story, it has been reported that the president assured soon-to-be acting homeland security secretary, Kevin McAleenan, that if he were to close the U.S. southern border with Mexico, and run afoul of the law, he would pardon him. It was not clear if Donald Trump was joking or serious, but the Department of Homeland Security spokesman states, "At no time has the president indicated, asked directed, or pressured the acting secretary to do anything illegal," **4/12/19**

■ The president, reacting to the horrific Notre Dame Cathedral fire in France decides to weigh in on how to battle the blaze, tweeting, "So horrible to watch the massive fire at Notre Dame Cathedral in Paris. Perhaps flying water tankers could be used to put it out. Must act quickly!" French fire officials respond to Trump's advice by posting a response on social media which states, "Hundreds of firemen of the Paris Fire Brigade are doing everything they can to bring the terrible #NotreDame fire under control. All means are being used, except for water-bombing aircrafts, which, if used, could lead to the collapse of the structure of the cathedral." **4/15/19**

▌ The president declares a desire to send asylum seeking immigrants to sanctuary cities to punish congressional districts represented by Democrats, who are not in favor with his policies on the U.S. southern border with Mexico. Although White House and Homeland Security officials say that the idea was considered but rejected, Donald Trump keeps it alive by tweeting, "Due to the fact that Democrats are unwilling to change our very dangerous immigration laws, we are indeed, as reported, giving strong considerations to placing Illegal Immigrants in Sanctuary Cities only." He adds, "The Radical Left always seems to have an Open Borders, Open Arms policy-so this should make them very happy." Responding to Trump, House Speaker Nancy Pelosi (D-CA) calls the idea "unworthy of the presidency of the United States and disrespectful of the challenges that we face as a country, as a people, to address who we are-a nation of immigrants." **4/16/19**

▌ Attorney General William Barr releases a heavily-redacted version of the Mueller report to Congress and the public, following a press conference, to once again state that no Russian collusion or obstruction of justice was found during the investigation. The report's 448 pages are quickly scrutinized by politicians, and the public at large, with both sides of the political aisle using portions of the report to either vindicate or implicate the president of wrongdoing. In the report are 10 instances of possible obstruction by Trump, where he may have "had a motive" to interfere with the investigation, because it could have led to troubling personal or business-related issues, including his attempts to build a Trump Tower in Moscow. Another area of concern with the Mueller Report, is Attorney General William Barr's assessment that the special counsel did not want Congress to make the final determination showing whether Donald Trump was guilty of obstruction. Muller makes it quite clear that Congressional oversight was possible, and that more than the attorney general's opinion should be taken into account. **4/18/19**

▌ A further look into the Mueller Report shows that when the president found out a special counsel was appointed to investigate possible ties with

Russia, Donald Trump reportedly said, "Oh my God. This is terrible. This is the end of my presidency. I'm fucked." Further information from the report shows that White House counsel Don McGahn refused to call the Department of Justice Attorney and have Robert Mueller removed from the Russia probe (without the order being tied to Trump), because it could have created another "Saturday Night Massacre" similar to Watergate and Richard Nixon. McGahn vowed to resign if he were forced to make the call, and Trump backed down. Also in the report, it was shown that the president was directly involved in a lie, claiming that former FBI director James Comey was fired on the recommendation of the Justice Department, when it was actually ordered by Trump himself. **4/18/19**

■ After devastating bomb attacks on churches and hotels in Sri Lanka on Easter Sunday, the president tweets his sympathies by posting, "Heartfelt condolences from the people of the United States on the horrible terrorist attacks on churches and hotels that have killed at least 138 million people and badly injured 600 more. We stand ready to help." The tweet is quickly deleted and re-posted to reflect a more accurate death toll, instead of one that claims the death toll was over six times the entire population of that nation. **4/21/19**

■ Donald Trump takes the unprecedented step of suing his own accounting firm, along with the Democratic chair of the House Oversight Committee, in order to prevent financial information about the Trump companies from being released. The lawsuit filed against Mazurs USA also is followed by a request from Trump to block a subpoena issued by Oversight Committee Chairman Rep. Elijah E. Cummings (D-MD) which seeks financial records from Mazars that address Trump's companies' Statements of Financial Condition, which could show financial improprieties by Trump and his business officials. **4/22/19**

■ During the annual Easter egg hunt on the South Lawn of the White House, the president chooses to mix politics and festivities by telling reporters that one of the children attending the event said "keep building that wall."

Trump also gives a shocking rebuke to reports of White House staffers not following his agenda, by proclaiming, "Nobody disobeys my orders." Trump was also asked if he was worried about possible impeachment and replied, "Not even a little bit." **4/22/19**

■ In an interview with the *Washington Post*, Donald Trump tells the newspaper that he opposes allowing current and former White House aides from testifying in front of Congressional panels. Trump cites the Mueller report as the limits of his cooperation, and claims that the additional interviews would be "very partisan." The defiant statement comes immediately after White House officials announce plans to fight a subpoena for Don McGahn, former White House counsel, to appear in front of the House Judiciary Committee. The Trump administration claims executive privilege as their reason for blocking McGahn's testimony. **4/23/19**

■ In a related story, the Trump administration orders former White House personnel security director Carl Kline not to cooperate with the House Oversight Committee. Kline was asked to appear to answer questions about recklessly granted security clearances for staffers with dubious backgrounds, or unanswered questions about personal or business dealings. **4/23/19**

■ Donald Trump posts a tweet congratulating Nick Bosa, an avid Trump supporter, and critic of former NFL quarterback Colin Kaepernick, as Bosa is drafted in the first round of the NFL college draft. Trump praises Bosa, as he ignores the first pick, Kyler Murray, who is African American, entirely. **4/27/19**

■ During a press campaign rally in Wisconsin, the president makes an outrageous claim about pending abortion laws in that state. Trump states, "The baby is born, the mother meets with the doctor. They wrap the baby beautifully and the doctor and the mother determine whether or not they will execute the baby." Trump's interpretation of the Republican-sponsored *Born–Alive Abortions Survivors Protection Act* is roundly criticized by medical experts and legal experts. **4/28/19**

■ According to the *Washington Post's* fact checker team, Donald Trump reaches the 10,000 lies told threshold during the month of April. **4/29/19**

■ The president and his family, along with the Trump Organization, unite to stop subpoenas from Congressional committees seeking financial information related to their various businesses. Trump files lawsuits against Deutsche Bank and Capital One to prevent them from providing loan information to the House Intelligence and Financial Services Committees, led by Reps. Adam Schiff (D-CA) and Maxine Waters (D-CA). **4/30/19**

CHAPTER 29

MAY IS A RELATIVELY uneventful one, by the usual Trump metric, but there are several items of note that stand out in ominous ways. May is a month that provides the words that will undoubtedly be carved on special counsel Robert S. Mueller III's tombstone (or maybe even Trump's)......"If we had confidence that the president clearly did not commit a crime, we would have said so."

The month is also very "taxing" in other ways, as the president and Congress play hide and seek with 45's financial information and tax returns. This comes on the heels of a *New York Times* report, revealing years of Trump Co's. business records that show over many years, the "very stable genius's" business acumen caused him to buy the Brooklyn bridge and trade the family cow for a handful of beans.

Jerry Falwell Jr., noted legal "scholar" and certified religious knucklehead, presents the notion in May that since Donald Trump has suffered the various slings and arrows of the Mueller Investigation, he needs to have his presidency extended by two years to compensate for the intrusion. Um, Jerry, after you finish reading the scriptures, you might want to peruse this little old document called THE U.S. CONSTITUTION!!! (Sorry, that was a Trumpian all caps moment).

Charges and counter-charges are the flavor of this month. Trump needs an "intervention" from his family, according to Nancy Pelosi, while the president claims that Pelosi has "lost it." Me thinks that a "time out" is really what both sides need, but as one might expect, it's not gonna' happen anytime soon.

■ Donald Trump retweets a social media post from Jerry Falwell Jr., president of Liberty University, which suggests that Trump should have his term in office extended by two years, based on time lost from the Russia investigation. **5/5/19**

■ Treasury Secretary Steven Mnuchin refuses an order from House Democrats to turn over six years of Donald Trump's tax returns, violating a 1924 U.S. law which stipulates that the Secretary "shall furnish" tax records if requested. Mnuchin claims that after consulting with the Justice Department, the Congressional order served no "legitimate purpose." **5/6/19**

■ The *New York Times* reveals 10 years of Donald Trump's tax information, showing that as a businessman, he squandered a vast fortune on failed ventures, and racked up a staggering $1 billion dollars of debt in the process. Trump responds to the story by claiming that his business moves were justified in the world of "rough and tumble" real estate, but side-by-side comparisons of other similar businesses show that Trump's deals were extremely poor ones, and depicts a man who used every conceivable tactic (some bordering on illegal) to obtain wealth. **5/7/19**

■ The president uses his powers of executive privilege over Robert Mueller's Russia report, in order to prevent its release to Congress, hours before the House Judiciary Committee votes to hold Attorney General William Barr in contempt of Congress for ignoring a subpoena issued by that body. The move is Donald Trump's first use of the powers of executive privilege as president. **5/8/19**

■ A federal judge rules against Donald Trump's attempts to defy a House subpoena of his business financial records. U.S. District Judge Amit Mehta finds that both the House Financial Services and Intelligence Committees had "valid legislative purposes" for seeking the information. **5/20/19**

■ A confidential IRS memo claims that the president must turn over his tax returns to Congress, unless he takes the unprecedented step of asserting executive privilege over them. The memo refutes the White House's position that Congress has no legislative purpose for requesting the returns, and states that the release of any president's tax returns, "is mandatory, requiring the Secretary of the Treasury to disclose returns, and return information requested by the tax-writing chairs." **5/21/19**

▌ The president storms out of a meeting with Democratic lawmakers which was scheduled to address an infrastructure bill, because he was reportedly angry about comments made by House Speaker Nancy Pelosi, who claimed that the president was engaged in a "cover-up," related to recent investigations into his finances, and the Russia probe. Trump then goes directly to the White House Rose Garden for a press briefing, complete with pre-written notes and handouts for the media to attack Pelosi and the Democrats. **5/22/19**

▌ Donald Trump launches into a full-scale attack on House Speaker Nancy Pelosi by posting a doctored video of her, highlighting missed words, and some slurred speech. Trump claims that Pelosi has "lost it," attacking the 79 year old's mental sharpness. Shortly thereafter, Pelosi calls for Trump's family and staff to "stage an intervention (with Trump) for the good of the country." **5/23/19**

▌ In the wake of Donald Trump's fiery exit from infrastructure talks with House leaders, the president uses aides to defend his actions during the contentious meeting. Trump tells staffers, one by one, to suggest to reporters that he was calm during the meeting with Pelosi, and did not throw a "temper tantrum," as was stated by Democrats. The president also takes the opportunity to re-state his manufactured self-praise, by reporting that he is an "extremely stable" genius. **5/24/19**

▌ North Korea fires short-range ballistic missiles, violating U.N Security Council resolutions, but Donald Trump denies such launches have taken place. During a press conference with Japan's Prime Minister Shinzo Abe, Trump directly counters reports of missile launches confirmed by John

Bolton, his national security adviser. In a related matter, the president sides with North Korean leader Kim Jong un, whose State media launches into an attack on Democratic presidential candidate Joe Biden, after the former vice president referred to Kim as a "dictator and a tyrant." The Korean-run media calls Biden "a fool of low IQ," to which Donald Trump adds, "Well, Kim Jong un made a statement that Joe Biden is a low IQ individual. He probably is, based on his record. I think I agree with him on that." **5/27/19**

▪ Robert Mueller makes a rare public address about the Russia investigation, as he departs his position as special counsel. Mueller's remarks clearly show that he disagrees with Attorney General William Barr's assertion that Donald Trump committed no crime of obstruction. Mueller states, "If we had confidence that the president clearly did not commit a crime, we would have said so." **5/29/19**

▪ Reports from the *Wall Street Journal* show that there was an attempt from the White House to hide the name of the warship USS John McCain from the president's view during his visit to Japan to meet with Prime Minister Shinzo Abe, by placing a tarp over the name of the ship, and by positioning a barge in front of the vessel, obscuring it so Donald Trump wouldn't have to see the name of the late U.S. Senator, with whom he battled in government, and disparaged in death. The tarp was removed from the ship after Navy personnel discovered what had occurred, and Trump was not aware of the goings on. **5/30/19**

▪ The president imposes a 5% tariff on all goods imported from Mexico, one of America's largest trading partners, unless that country takes drastic steps to stop illegal immigrants from entering the U.S. from its northern border. **5/30/19**

CHAPTER 30

SOMETIMES WHEN THE PRESIDENT favors an adjective, he uses it over and over. Whether it's calling someone a "dog" (usually a woman), or a "rat" (someone who says something bad about him), Donald Trump's voluminous vocabulary (just kidding, really), surfaces in the headlines every time he decides to erupt like Mt. Vesuvius when he's being attacked on social media or in the press (which is often, and usually the result of him tweet-serving the first volley).

June's word is "nasty," and is aimed at two British subjects of some notoriety. Trump refers to Meghan Markle, Duchess of Sussex as such when he tells a reporter "No, I didn't know she was nasty," (referring to comments she made about the president during the 2016 U.S. presidential election. Trump also throttles London's mayor Sadiq Khan by saying that he has been "foolishly nasty" to him, based on comments made to the British press. And for good measure, the president misspells Khan's name, and mocks his height in the same vicious tweet.

Other June dribs and drabs include Donald Trump predicting the collapse of the U.S. economy if he is not reelected in 2020, the Supreme Court blocking his administration's attempts to include a citizenship question on the 2020 Census (relax Melania, no one's going to find out), the fact that the moon is part of Mars (huh?), and his chilling admission to ABC News that he would consider taking opposition research on political opponents from foreign governments (a harbinger of things to come).

■ Donald Trump denies calling Meghan, Britain's Duchess of Sussex (nee Markle), "nasty" during an interview with U.K.'s *The Sun* newspaper. The Duchess made several disparaging comments about Trump during the 2016 U.S presidential election, and Trump was asked about her remarks. Trump reportedly tells a reporter, "No, I didn't know she was nasty." He later tries to walk back his comments on Twitter, posting, "I never called Meghan Markle 'nasty.' Made up by the Fake News Media, and they got caught cold." **6/2/19**

■ The president urges citizens to boycott AT&T, the parent company of CNN, due to the network's "unfair" coverage of him. Trump tweets, "I believe if people stoped (sic) using or subscribing to @AT&T, they would be forced to make big changes @CNN, which is dying with such bad Fake News! Why wouldn't they act. When the World watches CNN, it gets a false picture of USA. Sad!" **6/3/19**

■ Donald Trump, responding to criticism by London mayor Sadiq Khan during the president's visit to Britain, attacks the mayor via Twitter, posting, "@SadiqKhan, who by all accounts has done a terrible job as Mayor of London, has been foolishly 'nasty' to the visiting President of the United States, by far the most important ally of the United Kingdom. He is a stone-cold loser who should focus on crime in London, not me." Trump also goes on to mock the mayor's height (5'6") by tweeting, Kahn (sic) reminds me of our very dumb and incompetent Mayor of NYC, deBlasio, who has also done a terrible job-only half his height." **6/3/19**

■ During the president's stay in England, it is revealed that all of his adult children (including non-administration siblings Donald Jr., Eric, and Tiffany) traveled to that country as part of the U.S. delegation, which was funded by tax dollars. Trump also used the state visit to drop by his money-losing golf property in Ireland (Doonbeg), and schedules a brief last-minute meeting with the Irish Prime Minister to avoid appearances that the golf property visit was business-related. Trump's team also spends nearly $1 million dollars to rent limousines for the Secret Service protection for his family. **6/3/19**

▪ The president tries to make a point about U.S. space exploration, and ends up being mocked on social media. Trump argues that the U.S. should spend money on exploring Mars, rather than going back to the moon, by tweeting, "For all the money we are spending, NASA should Not be talking about going to the Moon-we did that 50 years ago. They should be focused on the much bigger things we are doing, including Mars (of which the Moon is part), Defense and Science!" Twitter immediately blows up with comments about the moon being part of Mars. **6/7/19**

▪ Former White House lawyer John Dean testifies before the House Judiciary Committee, and tells lawmakers that Donald Trump's actions in the Russia investigation were "worse than Watergate," by drawing parallels between Trump and attempts in 1974 of then-President Nixon to stop an investigation of illegal activity by his associates. Trump responds to Dean's testimony by calling him a "sleazebag, loser, and a rat." **6/10/19**

▪ The president states during an interview with ABC News's George Stephanopoulos that he would consider accepting information on his political opponents from foreign governments, if it were offered. During the interview, Trump suggests that "oppo research" from whatever source available is fair game. The president goes on to say that the FBI director who stated the Trump campaign should have contacted the bureau when Russian agents offered disparaging information on Hillary Clinton "is wrong" for coming to that conclusion. **6/12/19**

▪ Donald Trump, reacting to the controversy over his apparent willingness to accept information about political opponents, goes on Twitter to rant, and makes a gaffe about the name of a foreign country. Trump tweets, "I meet and talk to foreign governments every day. I just met with the Queen of England (U.K.), the Prince of Whales (sic), the P.M. of Ireland,

The president of France, and the President of Poland. We talked about Everything." **6/13/10**

■ The office of Special Counsel suggests that White House counselor Kellyanne Conway has violated the Hatch Act (executive branch employees engaging in political activities) on numerous occasions, and should be removed from government service. Donald Trump refuses to accept the Special Counsel's recommendations, claiming that Conway's "right of free speech" was being attacked. **6/13/19**

■ Donald Trump threatens U.S. voters by claiming that the economy would collapse if he is not reelected in 2020. Trump tweets, "The Trump economy is setting records, and has a long way up to go. However, if anyone but me takes over in 2020 (I know the competition very well), there will be a Market Crash the likes of which has not been seen before! KEEP AMERICA GREAT." **6/16/19**

■ Donald Trump schedules the mass deportation of "millions" of undocumented immigrants by Immigration and Customs Enforcement (ICE), and abruptly suspends the crackdown hours before it is scheduled to begin. Trump calls on Congress to solve the immigration crisis, and sets a two week period deadline for them to provide a suitable solution. **6/17/19**

■ Former White House Communications Director Hope Hicks refuses to answer 155 questions put to her during closed-door testimony before the House Judiciary Committee. Hicks does not testify, claiming executive privilege from the White House. **6/19/19**

■ The president suggests that a photographer would be sent to jail if he took a picture of a letter Trump had written involving the Mueller investigation. Trump tells the reporter/photographer, "Excuse me-Under Section II-well you can go to prison instead, because, if you use the photograph you took of the letter that I gave you—"When the reporter asks the president, "I'm sorry Mr. President, were you threatening me with prison time?" Trump then backs down on his threat. **6/21/19**

■ A legal team at a Border Patrol station near the U.S. southern border with Mexico finds inhumane living conditions for 250 teens, children, and infants. The team reports that children are ill, wearing soiled clothing, and in some instances, are denied soap or toothbrushes for basic hygiene. The U.S. State Department defends its treatment of the detained youths, claiming that soap and toothbrushes are not required, as they are not necessary to have "safe and sanitary" living conditions. **6/21/19**

■ The president schedules, and then suddenly calls off an airstrike against Iran in retaliation for that country's downing of a U.S. intelligence drone. Donald Trump has a change of heart when he learns at the "last moment" that the airstrike will result in hundreds of Iranian civilian deaths. **6/21/19**

■ An accusation of sexual assault is lodged against Donald Trump by New York-based writer E. Jean Carroll. The attack, which allegedly occurred in late 1995 or early 1996, happened in a dressing room of Bergdorf Goodman department store in Manhattan. Trump denies the assault ever happened, claiming that Carroll was "totally lying" and that she was "not his type." **6/21/19**

■ During the G-20 Summit in Osaka, Japan, the president jokingly tells Russian president Vladimir Putin, "Don't meddle in the election," (referring to information that supports previous interference by Russia in the 2016 U.S. presidential election). Trump also jokes with Putin that both countries should "get rid of" journalists, and then goes on to insult a 1951 war treaty with Japan, by telling FOX News, "If Japan is attacked, we will fight World War III. But if we're attacked, Japan doesn't have to help us at all. They can watch it on a Sony television." **6/27/19**

■ After the U.S. Supreme Court rules that the Commerce Department cannot place a question about citizenship on the 2020 Census form, Donald

Trump slams the ruling, calling it "ridiculous," and asks for a delay in the Census in order to provide more information to the Court in hopes that the ruling can be overturned. **6/27/19**

■ Following a stellar performance at the Democratic debates by Sen. Kamala Harris (D-CA), Donald Trump Jr. re-tweets a racist post about her from alt-right commentator Ali Alexander which states, "Kamala Harris is implying she is descended from American Black Slaves. She's not. She comes from Jamaican Slave Owners. That's fine. She's not even an American Black. Period." **6/28/19**

CHAPTER 31

JULY, 2019

THE REVOLUTIONARY WAR, ONE of the most difficult periods of America's history. Our troops fought for independence from Britain in the hills and valleys, mountains and fields. And, according to Donald Trump, we had one heck of a Continental Air Force. Yes, he actually said that, in front of America, during a stormy (not "that" Stormy), sweltering "Salute to America" celebration, complete with tanks, fireworks, and the "Baby Trump" balloon. Can this guy throw a shindig, or what?

And speaking of our former Colonial rulers, the British once again infuriate the president when leaked diplomatic cables from one of their ambassadors uses wonderfully alluring alliteration to describe Donald Trump in a way that only the stiff upper lip Brits could pull off, by referring to 45 as, "inept, insecure, and incompetent." The source of the cables, Sir Kim Darroch, is immediately hailed as the second coming of Winston Churchill for his candor, insight, and middle digit held aloft in distain of the resident White House "wanker."

July brings us the usual back and forth between the president and nearly everyone not named Lindsey Graham, as Trump picks fights with "the Squad," four freshmen Congresswomen (whose collective brightness look like halogen spotlights next to the 60 watt Sylvania bulb that is Trump), former House Speaker Paul Ryan (who got out while the getting' was good), and Rep. Elijah Cummings, (who presides over the "rat and rodent infested" city of Baltimore, where Trump's son-in-law manages "rat and rodent infested" properties… oops). So kick off your shoes, throw on the shades, and drink up the craziness of a Trump July!

- Donald Trump holds a 4th of July "Salute to America" celebration, complete with tanks, military flyovers, and a fireworks display in Washington, D.C. The gathering includes a GOP VIP section of politicians and donors, along with a smattering of protesters who oppose the president and his agenda. Also making an appearance at the event is the giant, mocking "Trump Baby" balloon. The gathering is held on a sweltering D.C afternoon and evening, punctuated by frequent downpours. During his address, the president presents a curious version of U.S. history, when he states the following item about U.S. forces during the Revolutionary War: "Our army manned the air, it rammed the ramparts, it took over the airports." Trump's comments, and the fact that airplanes were not in existence during the late 1700's, spur hundreds of social media memes about George Washington leading troops to "retake the concourses," and "seize the baggage claims" of various non-existent airports. The president tries to blame his remarks on a teleprompter malfunction caused by heavy rains. **7/4/19**

- One of Britain's lead ambassadors to the U.S. calls Donald Trump "inept, insecure, and incompetent," in memos leaked to the public. The ambassador, Sir Kim Darroch, also cables 10 Downing Street to inform them that the White House is "uniquely dysfunctional," and that Trump's presidency could end in "disgrace." The British government does not condemn Darroch's remarks, but offers that his views are not necessarily those of the British Government at large, and that they pay their ambassadors to be "candid," and express their judgments as they see fit. Donald Trump then launches into a Twitter attack on Darroch, saying that he had been told that the British diplomat was a "pompous fool," and a "very stupid guy." Trump then tells Britain that he will no longer deal with their ambassador, which causes Darroch to resign his post several days later. **7/7/19**

- The president shares a fake Twitter post claiming that Ronald Reagan predicted Donald Trump would be elected to the presidency one day in the future. The tweet features a picture of Trump and Reagan shaking hands at a White House reception in 1987, with the quote (supposedly from Reagan), "For the life of me, and I'll never know how to explain it, when I met that young man, I felt like I was the one shaking hands with a president." Reports from the *Washington Post*, as well as Snopes.com, find that no such comment was ever made by Reagan. **7/8/19**

■ Donald Trump, while speaking in front of a gathering held to honor an executive order signed to improve kidney dialysis, makes a statement to the assembled crowd that, "The kidney has a very special place in the heart," leaving many attendees scratching their heads, trying to make sense of the comment. **7/10/19**

■ Former House Speaker Paul Ryan says for the book *American Carnage*, by Politico reporter Tim Alberta, that his resignation from Congress was "an escape hatch" from Donald Trump's presidency. He also says that Trump "didn't know anything about government," and that he "wanted to scold him all the time." Predictably, the president launches into Ryan, calling him, "a baby," and a "terrible Speaker who didn't know what he was doing." **7/11/19**

■ In a scathing attack against certain members of the House of Representatives, the president tweets that the "Progressive Democrat Congresswomen should go back to their corrupt broken, and crime-infested countries." Donald Trump's comments are aimed at four freshman Congresswomen, Reps. Rashida Tlaib (D-MI), Ilhan Omar (D-MN), Ayanna Pressley (D-MA), and Alexandria Ocasio-Cortez (D-NY), because of negative comments the four had made about him at various times. All except Congresswoman Omar were born in the United States. **7/14/19**

■ The U.S. House of Representatives votes to condemn the president's racist remarks about the four minority Congresswomen known as "The Squad," who he told to "go back" to the countries of their origin. The vote was predictably down party lines, with only four Republicans joining the Democrats in condemning the president's remarks. Donald Trump posts a number of tweets in response, including one where he states, "I don't have a racist bone in my body." **7/17/19**

■ At a campaign rally in North Carolina, the president once again attacks Rep. Ilhan Omar, prompting the pro-Trump crowd to erupt into cheers of "send her back," aimed at the representative. The president allows the chants to continue for a full 13 seconds before he continues to speak. The next day, when asked about the chants, Trump says, "I disagree with it, by the way," and that he tried to suppress the chants by speaking "very quickly." Trump then reverses field the very next day, by calling the chanting crowd members at his rally, "incredible patriots." **7/17/19**

■ Donald Trump once again brings up his false allegations of voter fraud during the 2016 U.S. presidential election in California, when he addresses a group of young Conservatives about the dangers of Socialism. Trump tells the crowd, "Those numbers in California and numerous other states, they're rigged. They've got people voting that should not be voting. They vote many times, not just twice, not just three times. It's like a circle. They come back. They put a new shirt on. And in many cases, they don't even do that." Trump continues, "You know what's going on. It's a rigged deal." Trump also falsely tells the attendees from the Turning Point USA Teen Student Action Summit in Washington that he has been guaranteed absolute power to do as he pleases while serving as president, due to Article II of the U.S. Constitution. Trump states, "Then I have an Article II, where I have the right to do whatever I want as president." **7/23/19**

■ Also, during the president's appearance at the Turning Point USA event, a fake presidential seal is projected behind Donald Trump. The doctored seal features a two headed eagle (similar to Russia's seal). One of the eagle's claws is holding golf clubs (mocking Trump's penchant for excessive golf outings), and the other claw holds a wad of cash. The writing on the fake seal is in Spanish (an obvious reference to the U.S southern border affair), and reads, "45 is a puppet." Organizers for the event try to blame the incident on "a last-minute AV mistake," but ultimately fire the staffer responsible for it. **7/23/19**

▋ Donald Trump, showing frustration over Democrats pushing for his tax returns to be released, turns the table and attacks former president Obama by saying that his book deal (one he signed after he left office) is improper, and should be investigated. Trump suggests that Congress should "subpoena all of Obama's records." To add to the absurdity of Trump's comments, he goes on to tell reporters that the former president damaged the air conditioning in the White House's West Wing. Trump complains," Now it's freezing or hot in here." **7/26/19**

▋ The president attacks Rep. Elijah Cummings (D-MD) on Twitter, by insulting his Congressional district. Trump, within days of his controversial remarks aimed at four minority Congresswomen, tweets that Cummings' district is considered "the worst run and most dangerous anywhere in the United States. No human being would want to live there." He also goes on to call the city of Baltimore, which lies in Cummings' district, "a disgusting rat and rodent infested mess." In response, the *Baltimore Sun* writes a scathing editorial retort to Trump, calling him, "The useful idiot of Vladimir Putin," and that he is, "Still not fooling most Americans into believing he's even slightly competent in his current post, or that he possesses a scintilla of integrity." The *Sun* editorial ends by stating, "Better to have some vermin living in your neighborhood than to be one." **7/27/19**

▋ Coinciding with the president's comments about Baltimore, the *New York Times* releases a 2017 report from ProPublica showing that the company owned by Donald Trump's son-in-law Jared Kushner manages property in Baltimore that has been cited for health violations, including rats, mold, roaches, and other infestations. **7/29/19**

▋ After the Reverend Al Sharpton takes to Twitter to criticize Donald Trump's comments on Baltimore and Rep. Elijah Cummings, the president strikes back at the MSNBC television host by tweeting, "I have known Al for 25 years. Went to fights with him & Don King. Always got along well. He 'loved Trump!' He would ask for favors often. Al is a con man, a troublemaker, always looking for a score. Just doing his thing. Must have intimidated Comcast/NBC. Hates Whites and Cops!" **7/29/19**

∎ Donald Trump falsely claims that he assisted in the cleanup of the 911 tragedy by suggesting he was on scene and says, "I helped a little." Reports from workers cleaning up the debris confirm that Trump had workers assisting in the work, but that he did not participate in the cleanup efforts himself. **7/29/19**

CHAPTER 32

WHEN ONE LOOKS AT Trump's August, you get a sense just how clinically unfit a president he is while under the spotlight of public scrutiny. It almost seems as though he is someone who not only makes bad decisions when dealing with any sensitive issue, but seeks to double-down the confuzzled craziness almost immediately. To wit:

In dealing with the aftermath of the mass shootings in El Paso, Texas, and Dayton, (or is it Toledo?) Ohio, Trump chooses to visit wounded victims in the hospital, but no one wants to see him. Good decision? Take some quick photos of the doctors and nurses, and praise their efforts. Trump decision? Bring in a wounded infant who just became an orphan due to the massacre, and pose with the child while smiling and giving a thumbs up sign. Want more? Here goes:

You've successfully banned citizens of certain predominantly Muslim countries from entering the U.S., infuriating, well, you know, Muslims. Good decision? Talk about the benefits of why you believe this makes our country safer. Trump decision? Convince Israel's loose-cannon of a Prime Minister, Ben Netanyahu, to deny entry to U.S Congresswomen Ilhan Omar and Rashida Tlaib, both Muslims, from entering HIS country. Solid logic.

And there's more in August. To buy or not buy Greenland (Trump Tower Nuuk, anyone?), telling companies to stop doing business with China (then we won't have any more cheesy MAGA hats, will we?), or dropping bombs into hurricanes (I… just… can't). So read on and relive the righteous rigmarole of a Trump August.

■ Following deadly mass-shootings in Dayton, Ohio and El Paso, Texas, The president addresses the nation in its time of grief, to denounce white supremacy, but instead places blame on mental illnesses and violent video games, rather than addressing gun control legislation. Also, during his remarks, Trump, reading from a teleprompter, mistakenly refers to the shooting victims in "Toledo," rather than Dayton. **8/5/19**

■ Fast on the heels of the two mass shootings in El Paso and Dayton, video of a Trump rally from May, 2019 surfaces, when he asks the crowd, "How do you stop these people?" (referring to migrants crossing the U.S. border). The response from the crowd brings cries of "shoot them," which elicits a smile from Trump, but he does not address the comment directly. **8/6/19**

■ In the wake of recent mass shootings in Dayton and El Paso, Venezuela and Uruguay's foreign ministers issue advisories to their citizens who plan to travel to the U.S. The advisories warn citizens not to gather in places where large crowds assemble such as shopping centers, sporting events, and religious activities. Donald Trump then promises to lash out against any nation that issues travel advisories for the United States. Trump says, "We are a very reciprocal nation, with me as the head. When somebody does something negative to us in terms of a country, we do it to them." **8/6/19**

■ While making a Twitter comment about Google and social media influence elections, the president misspells his own last name. Trump tweets, "Lou Dobbs stated that this is a fraud on the American public.....and boosted negative stories on Donald Ttrump" (sic). **8/7/19**

■ The president and First Lady Melania Trump travel to El Paso, Texas to visit with wounded victims of a mass shooting and the first responders who attended to them, and find that none of the still- hospitalized survivors want to meet with them. Some of the wounded cite privacy concerns, but others refuse to see the president. The hospital (El Paso University Medical Center), quickly arranges to bring in two discharged shooting victims to meet with Trump, including a two-month old baby who was left orphaned by the tragedy. Donald Trump has a picture taken with the child, while smiling and giving a "thumbs-up" sign. Even though Trump makes it clear that he intends to stay away from politics during the Dayton and El Paso visits, he spends time attacking Democratic presidential candidate Beto O'Rourke, Senator Sherrod Brown (D-OH), Dayton mayor Nan Whaley, former Vice President Joe Biden, the *New York Times*, and FOX News. To make matters worse, the president is caught on cell phone video in the hospital, bragging about the size of the crowd at his recent El Paso rally, and how O'Rourke had smaller numbers at his own recently-held rally. It is later reported that following the El Paso hospital visit, Trump lashed out at his own staff for not having press coverage of his interaction with patients, even though a decision was made by the White House to not allow cameras or reporters inside the hospital. Finally, the president claims to a reporter, "My rhetoric brings people together." **8/9/19**

■ Donald trump retweets a conspiracy theory about the death of accused child rapist Jeffery Epstein. The tweet, from comedian Terrance K. Williams states, "Died of SUICIDE on 24/7 SUICIDE WATCH? Yeah right! How does that happen? #JefferyEpstein had information on Bill Clinton & now he's dead. I see #TrumpBodyCount trending but we know who did this! RT if you're not surprised #EpsteinSuicide #ClintonBodyCount #ClintonCrimeFamily." **8/11/19**

■ Former White House Communications Director Anthony Scaramucci, once a staunch supporter of the president, criticizes him openly by claiming that he is "off the rails." Scaramucci goes farther by stating in an interview that, "The honest people in the room know he is crazy." Donald Trump predictably responds via Twitter, attacking his former employee by posting, "Anthony Scaramucci, who was quickly terminated (11 days) from a position that he was totally incapable of handling, now seems to do nothing but television as the all-time expert on 'President Trump.' Like many other so-called television experts, he knows very little about me." **8/12/19**

■ The Trump administration, in its latest attack on immigrants to the U.S., announces that it will strongly consider denying green cards to legal immigrants who use public benefits, including housing assistance, food stamps, or Medicaid. The standards for their new policy, entitled "Inadmissibility on Public Charge Grounds, sets more difficult criteria for immigrants seeking permanent residency in the country. Acting U.S. Immigration Services Director Ken Cuccinelli makes a statement about the new directive, by adapting the Statue of Liberty poem by Emma Lazarus, to say, "Give me your tired, your poor, your people who can stand on their own two feet and who will not become a public charge," instead of the standard, "Give me your poor, your huddled masses, yearning to be free." **8/12/19**

■ In an unprecedented move, Israeli Prime Minister Benjamin Netanyahu denies entry to Israel for U.S. Congresswomen Rep. Ilhan Omar (D-MN) and Rashida Tlaib (D-MI), after Donald Trump tweets that the prime minister would, "show great weakness," by allowing them to enter his country, and that Omar and Tlaib, "hate Israel and all Jewish people, and there is nothing that can be said or done to change their minds." Netanyahu's order is met with widespread derision across the globe, from many political leaders. **8/15/19**

■ Donald Trump tells attendees at a rally in New Hampshire that he was once named Michigan's "Man of the Year," despite no proof that he was ever given such an award. Also, during the same rally event, Trump tells the audience that their financial security depends on his being elected to a second term as president. Trump boasts, "Whether you love me or hate me, you have to vote for me." **8/16/19**

■ Reports surface which claim that union workers at a Royal Dutch Shell's manufacturing facility in Pennsylvania were informed that they had to attend a speech by Donald Trump, or take the day off without pay. Workers who attend are told that they could not, "yell, shout, or protest" during the scheduled White House event. **8/17/19**

■ The president tells reporters that he is interested in purchasing the island of Greenland. At first, it is not known if Donald Trump is serious about the transaction, but the Greenland Ministry of Foreign Affairs posts a tweet in response that states, "We're open for business, not for sale." Later, after Denmark (the ruling government of Greenland) rebuffs Trump's "offer," the president cancels his scheduled trip to that country, calling Danish Prime Minister Mette Frederiksen's remarks, "not nice." **8/19/19**

■ The president downplays talk of the U.S. heading towards recession because he gave citizens a "tremendous tax cut," Trump then goes on to say that Americans are loaded up with money," and that "our consumers are rich." **8/19/19**

■ Donald Trump attacks four freshmen minority members of the House of Representatives (aka "The Squad") by declaring, "Any Jewish people that vote for a Democrat, it shows either a total lack of knowledge, or great disloyalty." **8/20/19**

■ The president, in the wake of mass shootings in Dayton, Ohio and El Paso, Texas backs off his promise to push stronger background checks for gun purchases after a phone conversation with the National Rifle Association's president, Wayne LaPierre. **8/21/19**

■ During a rambling press conference, Donald Trump states that he is the "chosen one," who is best equipped to take on China with his trade and tariff policies. Trump later tries to brush off his claim by saying he was just being sarcastic. **8/21/19**

■ Donald Trump retweets a social media post that claims he is a messiah for the world's Jewish population." Wayne Allan Root's post states, "President Trump is the greatest President for Jews and for Israel in the history of the world…and the Jewish people in Israel love him like he's the King of Israel. They love him like he is the second coming of God. But American

Jews don't know him or like him." In the retweet Trump writes, "Thank you Wayne Allyn Root for all the nice words." **8/22/19**

■ The president, exhibiting growing anger at the U.S. Federal Reserve, lunches into a Twitter attack at its chairman Jerome Powell for failing to lower interest rates. Trump posts, "As usual, the Fed did NOTHING. We have a very weak Fed. My only question is, who is our biggest enemy, Jay Powel (sic) or Chairman Xi?" **8/23/19**

■ Donald Trump, in continuing attacks on China with numerous trade tariffs, announces that he is demanding U.S. companies stop doing business with the Asian nation. Trump tweets, "Our great American companies are hereby ordered to immediately start looking for alternatives to China, including bringing…your companies HOME, and making your products in the USA." The president takes another snipe at China by announcing that he is ordering UPS, Federal Express, and Amazon to block any deliveries of the drug fentanyl from China. **8/23/19**

■ It is reported from several sources that the president asked Homeland Security and NSC officials to look into the practicality of dropping conventional bombs from the air into hurricanes, in order to stop them. Reports also surface that Donald Trump originally asked if a nuclear bomb could be used in the same capacity. The idea was quickly dropped. **8/25/19**

■ The president, speaking at the annual G7 summit in France, reiterates his claim that an obscure 1977 law would enable him to declare a national emergency and force U.S. businesses to leave China. Trump is then asked by a reporter if he had any second thoughts about imposing trade tariffs on China, and responds, "Yeah, sure, why not? I have second thoughts about everything." Shortly after Trump's comments are made public, the White House attempts to walk back the president's statement by claiming that reporters were misinterpreting his words. Trump also departs the G7 before talks on climate change and global warming are discussed. The president then floats the idea that the 2020 G7 summit scheduled to be held in the U.S., should be booked at his Doral Miami Golf Resort, sparking cries of conflict of interest. **8/25/19**

■ The president verbally attacks Puerto Rico in the wake of an oncoming hurricane by complaining about the island's misfortune on Twitter. Trump posts, "Wow! Yet another big storm heading to Puerto Rico. Will it ever end? Congress approved 92 Billion Dollars for Puerto Rico last year, an all-time record of its kind for 'anywhere.'" Trump continues his assault on the island with more tweets. "Puerto Rico is one of the most corrupt places on earth. Their political system is broken, and their politicians are either incompetent or Corrupt." He then goes on to claim, "And by the way, I'm the best thing that ever happened to Puerto Rico." It is also reported that the Trump administration diverted $155 million dollars from FEMA, which was earmarked for disaster relief, as the hurricane bears down on Puerto Rico. **8/27/19**

■ Donald Trump takes a swipe at Fox News, claiming that the network is no longer his ally. Trump lashes out after a DNC spokeswoman appears on FOX's *America's Newsroom* program. Trump posts on Twitter to show his displeasure by declaring, "The new @FoxNews is letting millions of GREAT people down! We have to start looking for a new News Outlet. Fox isn't working for us anymore." **8/29/19**

■ The president, in a rush to have his long-promised border wall built before the 2020 election, reportedly tells officials to do whatever it takes to finish the wall on the U.S. southern border with Mexico. Trump is said to have told officials to fast-track construction, seize private lands, and ignore current environmental laws in doing so. It is also reported that Trump promised pardons for those charged with crimes resulting from the project. The White House denies that Trump made such a promise to anyone. **8/29/19**

■ The Trump administration ends a program which allows immigrant families who have children with life-threatening illnesses such as HIV or cancer to stay in the U.S. while receiving treatment. **8/29/19**

■ The president chastises U.S. businesses that challenge his tariffs or are questioning other trade tactics he has initiated. Trump tweets, "Badly run and weak companies are smartly blaming these small tariffs instead of themselves for bad management…and who can really blame them for doing that? Excuses!" **8/30/19**

■ Donald Trump posts a picture of an Iranian rocket that was involved in a launch pad accident on Twitter. The image, most likely taken from a classified satellite or secret drone, shows the missile with a resolution that is far higher than any other known source, and raises concerns that the president is releasing classified military technology to the world. When questioned about this, Trump defiantly tells reporters, "We had a photo and I released it, which I have the absolute right to do." **8/30/19**

CHAPTER 33

THE MONTH OF SEPTEMBER is usually transitional, when summer makes way for fall. It's also a month for meteorological uncertainty, as turbulence in the upper atmosphere causes forceful, undisciplined bellowing of wind known as hurricanes. And, when it clashes with another forceful, undisciplined windbag in the White House, we get "Sharpie-gate." Yes, September gives us a view of a president using a 98 cent marking pen to draw a bogus storm path on a weather map generated by millions of dollars of state-of-the-art technology, just to show the world that although he's never heard of a Category 5 hurricane before, he knows more about their movements than almost anyone.

During the month we find that National Security Adviser John Bolton is fired (by Tweet, of course) because he "disagreed strongly" with many of Donald Trump's positions. This statement from the president immediately jettisons the mustachioed one from boot-licking sycophant, to brilliant visionary.

Trump's battles in September include a spat with *Will and Grace* star Debra Messing ("she's engaging in McCarthyism" and blacklisting his supporters), singer John Legend ("boring"), and his wife, actress Chrissy Teigen ("filthy-mouthed"), along with the late ABC News reporter Cokie Roberts ("She never treated me nicely"), and new environmentally-friendly light bulbs ("I always look orange").

But despite all of the balderdash and kerfuffle of a traditionally sleepy transition month, things are about to get "woke," as all the hip kids say, as Nancy Pelosi puts DJT in her impeachment crosshairs.

■ In the shadow of Hurricane Dorian (a major Category 5 storm) bearing down on Florida, the president tells reporters that he's "not sure that (he's) ever heard of a Category 5 hurricane," despite four Category 5 storms endangering the U.S. since he took office. Donald Trump also tweets that Hurricane Dorian could possibly impact Alabama during its rampage, but he is quickly rebuked by the National Weather Service, who tweets, "Alabama will NOT see any impacts from #Dorian. We repeat, no impacts from Hurricane #Dorian will be felt across Alabama." **9/2/19**

■ In a related story, the White House issues an apparently altered National Weather Service map, showing that Alabama was at one time in the path of Hurricane Dorian. The new picture, displayed by the president shows a hurricane map showing Alabama to be included in Dorian's path, which was hand drawn with a black marking pen. **9/4/19**

■ The Trump administration diverts $3.6 billion dollars from planned military projects in order to begin work on the president's long-promised border wall with Mexico. Reports indicate that no less than 127 projects will be plundered in order to secure enough funds to build 175 miles of barrier. Senator Charles Schumer (D-NY) charges that Trump is trying to "usurp exclusive power of the purse and loot vital funds from our military." **9/4/19**

■ It is discovered that Vice President Mike Pence lodged far away from scheduled diplomatic meetings in Dublin, Ireland in order to stay at a Trump-owned property. The resort, Doonbeg, is located 125 miles away from the Irish capital, and was reportedly suggested by the president for Pence's visit. **9/4/19**

■ Donald Trump engages in a spat with *Will and Grace* star Debra Messing after the NBC sitcom star questions the mental acuity of African Americans who voted for Trump by saying that they were "mentally ill." Trump responds to Messing's statement (which was later retracted by the actress), by claiming that she is engaging in "McCarthyism" by creating a "black-list" of Trump's supporters. **9/4/19**

▮ The House Oversight Committee investigates whether the U.S. Air Force is diverting airplane refueling stops to a small airport in Prestwick, near Donald Trump's failing luxury resort in Scotland. The refueling stops also reportedly include overnight stays at Trump's resort, which are considerably more expensive than other local accommodations nearby. Stops at Prestwick reportedly rose from 95 in 2015, to 259 during the first 9 months of 2019 resulting in fuel purchases at considerably higher rates than other airports in the region. **9/7/19**

▮ It is revealed that employees of the National Oceanic and Atmospheric Administration (NOAA) were warned not to contradict the president's statements about Hurricane Dorian impacting Alabama. This creates a rift between NOAA and its division of the National Weather Service, who originally tweeted that the president was incorrect about his statement regarding the hurricane's path. Reports also surface that the Secretary of Commerce, Wilbur Ross, threatened to fire top NOAA officials unless they publically supported the president's version of events regarding Dorian. **9/7/19**

▮ Republican leaders in several states consider cancelling GOP primaries in advance of the 2020 U.S. presidential election, in order to give full party support to Donald Trump. Trump faces official challenges from former Massachusetts governor William Weld, along with former Congressional representative Joe Walsh. **9/7/19**

▮ Donald Trump takes personal offense that an *NBC Nightly News* special program on prisons makes no mention of his First Step Act, which was a criminal justice reform bill that received strong bi-partisan support in Congress. The two hour program, narrated by NBC's Lester Holt, draws a four tweet barrage from Trump, aimed at Holt and singer John Legend, who also appears on the program. Trump tweets, "I SIGNED IT INTO LAW, no one else did, & Republicans deserve much credit." Trump continues to personally attack Legend and his wife Chrissy Teigen by posting, "Guys like boring…musician @johnlegend and his filthy-mouthed wife are talking about how great it is (crime bill), but I didn't see them around when we needed help getting it passed." **9/8/19**

▪ The president announces that he is cancelling a meeting with Taliban leadership at Camp David after he is criticized by members of both Democratic and Republican parties for offering to bring the extremist Islamic organization to the U.S. just days before the 18th anniversary of the 9/11 attacks. **9/9/19**

▪ Reports surface that the United States successfully extracted a high-level Russian asset, from that country, partly due to a concern that Donald Trump revealed classified information to Russian Foreign Minister Sergey Lavrov, and also to then-Russian Ambassador to the U.S., Sergey Kislyak, which compromised the foreign agent's cover. Both the White House and CIA deny that the president handled sensitive information improperly, leading to the extraction of the agent in question. **9/9/19**

▪ The president fires national security adviser John Bolton by tweet. Donald Trump says that Bolton, "disagreed strongly with many of my suggestions," and after clashing with the president on numerous foreign policy positions. Bolton was Donald Trump's third security adviser in 2 ½ years in office. **9/9/19**

▪ The White House confirms that acting chief of staff Mick Mulvaney contacted Commerce Secretary Wilbur Ross about the National Weather Service rebuke of the president's erroneous statement about Hurricane Dorian striking Alabama, but stops short of admitting that Mulvaney applied pressure on Ross to have the National Oceanic and Atmospheric Administration (NOAA) release a statement which supported the president's claims under threats of firings, as some media outlets had reported. **9/11/19**

▪ The U.S. Supreme Court let stand a Trump administration rule requiring asylum-seekers from Central American countries attempting to enter the U.S. from its southern border to first apply for asylum in Mexico. The court's ruling, which effectively bans refugees from entering the U.S., is challenged by opponents of Trump's immigration policies. **9/11/19**

■ The Trump administration repeals major Obama-era clean water regulations, which had created protections to prevent polluting streams, water bodies, and wetlands with chemical contamination. The 2015 legislation, known as the Clean Waters of the United States rule, had been derided by Donald Trump as a federal land-grab that hampered the efforts of farmers and developers, but was strongly supported by numerous environmental groups. **9/12/19**

■ Following his rollback of Obama-era energy efficiency rules pertaining to light bulbs, Donald Trump says that the new environmentally friendly lights cause him to have an unacceptable skin tone, Trump tells reporters, "And I looked into it, the bulb that we're being forced to use, number one to me, most importantly, the light's no good. I always look orange. And so do you. The light is the worst." **9/13/19**

■ Reports surface that a serious accusation from a government whistleblower, possibly involving high-ranking members of the Trump administration, was being withheld from Congress. According to House Intelligence Committee Chairman Adam Schiff, (D-CA) a subpoena was presented to acting Director of National Intelligence (DNI) Joseph Maguire, stating that due to the "credible" nature of the complaint, which created "urgent concern," The DNI should cooperate with the subpoena. **9/16/19**

■ The president blocks his former staff secretary and senior adviser Rob Porter from testifying before Congress about issues related to Special Counsel Robert Mueller's Russia investigation. Donald Trump prevents his former staffer from cooperating with the House Judiciary Committee's probe into potential obstruction of justice and corruption. The president once again uses the "absolute immunity" argument to block testimony, as he had previously done with former White House Counsel Don McGahn, and former Communications Director Hope Hicks. **9/17/17**

■ Donald Trump, reacting to the ongoing investigations into his business profiting from the presidency, lashes out at former President Obama. Trump tweets, "House Judiciary, sadly for them after two years and $40,000,000 spent-ZERO COLLUSION, ZERO OBSTRUCTION. So they say, OK, lets (sic) look at everything else, and all of the deals that 'Trump' has done over his lifetime. I have a better idea. Look at the Obama Book Deal, or the ridiculous Netflix deal." **9/16/19**

■ New York State prosecutors subpoena the president's accounting firm in order to obtain eight years of personal and corporate tax returns, to begin investigating him, along with his family members, for any role they may have played in hush-money payments made to cover illicit affairs the president allegedly had before taking office. **9/16/19**

■ ABC News reporter Cokie Roberts dies at age 74 from breast cancer and her career draws praise from former presidents Bush and Obama, calling her a "role model" for young women professionals, at a time when journalism was largely dominated by men. Donald Trump, when asked about Roberts exclaims, "She never treated me nicely." **9/17/19**

■ A major controversy erupts for the White House, as news of a government whistleblower's claim of improprieties regarding Ukraine stem from the Executive Branch, result in an official complaint being filed with the Department of National Intelligence (DNI). The department's acting director, Joseph Maguire does not hand over the complaint to Congress, as specified by law, because he was being prevented from doing so by the White House. According to sources, the whistleblower was made aware of an offer by Donald Trump to Ukraine's President Volodymr Zelensky that $250 million dollars of military aid would be given to his country in exchange for an investigation on Democratic presidential candidate Joe Biden, and his son Hunter, who was on the board of directors of a Ukrainian gas company. Trump, during a press briefing, denies any wrongdoing during a phone conversation with Zelensky, calling the whistleblower's claims, "a ridiculous story." Trump later fires off several tweets criticizing news reports, calling it, "Fake News." **9/19/19**

■ The president admits that he had phone conversations with Ukrainian President Volodymyr Zelensky, but denies that any improper offer of military aid for an investigation into Joe Biden was discussed. Trump states, "No quid pro quo. There was nothing." The comment refers to the whistleblower complaint that pressure was applied to Ukraine for action against the president's Democratic presidential opponent. **9/22/19**

■ Donald Trump briefly attends a climate change summit of world leaders which is held at the United Nations General Assembly (UNGA), sitting with Vice President Mike Pence. After 10 minutes, Trump and Pence leave to attend a meeting on worldwide religious persecution, which was arranged by the White House to occur at roughly the same time. **9/23/19**

■ The president posts a sarcastic tweet aimed at youthful climate change advocate Greta Thunberg, who had just delivered a forceful speech to the United Nations, by posting, "She seems like a very happy young girl looking forward to a bright and wonderful future… So nice to see." **9/24/19**

■ House Speaker Nancy Pelosi (D-CA) initiates an impeachment inquiry of the president, accusing him of violating his oath of office by seeking assistance from Ukraine in obtaining disparaging information on former Vice President Joe Biden, who is a leading Democratic candidate for the 2020 U.S. presidential election. Pelosi takes the monumental step of impeachment after Donald Trump acknowledges that he urged Ukrainian President Volodymr Zelensky to begin an investigation on Biden. Immediately after Pelosi makes her announcement, the president tweets, "PRESIDENTIAL HARASSMENT!" **9/24/19**

■ The White House releases a five-page memorandum of Donald Trump's July 2019 phone conversation with Ukrainian President Zelensky. In the transcript, Trump urges the foreign leader to "look into" Democratic rival Joe Biden, and asks him to work with the U.S. attorney general and Trump personal lawyer Rudy Giuliani in uncovering any potential wrongdoing by Biden or his son, Hunter. At one point, Trump tells Zelensky that he would like him to "do a favor for us." **9/25/19**

▪ The U.S. Senate, in a stunning 59-41 vote, overturns the president's national emergency border declaration, which would have allowed him to divert military funds to build a wall on the U.S. southern border with Mexico. The White House promises a presidential veto later in the week. **9/25/19**

▪ A whistleblower's accusations against the President of the United States are revealed, and acting Director of National Security Joseph Maguire testifies in front of the House and Senate Intelligence Committees. The complaint, allegedly filed by a CIA agent assigned to the White House, details a widespread and systemic attempt by Donald Trump to leverage U.S. military aid in exchange for delivering compromising information on former Vice President Joe Biden, and his son, Hunter. The complaint also reveals repeated attempts by White House staffers to "lock down" records of phone calls Trump made to Ukraine's President Volodymr Zelensky, by moving them to a separate secure computer server designated for sensitive classified information. Such a move would protect communications from additional scrutiny. Donald Trump fires off numerous tweets, including one that reads, "THE GREATEST SCAM IN THE HISTORY OF AMERICAN POLITICS." **9/26/19**

▪ Donald Trump, reacting to the whistleblower report which was presented to the House and Senate, allegedly tells a private gathering, "I want to know who's the person who gave the whistleblower the information, because that's close to a spy. You know what we used to do in the old days when we were smart, with spies and treason, right? We used to handle it a little differently than we do now." Trump goes on to post more about the whistleblower, claiming, "THE DEMOCRATS ARE TRYING TO DESTROY THE REPUBLICAN PARTY AND ALL THAT IT STANDS FOR. STICK TOGETHER, PLAY THEIR GAME AND FIGHT HARD REPUBLICANS. OUR COUNTRY IS AT STAKE." **9/26/19**

■ Facing increasing pressure from Democrats over impeachment proceedings, the president launches into a torrid tweetstorm. Including a post from Trump that says he wants, "to meet not only my accuser, who presented SECOND AND THIRD HAND INFORMATION, but also the person who illegally gave this information, which was largely incorrect, to the 'whistleblower.' Was this person SPYING on me, the U.S. President? Big Consequences!" Trump also questions whether House Intelligence Committee Chairman Adam Schiff (D-CA) should be arrested for "treason." Finally, the president sends one more tweet, claiming that his impeachment would provoke a "Civil War-like fracture" in the U.S. Representative Adam Kinzinger (R-IL) criticizes Trump's comment, calling it, "beyond repugnant." **9/30/19**

CHAPTER 34

UKRAINE, THAT RAGAMUFFIN COUNTRY of 42 million people, is a European nation bordered by Russia, Belarus, Poland, Slovakia, Hungary, Romania, and Moldova. Their national anthem goes along the lines of, "The glory and the will of Ukraine have not yet died." That's really enough information about the country for anyone not named Putin or Giuliani to know. But Ukraine will go down in history as the nation that gobsmacked Donald J. Trump right down to his orange-tinted core.

When one looks back at October, Ukraine will become the center of a narrative that plays in the minds of Americans like a B-rated movie one can't escape from. The investigation of Trump's involvement with Ukraine will bring us the accusation of it being a "coup" (Trump's words), a "lynching" (Trump's cringe-worthy words), and that the American public should "get over it" (Mick Mulvaney's words, that he retracted faster than a two-year old burning his hand on a stove). When Merriam-Webster publishes its most used words and phrases of 2019, "Ukraine" should occupy the top spot, closely followed by "quid pro quo."

Rounding out the month, our 45th president goes a bit medieval by suggesting that the U.S. border with Mexico should be surrounded by a moat, complete with dangerous reptiles and alligators (wouldn't you LOVE to see the government bid that one out?), along with an electrified fence backup, and military sharpshooters standing by to shoot migrants "in the legs." We're not sure if this skullduggery includes measures in Colorado, which Trump maintains, borders Mexico.

■ Secretary of State Mike Pompeo, who was found to have listened in on the phone conversation between Donald Trump and Ukraine President Zelensky, defiantly tells House Democrats investigating potential impeachment, that he will not allow current and former government staffers in his orbit to testify during the hearings. Pompeo states that the hearings were "not feasible," and accuses Democrats of "bullying." But special envoy Kurt Volker and former ambassador to Ukraine, Marie Yovanovitch, agree to appear, in defiance of the Secretary. Meanwhile, the president tweets that he feels he has come to the conclusion that actions against him are not an impeachment, but rather, "a coup." **10/1/19**

■ According to the *New York Times*, the president, frustrated with his inability to shut down the U.S. southern border with Mexico, allegedly speaks with immigration advisers about ways to stem the tide of migrants seeking asylum in the U.S. which were impractical, immoral, or illegal. Trump tells aides that the border should be protected with a moat-like structure, stocked with reptiles or alligators, which could be electrified, or that migrants should be "shot in the legs," in order to slow down border crossings. Ultimately, his staff informs the president that none of these measures could possibly be undertaken. **10/1/19**

■ Donald Trump, still raging against Democrats who are investigating the possibility of his impeachment, airs a profane tweet to vent his frustration. Trump posts, "The Do Nothing Democrats should be focused on building up our country, not wasting everyone's time and energy on BULLSHIT, which is what they have been doing since I got overwhelmingly elected in 2016, 223-306. Get a better candidate this time, you'll need it." **10/2/19**

■ The president, addressing reporters on the White House lawn, tells reporters that China should get involved with the investigation of former Vice President Joe Biden. Trump comments, "China should start an investigation into the Bidens because of what happened with China is just about as bad as what happened with Ukraine. I'm sure that President Xi (Jinpang) does not like being under that kind of scrutiny where billions of dollars is taken out of his country by a guy that just got kicked out of the navy." Trump's claims involve an accusation that Hunter Biden, Joe Biden's son, used a 2013 trip to China with his father and left with $1.3 billion dollars for a private equity fund. The president however, offers no proof of this claim. **10/3/19**

■ House investigations reveal that senior State Department officials cooperated with the Ukrainian president's top aide, and also with Donald Trump's personal lawyer, to exert pressure on Ukraine in order to have them commit to an investigation of Joe and Hunter Biden, using a potential meeting with the U.S. as leverage. **10/3/19**

■ A second whistleblower complaint is filed from an Internal Revenue Service official that points out interference with annual audits of the president or vice president's tax returns. The White House dismisses the complaint as "flimsy" due to its second-hand sources, but Democrats flag it in a federal court filing to warrant further investigations. **10/3/19**

■ The White House issues a proclamation denying visas to immigrants who cannot prove they will be able to afford to pay for health care as they apply to enter the U.S. The Trump administration states that it wants to prevent immigrants who will "financially burden" the U.S. healthcare system. **10/6/19**

■ Donald Trump continues his attacks on Senator Mitt Romney (R-UT), based on Romney's failure to support him on his controversial call with Ukraine's president Zelensky. Trump tweets, "Somebody please wake up Mitt Romney and tell him that my conversation with the Ukrainian President was a congenial and very appropriate one, and my statement on China pertained to corruption, not politics. If Mitt worked this hard on Obama, he could have won. Sadly, he choked!" Trump also sends out other tweets attacking the former 2012 GOP presidential nominee, calling him a "pompous ass," and falsely claims that the "Great people of Utah are considering their vote for their Pompous Senator, Mitt Romney, to be a big mistake," and ends with "#IMPEACHROMNEY." There is immediate blowback as Trump's comments are roundly criticized, with some critics pointing out to the president that a member of the Senate cannot be impeached. **10/5/19**

■ The president calls for a withdrawal of military troops from Syria's border with Turkey, abandoning Kurdish fighters who assisted the U.S. forces in fighting ISIS during a long-running conflict. Donald Trump is criticized by ranking members of both parties, including Republicans Mitch McConnell (R-KY) and Lindsey Graham (R-SC). Trump strikes back at criticism of his action by tweeting, "As I have stated strongly before, and just to reiterate, if Turkey does anything that I, in my great and unmatched wisdom, consider to be off limits, I will totally destroy and obliterate the Economy of Turkey (I've done before)." **10/7/19**

■ The Trump campaign forces the Target Center in Minneapolis to withdraw their request that they be paid $530,000 to cover security costs for a Trump rally scheduled for October 10th. The arena makes a request after Mayor Jacob Farley (D), informs the campaign that the city of Minneapolis will not pay for security. Donald Trump attacks the mayor for his attempted action, and calls Frey "a lightweight." He then posts a map of the counties he won in Minnesota during the 2016 U.S. presidential election. **10/8/19**

■ The White House notifies House Democrats that they will not offer any cooperation in the ever-widening impeachment inquiry. The Trump administration, which previously blocked testimony from U.S. ambassador to the E.U. Gordon Sondland before the House of Representatives, maintains that the inquiry violates due process, as the entire House was not called on to vote to begin the action, which is not required. **10/8/19**

■ Former Vice President Joe Biden calls for Donald Trump's impeachment for the first time, citing Trump's blatant disregard for Democracy, and for "shooting holes in the Constitution." Biden joins other Democratic presidential candidates in calling for Trump's impeachment. The president responds via Twitter, responding, "Joe's failing campaign gave him no other choice." **10/9/19**

■ Defending his order to withdraw U.S. troops from Syria, leaving Kurdish forces to face Turkey's military who will seek to obliterate them, Donald Trump explains that betraying the Kurds, former U.S. allies, was acceptable because "they didn't fight with us in World War II," and also because, "they didn't help us with Normandy." **10/9/19**

■ Reports surface that claim Donald Trump pressured then-Secretary of State Rex Tillerson to drop a criminal case against a client of Rudy Giuliani, who was accused of evading U.S. sanctions against Iran's nuclear program. Tillerson refused to drop the case, citing that doing so would be illegal. **10/11/19**

■ A violent parody video of Donald Trump shooting figures representing his political rivals and news organizations surfaces at the American Priority Conference, which is held at a Trump property in Florida. The video is edited to superimpose the president's face on a character from the 2014 film *Kingsman*, and depicts him massacring victims whose faces are replaced by news organizations' logos such as CNN and the *Washington Post*. The video also shows Trump attacking political enemies Adam Schiff and former presidents Clinton and Obama, along with the late Senator John McCain (R-AZ). The White House issues a statement that Trump did not view the video, but that he "strongly condemns it." Trump himself makes no public comment. **10/14/19**

■ Donald Trump goes on Twitter to brag about the state of the U.S. economy, and ends the post with a self-indictment that has many political observers questioning its purpose. Trump Tweets, "THE MEDIAN HOUSEHOLD INCOME IS AT THE HIGHEST POINT EVER, EVER, EVER!" He continues, "MORE PEOPLE WORKING TODAY IN THE USA THAN ANY TIME IN HISTORY! Tough numbers for the Radical Left Democrats to beat!" Trump then adds a bizarre end to the tweet by posting, "Impeach the Pres." **10/16/19**

▮ The president tries to justify his decision to pull U.S. troops out of Syria, leaving former allies, the Kurds, to fend for themselves against a hostile Turkish military. Trump states that the Kurds are "no angels," and that "there's a lot of sand they can play with." The president, who is under fire for his decision, is faced with a mostly unified bi-partisan House of Representatives, who vote 354-60 to rebuke his action. Later, members of Congress meet with Trump to discuss Syria, and the meeting ends in an explosive exchange between the president and House Speaker Nancy Pelosi (D-CA). Pelosi accuses Trump of having a "meltdown" during the brief meeting, and it is reported that Trump either called the Speaker a "third-rate politician," or a "third-grade politician." **10/16/19**

▮ The president sends a personal letter to Turkey's President Erdogan, urging him to cease any military actions against the Kurds. The letter, which Donald Trump releases to members of Congress, tells the Turkish leader that the world "will look upon you forever as the devil if good things don't happen. Don't be a tough guy. Don't be a fool." Sources tell BBC News that Erdogan threw Trump's letter in the trash. **10/16/19**

▮ Gordon Sondland, U.S. envoy to the European Union, tells a closed-door House committee that the president directed him to work with his personal lawyer, Rudy Giuliani, on matters related to Ukraine. **10/17/19**

▮ The White House announces that the 2020 G-7 meeting will be held at Donald Trump's Doral International Resort in Miami, raising questions about the president and his family potentially profiting from an event of such magnitude at one of his properties. **10/17/19**

▮ Acting Chief of Staff Mick Mulvaney admits that Donald Trump with-held military aid from Ukraine unless they did not agree to cooperate by holding an investigation of his political rivals. Mulvaney, in a stunning press conference, tells reporters that, "We do that all the time with for-eign policy" He continues, "I have news for everybody: get over it. There is going to be political influence in foreign policy." Mulvaney later tries to walk back his comments, saying, "There was absolutely no quid pro quo," but could not escape the controversy his comments create. **10/17/19**

∎ The president changes course on holding the G-7 at his resort at Doral International Resort, due to increased pressure from critics, who point out that Trump stands to profit from the meeting being held at his property. In making the about-face, Trump tweets, "Doral in Miami would have been the best place to hold the G-7, and free, but too much pressure from the Do Nothing Radical Left Democrats & their Partner, the Fake News Media." **10/18/19**

∎ Still reeling from his reversal on holding the G-7 meeting at Doral International, the president takes aim at the emoluments clause of the U.S. Constitution. Donald Trump tells reporters that he's the victim of the "phony emoluments clause," and tries to distance himself from being seen as profiting from the presidency by attacking former President Obama's multiyear deal with Netflix, and his book deal, both of which were signed after Obama left office. **10/21/19**

∎ U.S. ambassador to Ukraine, William Taylor, testifies in front of the House Intelligence Committee that he believes Donald Trump explicitly offered a quid pro quo of military assistance in exchange for an investigation into Hunter Biden and his involvement with Burisma, a Ukraine gas company. Taylor, a lifetime U.S. diplomat who served under presidents from both parties, claims that he was told by U.S. ambassador to the E.U., Gordon Sondland, that Donald Trump wanted to place Ukrainian President Volodymr Zelensky "in a public box" by forcing him to announce an investigation before military funds would be released. **10/21/19**

∎ Donald Trump falsely claims that former President Obama tried to call North Korean leader Kim Jong un 11 times during his two terms in office, but due to Kim's "lack of respect" for the former president, he never took any of his phone calls. Ben Rhodes, National Security Council spokesman under Obama posts a response on Twitter shortly thereafter, calling

Trump a "serial liar and not well," and that his claims about Obama and Kim were wrong. **10/21/19**

■ The president calls the House impeachment inquiry a "lynching," drawing criticism from politicians on both sides of the aisle, who point out that the term is most associated with the murders of blacks during the early years in America after the Civil War. **10/22/19**

■ The president, still under fire for his decision to withdraw U.S. troops from Syria, delivers remarks to the press that are jaw-droppingly false, causing blowback from many media outlets. First off, Donald Trump tells reporters that Turkey has agreed to a "permanent" cease fire, and that the original Syrian mission was supposed to only last for 30 days, but lasted for 10 years. There was no agreement with Turkey, and the mandate in Syria had no such timeline. Trump also falsely claims that ISIS fighters who were imprisoned in Syria were under "very, very strict lock and key," and that the few who had escaped were "largely recaptured." The U.S. Secretary of Defense, Mark Esper, reports that more than 1,000 ISIS fighters had escaped, and their whereabouts were unknown. **10/23/19**

■ Former Acting Attorney General Matt Whitaker tells FOX News's Laura Ingraham that Donald Trump has not committed a crime by suggesting a quid pro quo with Ukraine because "abuse of power is not a crime." Reaction on social media is swift, and numerous news outlets jump on Whitaker's comments as inaccurate. **10/23/19**

■ During a hearing of the 2nd U.S. Circuit Court of Appeals concerning the release of Donald Trump's tax returns his attorney, William Consovoy, informs judges hearing the case that the president couldn't be prosecuted by authorities even if he shot someone in the street. The claim, based on Trump's 2016 campaign remarks that he could "stand in the middle of Fifth Avenue and shoot somebody and (I) won't lose any voters," has been a contention of the president's legal team, stemming from a Department of Justice policy which protects a sitting president from prosecution. **10/23/19**

∎ A group of 25 members of the U.S. House of Representatives storms into a secure basement meeting area to protest that House Democrats were holding impeachment hearings in closed quarters. The Republican-led protest is orchestrated by Rep. Matt Gaetz (R-FL), and is reportedly endorsed by GOP leadership, including the president. Republican representatives also reportedly brought cell phones into the Sensitive Compartmented Information Facility (also known as the SCIF), which violates security laws. **10/23/19**

∎ The President of the United States attacks members of his own party who do not fully support him, on Twitter. Trump posts, "The Never Trumper Republicans, though on respirators with not many left, are in certain ways worse and more dangerous for our Country than the Do Nothing Democrats. Watch out for them, they are human scum." **10/23/19**

∎ During a speech at an energy conference in Pittsburgh, Donald Trump makes a dumbfounding claim about a U.S. border wall being built in Colorado. Trump tells those gathered at the conference, "We're building a wall on the border of New Mexico, and we're building a wall in Colorado. We're building a beautiful wall, a big one that really works, that you can't get over, you can't get under." Trump continues, "And we're not building a wall in Kansas, but they get the benefit of the walls that we just mentioned." Trump later tries to claim that he was joking, but his remarks were routinely mocked on social media and late-night television programs. **10/23/19**

∎ The Department of Justice announces it is opening a criminal investigation into the government's Russia probe, raising criticism from Democrats that the president is "weaponizing" a federal bureau to go after his opponents. Trump comments on the probe, stating that it will reveal "very bad things." **10/25/19**

∎ The president attends game five of the 2019 World Series in Washington and when introduced, receives a loud chorus of boos from the sold out crowd, with some people chanting "Lock him up." **10/27/19**

■ The president announces that U.S. Special Operations forces have killed ISIS leader Abu Bakr al-Baghdadi in Idlib Province, Syria. Donald Trump, in revealing details about the mission, says that al-Baghdadi died in a state of "utter fear, total panic, and dread." He goes on to say that the ISIS leader "died like a dog. He died like a coward." Trump also uses his press conference to downplay the vital role Kurdish intelligence played in the operation, although reports indicate they were vital to the mission's success. The president then raises eyebrows with military and intelligence agencies, as he tells reporters that his view of the raid was like "watching a movie," which reveals to the worlds' intelligence communities more advanced surveillance techniques than had been previously known. **10/27/19**

■ Lt. Colonel Alexander Vindman, top Ukraine expert on the National Security Council, testifies in the House impeachment hearings, and reveals that he was very concerned the president's call to Ukraine President Volodymr Zelensky was "inappropriate." Vindman also tells the committee that he, along with Dr. Fiona Hill of the National Security Council (NSC), informed U.S. Ambassador Gordon Sondland that they were both concerned about the direction of relations between the U.S. and Ukraine. Sondland, in earlier testimony to the House, denied that anyone within the NSC or White House had expressed such worries to him. **10/28/19**

■ Donald Trump suggests that his wife Melania wouldn't cry if he were shot during an assignation attempt. Trump makes the comments during a private fundraiser, as he was discussing how hard Rep. Steve Scalise's (R-LA) wife cried when he was shot during a Congressional baseball practice in 2017. Trump says, "She cried her eyes out when I met her at the hospital that fateful day. I mean, not many wives would react that way to tragedy. I know mine wouldn't." **10/29/19**

■ Donald Trump tweets a fake picture of himself "awarding" a medal to a Belgian Malinois canine, named Conan, who helped capture and kill ISIS leader Abu Bakr al-Baghdadi. The picture was doctored from an Associated

Press photo of Trump previously awarding a Medal of Honor to James McCloughan, photo shopped to replace him with the dog. **10/30/19**

■ The U.S. House of Representatives votes to formally begin an impeachment inquiry surrounding the actions of the President of the United States, concerning his actions involving Ukraine. The vote, which passes 232-196, and is largely along party lines, starts in motion the third such action against a U.S. president in the history of the nation. **10/31/19**

■ The president announces that he is changing his primary residence from New York to Florida. Donald Trump files documents to show his relocation from Trump Tower in New York to his Mar-a-Lago resort in Palm Beach, Florida. Trump tweets about the change, claiming that he has been "treated very badly" by both (New York) state and city political leaders, which influenced his decision. In response, New York's Governor Andrew Cuomo responds via Twitter, "Good riddance. It's not like @realDonaldTrump paid taxes here anyway. He's all yours, Florida." **10/31/19**

CHAPTER 35

IF YOU THOUGHT THAT the Kavanaugh hearing and Mueller probes were contentious, mean-spirited, and downright decrepit, you might want to remember those as the "good old days" in D.C. November brings us the warp-speed brouhaha known as "the impeachment." It's a sorry tale of woe that includes Congressional subpoenas met with middle fingers held aloft, shadowy whistleblowers, "drug deals and hand grenades" (thank you, Rudy Giuliani, you're the gift that keeps on giving), foreign leaders loving someone's ass, and yes, more of 2019's word(s) of the year, "quid" (I have)" pro" (you want), and "quo" (maybe you get, if you're nice to me). There are hearings, testimony, attacks, and counter-attacks. Wash, rinse, and repeat.

But as many a TV product huckster has said, "But wait, there's more!" November brings us a continuation of the acrimonious behavior we've been cringing from these past 30+ months, such as: White House staffers creating junior wall-builders during Halloween festivities for impressionable tots, the $2 million dollars paid to charities to cover Trump's skullduggery involving other charities, Ivanka Trump miraculously creating 14 million jobs ("Oh look, Daddy, I'm helping those unemployment numbers for you"). And who could forget Donald Jr.'s contribution to November, when the budding literary genius released *Triggered*, also known as, *Daddy, Please Love Me*.

So let's travel together down the long, dark path of November, and embrace the hullabaloo that's soon to follow.

■ The White House hosts a Halloween party in the Eisenhower Executive Office Building, which holds the offices of the president and vice president. One of the festivities allows visiting child guests to help build a "wall" with brick-colored paper cards, and slogans such as "America First" printed on them. **11/1/9**

■ A federal judge in Oregon blocks the Trump administration's rule which requires immigrants applying for U.S. visas to provide proof that they either have health insurance, or can financially afford to pay medical expenses before their applications would be processed. U.S. District Judge Michael Simon grants a temporary restraining order, while a federal lawsuit against the policy is being considered. **11/2/19**

■ A U.S. federal court rules that Donald Trump's tax returns must be turned over to a New York grand jury. The tax records, which were subpoenaed by Manhattan District Attorney Cyrus Vance, are critical to the grand jury investigation of hush-money payments allegedly made by Trump's team to two women in advance of the 2016 U.S. presidential election. **11/4/19**

■ Donald Trump faces a barrage of criticism after he publicly promotes his son's new book on Twitter. Trump posts, "My son @DonaldTrumpJr is coming out with a new book, 'Triggered: How the Left Thrives on Hate and Wants to Silence Us'-available tomorrow, November 5th!" Trump Sr. continues, "A great new book that I highly recommend for ALL to read. Go order it today!" Response to the tweet is swift, especially in light of Donald Trump's claims of nepotism aimed at former Vice President Joe Biden's son working for a Ukrainian gas company while he was in office. **11/5/19**

■ Four senior White House officials refuse to honor subpoenas ordering them to testify before the House Intelligence Committee. White House lawyer John Eisenberg, National Security Council lawyer Michael Ellis, security aide Robert Blair, and budget official Brian McCormack claim that they are prohibited from testifying before the House due to White House directives. **11/5/19**

- U.S. ambassador to the E.U., Gordon Sondland, makes detailed changes to his testimony before House impeachment investigators, stating that he now remembers telling a top aide to Ukrainian President Volodymyr Zelenesky that U.S. military aid would be withheld unless they committed to investigate the 2016 U.S. presidential election, and former Vice President Joe Biden. Sondland delivers the change of position in a three page declaration, claiming that his memories of the events surrounding Ukraine were "refreshed," after reviewing the opening statements given to Congress by acting ambassador to Ukraine, Bill Taylor, and former adviser to Donald Trump on Russia and Europe, Tim Morrison. **11/5/19**

- U.S. Senator Lindsey Graham (R-SC) claims that the president should not be subject to impeachment for involvement with Ukraine because there's little chance that the Trump administration was savvy enough to carry out a quid pro quo involving military aid for anti-corruption investigations. Graham also states that Donald Trump's administration's policy towards Ukraine was "incoherent." **11/6/19**

- It is reported that the president wanted Attorney General William Barr to hold a news conference in order to clear him from any illegal activity revolving around his July 25th phone call with Ukrainian President Zelensky. Barr reportedly refused to do so, and the president denies the validity of the report, calling it "pure fiction," **11/6/19**

- A federal judge orders Donald Trump to pay $2 million dollars to various charities as a fine for misusing funds from his charitable foundation, which he used for personal and political interests instead of assisting charities, as promised. **11/7/19**

- Senator John Kennedy (R-LA), slams House Speaker Nancy Pelosi during a rally for Donald Trump in Louisiana. Kennedy, in front of a cheering crowd of Trump supporters, tells the assembled throng, "In three short years, President Trump had doubled the growth in the greatest economy in all of human history. And do you know what our Democratic friends have done for him? Speaker Nancy Pelosi is trying to impeach him." Kennedy then states, "I don't mean any disrespect, but it must suck to be that dumb." **11/8/19**

∎ An attorney for the whistleblower who raised concerns about activities in the White House involving Ukraine, which resulted in charges being filed against Donald Trump, sends a cease and desist letter to the White House, calling for a halt to the demands that his client's name be released to the public. Despite the letter being issued, the president continues to call for the whistleblower's name to be made public, stating, "The whistleblower is a disgrace to our country. A disgrace. And because of that, should be revealed." **11/8/19**

∎ Acting White House Chief of Staff Mick Mulvaney refuses to comply with a subpoena issued by the House committee investigating Donald Trump's involvement with Ukraine. Mulvaney, claiming that the White House has granted him "total immunity," joins Senior Adviser Robert Blair, National Security Council lawyers John Eisenberg and Michael Ellis, and Brian McCormack, associate director for natural resources, energy, and science at the Office of Management and Budget, in refusing to testify before the House. **11/8/19**

∎ Excerpts from Donald Trump Jr.'s newly-published book *Triggered: How the Left Thrives on Hate and Wants to Silence Us,* reveal that Trump Jr. describes the "sacrifices" the family supposedly made while his father has served as president. Trump writes about visiting Arlington National Cemetery with this missive, "At that moment, I also thought of all the attacks we'd already suffered as a family, and about all the sacrifices we'd have to make to help my father succeed-voluntarily giving up a huge chunk of our business and all international deals to avoid the appearance that we were 'profiting off the office.'" **11/8/19**

■ Former U.S. United Nations ambassador Nikki Haley claims that two of Donald Trump's senior cabinet members tried to recruit her in a coordinated effort to ignore the president, in order to "save the country." Hailey, in her new book, titled, *With All Due Respect*, writes that former Secretary of State Rex Tillerson and former White House Chief of Staff John Kelly tried to encourage her to work around the president, and that she refused to do so. **11/10/19**

■ Donald Trump claims to the Economic Club of New York that his daughter Ivanka has created 14 million jobs in the U.S. during the past 2 ½ years. The claim is immediately debunked by economic experts, who show that Trump's administration has only created 6 million total jobs during his term in office. **11/12/19**

■ The president discusses firing the intelligence community's inspector general, Michael Atkinson, because he reported that the whistleblower complaint about Trump's involvement with Ukraine was credible. **11/12/19**

■ According to testimony from State Department official Christopher Anderson, the president called then-National Security Advisor John Bolton after seeing a report on CNN that the U.S. planned to send a naval vessel into the Black Sea, in order to demonstrate freedom of navigation in those waters. Trump reportedly complained that the maneuvers would provoke Russia, and the plans were subsequently scrapped. **11/12/19**

■ During Marie Yovanovitch's televised testimony before the House Intelligence Committee investigating Donald Trump's involvement with Ukraine, the president fires off an intimidating tweet attacking the former U.S. envoy to that country. Trump posts, "Everywhere Marie Yovanovitch went turned bad. She started off in Somalia, how did that go? Then, fast-forward to Ukraine, where the new Ukrainian President spoke unfavorably about her in my second phone call with him." Trump continues, "It is a U.S. President's absolute right to appoint ambassadors." House Intelligence Committee Chairman Adam Schiff interrupts the impeachment proceedings in order to read the president's tweet live and directly to Yovanovitch, who responds that the remarks were, "very intimidating." The president responds by saying that he has "freedom of speech" to issue such comments. **11/15/19**

■ According to an ABC News/Ipsos poll, 70% of Americans believe Donald Trump acted improperly in asking a foreign leader to investigate a political opponent. The same poll finds that 51% favor impeachment and removal from office. **11/18/19**

■ Ambassador Gordon Sondland admits to House impeachment investigators that there was an attempted exchange of political information for the release of military funding for Ukraine. Sondland, U.S. ambassador to the E.U., testifies that the president and his personal attorney Rudy Giuliani sought a "quid pro quo" arrangement, involving an investigation of political rival Joe Biden. **11/20/19**

■ Dr. Fiona Hill, former top Russian expert on the National Security Council, and David Holmes, an embassy aide serving in Ukraine, both testify before the House Intelligence Committee, and offer more damning testimony about the actions of Donald Trump and members of his administration, with regards to Ukraine. Hill states that those serving Trump were engaged in a "domestic political errand" concerning Ukraine, and that the actions sharply diverged from U.S. policy goals. Dr. Hill also tells the committee that Republicans were pushing a "fictional narrative" about Ukraine playing a role in the 2016 U.S presidential election, which had its roots in Russian propaganda efforts. She also confirms her previous closed-door testimony before the House that then-National Security Adviser John Bolton wanted no part of the "drug deal" that Ambassador Sondland and White House Chief of Staff Mick Mulvaney were "cooking up," and that Bolton called Trump personal lawyer Rudy Giuliani a "hand grenade who's going to blow everybody up." Holmes confirms his similar previous testimony that he overheard part of a phone conversation between Donald Trump and Sondland while in Kyiv, in which he asked the ambassador if Ukraine President Zelensky was "going to do the investigation," and how Sondland told Holmes that the president is only interested in "big stuff that benefits the president, like the Biden investigation." Holmes also testifies that Sondland told Trump that Zelensky "loves your (Trump's) ass, and would do anything you asked him to." In response to the testimony, the president resorts to Twitter, referring to those involved with the impeachment hearings as "human scum." **11/21/19**

▮ It is reported that Rep. Devin Nunes (R-CA) of the House Intelligence Committee, may have met with Ukrainian officials in 2018 in order to dig up compromising information on former Vice President Joe Biden. The claim, floated by Lev Parnas, who is facing numerous charges of fraud and conspiracy, is denied by Nunes. **11/24/19**

▮ The president orders Defense Secretary Mark Esper to stop a disciplinary review of Navy SEAL Chief Petty Officer Edward Gallagher, which could have resulted in him losing his SEAL status, and Trident pin. Gallagher, who was initially charged with military misconduct by posing for a picture with a dead ISIS fighter, was pardoned by Donald Trump earlier in November, resulting in protests from U.S. Navy officials. The subsequent fallout results in the firing of Navy Secretary Richard V. Spencer, who is forced to resign. **11/25/19**

▮ U.S Federal District Court Judge Ketanji Brown Jackson rules that former White House counsel Don McGahn must testify before House impeachment investigators about the president's efforts to obstruct justice in the Muller Russia investigation. In a 120 page decision, Jackson rules that senior presidential aides must comply with Congressional subpoenas, and that "presidents are not kings." **11/25/19**

▮ During a campaign rally in Sunrise, Florida, the president makes numerous bizarre claims, including that liberals are trying to rename the Thanksgiving holiday. Trump states, "You know, some people want to change the name 'Thanksgiving'. They don't want to use the term 'Thanksgiving.'

He continues, "We're not changing it. We're going to have to do little work on Thanksgiving." Trump also claims during the event that during an unscheduled visit to Walter Reed National Military Medical Center, doctors complimented his physique by saying, "Take off your shirt, sir, and show us that gorgeous chest. We've never seen a chest quite like it." To add to the bizarre comment, Trump posts a picture the next day on Twitter with his head superimposed on the muscular body of movie star Sylvester Stallone, posing for his motion picture, *Rocky*. **11/25/19**

■ First Lady Melania Trump is soundly booed at a middle and high school event in Baltimore. Trump, who delivers a speech to students at the B'More Youth Summit on Opioid Awareness, encouraging them to steer clear of drugs, is booed throughout her five minute address. **11/26/19**

■ Donald Trump Jr. urges his followers to record themselves ruining their families' Thanksgiving gatherings by bringing up politics at the dinner table. Trump offers a signed copy of his book *Triggered*, and a MAGA hat as a prize to whomever sends him the best photo or video of the family conflict. **11/27/19**

CHAPTER 36

REMEMBER WHEN CHRISTMAS HOLIDAY movies were something you looked forward to every December, when you could engage in escapism for a short while, and let the warm cloak of joy wash over you while gleefully watching a nostalgia-draped classic? Well, you can't even rely on that pleasure anymore, because Trump-world believes there is a world-wide conspiracy to remove 45's less-than-memorable cameo appearance in *Home Alone 2*. Bah Humbug!

Meanwhile, at the NATO summit in London, the president is treated like the pimply-faced kid in junior high when world leaders Trudeau, Macron, and Johnson, mock Trump in an impromptu huddle, and plan to see which one of them can put the "kick me" sign on 45's back.

And if you think that those heads of state are engaging in "bathroom humor" at Donald Trump's expense, you may be right. However, he just adds to the hullabaloo when he uses his pulpit to attack the common commode when he declares that one has to flush, "10 times, 15 times," to accomplish what we all do in one handle pull. And then there's another country for Trump to tick off, place tariffs on, or otherwise threaten, as the USDA declares Wakandia from the *Black Panther* movie to be a real nation.

Rounding out December we have Trump crossing the 15,000 false or misleading claim threshold, golf costs of over $118 million, windmills that spew "fumes and gasses," two articles of impeachment, and tweeting one QAnon conspiracy. (The last two are sung to the tune of the *12 days of Christmas*). Happy Impeachment, everyone, or is that Merry Impeachmas?

■ While at a NATO summit in London, French President Emmanuel Macron fact-checks Donald Trump's false claims about many captured ISIS fighters in Syria being from Europe. Trump, who jokes that the U.S. could send France "some nice ISIS fighters," if they wanted them, soon turns dour when Macron corrects him, telling the U.S. president that European-bred ISIS fighters represent a "tiny minority" of their fighters. The riff is a continuation of contentious remarks between the two world leaders, over the perceived U.S. failure to support NATO. Also, during a break in the summit, cameras catch Canadian Prime Minister Justin Trudeau (whom Trump had earlier called "two-faced"), British Prime Minister Boris Johnson, and Macron mocking Trump and laughing at his antics. **12/3/19**

■ With the holiday season approaching, the Trump administration finalizes a rule which tightens work requirements for recipients of Supplemental Nutrition Assistance Program (SNAP) benefits. The move will cut off nearly 700,000 food stamp patrons, who are able-bodied adults with no dependents. **12/4/19**

■ According to records revealed by the House Intelligence Committee, the president routinely used unsecure cell phones to communicate with personal lawyer Rudi Giuliani and other individuals. These lines are vulnerable to foreign intelligence sources and may very well have been monitored by governments such as Russia. **12/6/19**

■ More than 500 legal scholars sign an open letter claiming that the President of the United States committed "impeachable conduct" with regards to his actions on Ukraine, and state that lawmakers would be within their rights to vote for impeachment. The scholars, from prestigious universities such as Harvard, Yale, Columbia, UC Berkeley, among others, publish their letter online, through the nonprofit advocacy group, Protect Democracy. **12/6/19**

■ The president orders the Environmental Protection Agency to investigate claims that low flow toilets in the U.S. are causing Americans to flush toilets, "10 times, 15 times, as opposed to once." He also states that other bathroom appliances have allowed water to slow to a trickle, causing people to have to use more water while showering or washing their hands. **12/6/19**

▌ The Justice department releases its report into FBI involvement of the Russia investigation. Inspector general Michael Horowitz finds that the bureau acted properly in conducting its probe, but finds that several significant errors were made in the process. Attorney General William Barr disputes Horowitz's findings, and claims that the FBI acted in "bad faith" when they investigated the Trump presidential campaign in 2016. **12/9/19**

▌ Donald Trump criticizes FBI Director Christopher Wray for saying that he (Wray) supports the investigator general's report on the FBI's role in the Russia investigation. Trump posts on Twitter, "I don't know what report current Director Christopher Wray was reading, but it sure wasn't the one given to me." He continues, "With that kind of attitude, he will never be able to fix the FBI, which is badly broken despite having some of the greatest men & women working there." **12/10/19**

▌ House Democrats release two articles of impeachment against the president, based on his involvement with Ukraine. The articles include abuse of power, and obstruction of Congress. Judiciary Chairman Jerrold Nadler, along with House Speaker Nancy Pelosi, read the articles during a statement to the press, but take no questions from reporters. The articles of impeachment precede a vote by the Judiciary Committee, and ultimately the full House, before Christmas. **12/10/19**

▌ During a political rally in Pennsylvania, Donald Trump attacks Democrats for their efforts to impeach him, as well as the FBI, (whose members he praised the day before) for perceived actions to undercut his 2016 U.S. presidential campaign. Trump saves the most venom for the FBI by stating, "And the FBI also sent multiple undercover human spies to surveil and record people associated with our campaign." He continues, "Look how they've destroyed the lives of people that were great people.

That are still great people. Their lives have been destroyed by scum, ok? By scum." **12/10/19**

■ Donald Trump launches into yet another tirade against teen climate change activist Greta Thunberg, after Time Magazine announces that she is that publication's "Person of the Year." Trump, who has routinely attacked Thunberg in the past, takes aim at the 16 year-old by tweeting, "So ridiculous. Greta must work on her Anger Management problem, then go to a good old fashioned movie with a friend! Chill, Greta, Chill!" In response, Thunberg changes her Twitter bio to say that she is a "Teenager working on her anger management problem. Currently chilling, and watching a good old fashioned movie with a friend." **12/12/19**

■ The House Judiciary Committee, after contentious hearings, votes to send two articles of impeachment to the full House of Representatives for a vote, which would be only the third time in history that impeachment will be voted on, involving a seated U.S. president. In response, the president fires off 115 tweets and retweets criticizing the process. **12/13/19**

■ Donald Trump, continuing to show his frustration over the scheduled impeachment vote, tweets an attack on House Speaker Nancy Pelosi (D-CA). Trump claims on Twitter that Pelosi didn't answer a question about including bribery as an article of impeachment, "because Nancy's teeth were falling out of her mouth, and she didn't have time to think." **12/17/19**

■ According to fact checkers, the president has made 15,413 false or misleading claims during his first term on office. The new total includes a significant uptick of false statements during 2019, mostly attributed to his uproar over the impeachment proceedings over his involvement with Ukraine. **12/17/19**

■ Numerous pro-impeachment rallies are held across the U.S. on the eve of the House vote on impeachment. Protesters carry signs and listen to speeches in support of impeaching Donald Trump. **12/17/19**

■ Donald Trump sends House Speaker Nancy Pelosi a six page letter criticizing her leadership, and slamming the articles of impeachment being brought against him by House Democrats. The rambling missive blasts the Democrats for their "partisan impeachment crusade," and accuses them of "unfettered contempt" for the U.S. system of government. Trump also takes a personal jab at Pelosi, disputing her claim that she prays for him by saying, "You are offending Americans of faith by continually saying 'I pray for the President,' when you know this statement is not true, unless it is meant in a negative state." Speaker Pelosi brushes off the letter, calling it "sick." **12/17/19**

■ Over 700 historians sign an open letter urging the House of Representatives to impeach Donald Trump. The letter, which references the president's "attempts to subvert the Constitution," and launching investigations to "advance his own re-election," is signed by prominent historian Jon Meacham, filmmaker Ken Burns, and many others. **12/17/19**

■ The U.S. House of Representatives votes to approve two articles of impeachment against Donald Trump. The votes occur largely down party lines. The first article (Abuse of Power) passes 230-197, and the second (Obstruction of Congress), passes by a vote of 229-198. The result of the vote will insure that Trump will be only the third U.S. president to suffer impeachment while in office, joined by past presidents Andrew Johnson and Bill Clinton, both of whom were cleared by the Senate. Leading up to the final vote, Republican Congressmen take turns deriding the impeachment, with two representatives calling the actions of the House worse than the Japanese attack on Pearl Harbor, or Pontius Pilate's judgment of Jesus Christ. The president weighs in on the proceedings with numerous tweets during the hearings and vote, including one that states, "ASSAULT ON AMERICA AND AN ASSAULT ON THE REPUBLICIAN PARTY!!!" House Speaker Pelosi also announces she will not send the articles of impeachment directly to the Republican-controlled Senate until details of the ensuing trial are settled upon. **12/18/19**

∎ A Conservative Denver radio talk show host is fired after telling his listeners that he wished for a "nice school shooting" to distract from media coverage of the Trump impeachment. Chuck Bonniwell makes the comments on 710KNUS's *Chuck and Julie* afternoon program. Bonniwell's wife, co-host Julie Hayden attempts to walk back her husband's remark, but the program is terminated by station management "immediately." **12/18/19**

∎ During a political rally in Battle Creek, Michigan following the vote to impeach him, the president makes a reprehensible comment involving beloved late Congressman John Dingell, (D-MI) who died earlier in the year. Donald Trump laments that Dingell's widow, Debbie Dingell, voted to impeach him after Trump gave the Dingell family the "A plus treatment" after learning of his death, and that the late lawmaker would be "thrilled" by the respect shown during his funeral. Trump then continues on to say that he would be "looking down" at the ceremony, or maybe that he would be "looking up," suggesting that Dingell might be in hell instead. Loud groans are heard from the audience after Trump's remark, and he is loudly condemned by other members of Congress. Debbie Dingell tells MSNBC during an interview that Trump's callous comment hurt her deeply. **12/18/19**

∎ The U.S. Department of Agriculture (USDA) removes the fictional country of Wakandia from its online list of free trade countries that have agreements with the U.S. government. The country, which is from the Disney Movie *Black Panther*, reportedly trades such items as livestock, dairy goods, tobacco, and alcohol with the U.S., is removed from the list after the USDA claims making a "mistake." **12/18/19**

∎ A leading Christian publication, *Christianity Today*, calls for the removal of Donald Trump from office following his impeachment by the U.S. House of Representatives. In an editorial by the magazine founded (and estranged from) the Rev. Bill Graham, Editor-in-Chief Mark Galli writes that although Democrats have "had it out for" Trump since he took office, his actions involving Ukraine are "unambiguous," and calls for his ouster.

Trump strikes back by tweeting *Christianity Today* "would rather have a Radical Left non believer, who wants to take your guns, rather than Donald Trump as your President." **12/19/19**

■ Following the vote to impeach Donald Trump, the president posts a daunting image of himself on Twitter. The image is of a menacingly-lit black and white photo of Trump seated in a chair, hands folded. The words in text above and below the picture read, "In reality they're not after me, they're after you. I'm just in the way." **12/19/19**

■ Former White House press secretary Sarah Huckabee Sanders issues an apology to former Vice President Joe Biden, after she mocks Biden's stutter in a tweet during the Democratic presidential debate. Sanders posts, "IIIIIIIIIIIII hhhave absolutely no idea what Biden is talking about #DemDebate." Biden is quick to respond to Sanders by tweeting, "I've worked my whole life to overcome a stutter. And it's my great honor to mentor kids who have experienced the same. It's called empathy. Look it up." Huckabee Sanders tweets a response to Biden which states, I actually didn't know that about you and that is commendable. I apologize and should have made my point respectfully." **12/20/19**

■ It is reported that White House officials requested that military aid to Ukraine be held 1 ½ hours after Donald Trump's phone call to Ukrainian President Volodymyr Zelensky on July 25th, according to documents obtained through a Freedom of Information Act request to the Department of Defense (DoD) and Office of Management and Budget (OMB), by the Center for Public Integrity. The emails, although heavily redacted, clearly show that aid was paused pending "further review." **12/22/19**

■ Donald Trump's holiday golf vacation to Mar-a-Lago push the total cost of such outings to over $118 million dollars during his presidency. The amount represents the equivalent of 296 years of presidential salary that Trump is not taking. It is reported that some of the millions of dollars are being funneled back to Trump's businesses, because many Trump aides are staying at his properties. **12/22/19**

∎ The president once again launches into an attack on windmills while speaking to attendees of the Turning Point USA conference in Florida. Donald Trump claims that windmills create "tremendous fumes and gasses (that) are spewing into the atmosphere" and that they impact the "carbon footprint" of the planet. There is no proof of Trump's claims that can be backed up by the scientific community. **12/22/19**

∎ The president invites Chief Petty Officer Edward Gallagher, a Navy SEAL convicted of posing for a picture with the body of a dead ISIS fighter in 2017, to his Mar-a-Lago resort for a Christmas celebration. Several days later, a leaked video of interviews with Gallagher's Navy SEAL team claim that their former platoon leader was "evil" and "toxic" and his behavior in the Middle East and he was "positively OK" killing anybody that was moving. **12/24/19**

∎ A map that tracks pollution in the U.S. disappears from the Internet, preventing valuable information on pollution from being easily referenced by scientists. TOXMAP's demise is blamed on the Trump administration's pattern of obfuscation and regulatory rollbacks of environmental policies. **12/26/19**

∎ It is discovered that Donald Trump's cameo in the 1992 movie *Home Alone 2* was not included in the CBC's (Canadian Broadcasting Corporation) airing of the popular movie. Trump himself takes to Twitter to blame Canadian Prime Minister Justin Trudeau for the omission, and Trump's son Donald Jr. blasts the CBC in a tweet that reads, " 'Pathetic': Canada's CBC under fire when Trump's cameo in 'Home Alone 2' disappears from Christmas broadcast." The CBC later explains that the Trump scene was removed in 2014 when the network acquired rights to broadcast the movie, and was edited for time. There was no political motive. **12/26/19**

▌ Actor Jon Voight posts an online video insinuating that Donald Trump's presidency is mandated by God, and receives a praising tweet from the president who posts that the actor "delivers big. Also, LOVES THE USA!" **12/27/19**

▌ Donald Trump retweets a video message featuring hashtag referencing a pro-Trump conspiracy theory known as QAnon. The fringe group's tweet, which includes the slogan #WWG1WGA which stands for "Where we go one, we go all," is part of the QAnon philosophy that claims an individual inside the U.S. government known as "Q" knows of information on a secret plot to overthrow Trump, and is led by prominent politicians, who are pedophiles. **12/27/19**

▌ The president goes after leadership of New York State and California, both of which have high rates of homelessness by saying that the governors should call him if they "can't handle the situation." Trump goes on to tweet that the governors of the states "must call and 'politely' ask for help." **12/28/19**

▌ Donald Trump faces backlash for retweeting a post that reveals the supposed name of the government whistleblower, whose complaint triggered the president's impeachment investigation. Although Trump's retweet is taken down, the White House defends the president, saying that it is not a violation of law for him to name the whistleblower. **12/30/19**

CHAPTER 37

JANUARY MAY VERY WELL be the most defining month of the Trump presidency. Beginning with the mafia hit on Iraq's General Qasem Soleimani, and ending with the kangaroo court proceedings in the U.S. Senate; formerly-known-as the "world's greatest deliberative body." January offers a cornucopia of madness that never seems to end.

Facts matter in the month of January, and once again the former TV-host-turned-politician-turned-Caesar, presents some mind-numbing statistics. Trump breaks the all-time lie threshold by spinning 16,000 mistruths and fantasies since his inauguration, bypassing all other U.S. presidents, combined, with one year left in his term. As far as lying is concerned, DJT is the Ted Williams of politics. No one can catch him.

The president traverses uncharted waters of his expertise during the first month of 2020, when he becomes a medical expert, declaring that U.S. military personnel who were shelled by Iranian missiles and suffered severe traumatic head injuries only had "headaches." ("Hey kid, you're OK, just rub some dirt on it and get back in there. We need you. The Saudis are sending us some serious bank for protection, and they pay CASH! You gotta' serve me…I mean us.")

"So, how's your 409K's doing?" "We have to protect Thomas Edison." "Do you think Americans care about Ukraine?" "Satanic pregnancies." "We're not leaving (Iraq) unless they pay us." "I wouldn't go to war with you people." Losers." "Dopes and babies." "Get rid of her. Get her out tomorrow. I don't care. Take her out, OK? Do it!" "Vote against the president, and your head will be on a pike."

▮ The United States military uses a drone strike to Kill General Qasem Soleimani, head of Iran's elite Quds military force at Baghdad's International Airport. The president does not brief any Democratic Congressional leaders of the strike, but does provide pre-attack information to Senate Majority Leader Mitch McConnell (R-KY) and Senator Lindsey Graham (R-SC). Donald Trump also reportedly tells guests at his Mar-a-Lago resort (where he was vacationing) that he was working on a "big" response to Iranian aggression and that they would be hearing about it "very soon." **1/2/20**

▮ Vice President Mike Pence makes a claim that Iran's General Soleimani who was recently killed in a U.S. drone strike in Iraq, was involved with 10 of the 19 terrorists responsible for the 9/11 attacks in the United States. Pence tweets that the terrorists traveled through Iran on their way to the U.S., but there is no proof Soleimani worked with, or knew anything about the planned attacks or the men who carried them out. **1/3/20**

▮ Donald Trump uses his personal Twitter account to notify Congress of his plans to retaliate against Iran if they attack U.S. personnel or assets. Trump posts, "These Media Posts will serve as notification to the United States Congress that should Iran strike any U.S. person or target, the United States will quickly and fully strike back, & perhaps in a disproportionate manner. Such legal notice is not required, but it is given nonetheless!" The president appears to be mocking the War Powers Act of 1973, which checks the president's power, taking aim at Democrats who challenged him on the decision to kill Iran General Qasem Soleimani. The House Foreign Relations Committee sarcastically responds to the president with a tweet of its own, posting, "This Media Post will serve as a reminder that war powers reside in the Congress under the United States Constitution. And that you should read the War Powers Act. And that you're not a dictator." **1/5/20**

▮ The president threatens to bomb 52 cultural sites in Iran (the number derived from the 52 U.S. hostages taken by Iran in 1979) if that country retaliates against the U.S., as tensions escalate following the killing of a top Iranian general. Donald Trump, in remarks made aboard Air Force One says, "They're allowed to kill our people. They're allowed to torture and maim our people. And we're not allowed to touch their cultural sites. It doesn't work that way." Attacking cultural sites is illegal under the 1954 Hague Convention and the 1972 World Heritage Convention, which both the U.S. and Iran have ratified. **1/5/20**

∎ Donald Trump threatens to impose deep sanctions on Iraq and force them to reimburse the U.S. for military expenditures if they force the withdrawal of troops from their country. Trump tells reporters while flying on Air Force One, "We've spent a lot of money on Iraq. We have a very extraordinarily expensive air base that's there. It cost billions of dollars to build. We're not leaving unless they pay us back for it." **1/5/20**

∎ Questions arise surrounding the killing of General Qasem Soleimani as the White House does not release specific threats posed by the Iranian commander, other than saying that there was an "imminent" attack being planned by him. After being briefed by the Trump administration on Soleimani's death, several senators criticize the reasons given, including Rand Paul (R-KY) and Mike Lee (R-UT), who calls the briefing the "worst I've ever seen." **1/7/20**

∎ In an attempt to deflect blame from the Soleimani death, Donald Trump tries to blame former president Obama for funding Iran's military operations, including the retaliatory missile strikes on a U.S. base. During a press briefing at the White House, Trump remarks, "Iran's hostilities substantially increased after the foolish Iran nuclear deal was signed in 2013, and they were given $150 billion, not to mention $1.8 billion in cash." Trump continues, "The missiles fired last night at us and our allies were paid for with funds made available by the last administration." **1/8/20**

∎ A federal appeals court declines to lift an injunction on the "public charge" rule used by the Trump administration to restrict green cards for immigrants who may become reliant on public assistance. The rule would revoke green card status to any immigrant who receives Supplemental Security Income (SSI), Temporary Assistance for Needy Families (TANF), Supplemental Nutrition Assistance Program (SNAP), as well as most forms of Medicaid. **1/8/20**

■ Treasury Secretary Steve Mnuchin refuses to release Secret Service spending information relating to travel of the president and his family until 2021, which would be after the 2020 U.S. presidential election. Mnuchin, in a battle with Democrats over re-assigning the Secret Service to the Treasury Department from the Department of Homeland Security, rejects the offer made to have Secret Service financial records released within 120 days of the agreement to re-assign the agencies. **1/9/20**

■ Donald Trump, in a tweet attempting to tout his economic growth policies, misstates the name of a popular investment program used by many Americans to save for retirement. Trump tweets, "STOCK MARKET AT ALL-TIME HIGH! HOW ARE YOUR 409K'S DOING? 70%, 80%, 90% up. Only 50% up! What are you doing wrong?" **1/9/20**

■ The U.S. House of Representatives approves a measure relating to the War Powers Resolution of 1983, which would restrict the president's authority to attack Iran without first receiving Congressional approval. The resolution passes 224-194 and proceeds to the Senate. The bill is known as a "concurrent resolution," and is more symbolic in nature, as the Senate will likely vote it down. Donald Trump responds to the action by House Democrats as "Just another Democrat fraud," and "Presidential Harassment." Trump also tweets, "Crazy Nancy Pelosi's War Powers Resolution." **1/9/20**

■ The Trump administration announces that they will be rolling back decades-old regulations that could have an adverse effect on combating climate change. The revisions are to the National Policy Act which requires federal oversight in assessing the environmental impact of projects such as infrastructure, mines, and highways. The president comments on the proposed rollbacks by stating, "These endless delays waste money, keep projects from breaking ground and deny jobs to our nation's incredible workers. From day one, my administration has made fixing this regulatory nightmare a top priority." The new regulations are guaranteed to be fought with legal challenges from numerous environmental groups. **1/9/20**

■ Donald Trump takes to Twitter to boast that the nation's cancer death rate is the lowest in history. Trump Tweets, "U.S. Cancer Death Rate Lowest in Recorded History! A lot of good news coming out of this Administration." In fact, U.S. cancer death rates have been declining every year since 1991 and cannot be attributed to actions taken by the Trump administration. **1/9/20**

■ Donald Trump implies that he should have won the Nobel Peace Prize over eventual winner Abiy Ahmed. During a campaign event in Toledo, Ohio Trump comments, "I made a deal, I saved a country, and I just heard that the head of that country is now getting the Nobel Peace Prize for saving the country." Trump continues, "I said what, did I have something to do with it?" **1/10/20**

■ The president says that he will prevent former national security adviser John Bolton from testifying at the Senate impeachment trial. Donald Trump indicates he will use the powers of executive privilege to block Bolton's potential testimony. Trump claims that his actions are "for the sake of the (presidential) office." **1/11/20**

■ During an interview with FOX News' Laura Ingraham, the president reveals that his administration is accepting cash payments for troops in Saudi Arabia. Trump tells Ingraham, "We have a very good relationship with Saudi Arabia. I said listen, you're a very rich country. You want more troops? I'm going to send them to you, but you're going to have to pay us." Trump continues, "They're paying us. They've already deposited $1 billion in the bank." Also during the same interview, Trump doubles down on his administration's claim of "taking Syria's oil," and holding it for an undetermined amount of time. Trump leaves open the possibility of the U.S. keeping the oil, saying, "Maybe we will, maybe we won't. I don't know, maybe we should take it." **1/11/20**

- Facing increased scrutiny at home for the drone attack and death of General Qasem Soleimani, the president claims that the former Iranian leader was planning attacks on four American embassies, and a decision was made to prevent these "imminent" attacks. Secretary of Defense Mark Esper counters Trump's claims, saying that he saw no specific evidence to support the president's view. Trump then changes his story on Soleimani, stating "it doesn't really matter" if he were actively planning attacks. **1/12/20**

- Donald Trump retweets an incendiary picture of House Speaker Nancy Pelosi (D-CA) and Senate Minority Leader Charles Schumer (D-NY) dressed in Muslim attire, with an Iranian flag in the background. The tweet's commentary states, "The corrupted Dems trying their best to come to the Ayatollah's rescue." **1/13/20**

- Donald trump tries to claim that he protected insurance coverage for millions of Americans with pre-existing conditions, which fails to align with his administration's record on healthcare. Trump has repeatedly attempted to dismantle the Affordable Care Act (also known as Obamacare), which made protecting pre-existing conditions a cornerstone of the legislation. **1/13/20**

- Lev Parnas, a former associate of Trump lawyer Rudy Giuliani, releases documents and text messages to House Democrats, which reportedly shows extensive involvement in dealings with Ukraine, and attempts to gather information on Hunter Biden, in order to discredit Joe Biden's presidential campaign. **1/15/20**

- Following up on Lev Parnas's release of documents surrounding the Ukraine issue, the indicted associate of Donald Trump's lawyer Rudy Giuliani gives an interview to MSNBC'S Rachel Maddow. During the program Parnas tells Maddow that then-National Security Adviser John

Bolton, Vice President Mike Pence, and the president all knew of the activities related to Ukraine, and the attempts to gather information on Joe Biden. **1/16/20**

■ The U.S. House of Representatives delivers two articles of impeachment to the Senate, starting in motion the trial of Donald John Trump, the 45th president of the United States. The House's action officially makes Trump only the third president in American history to face removal from office. **1/16/20**

■ The General Accountability Office issues a report that claims the White House violated federal law by withholding security assistance to Ukraine. The GAO says in its report that the Office of Budget and Management (OBM) broke the law when it held up funds issued by Congress under orders from the president. Democrats quickly point out that the violation is another example of a lawless Trump administration, while Republicans claim the president was within his right to control funding, based on his "priorities." **1/17/20**

■ The U.S. Department of Agriculture announces new proposed nutritional guidelines for school breakfasts and lunches. The revised standards would allow schools to cut the amount of fruits and vegetables served to students, allowing them to substitute higher calorie foods such as French fries, burgers and pizza. The change is announced on former First Lady Michelle Obama's birthday. Mrs. Obama championed healthier school nutrition while in the White House, and it was considered to be her signature achievement. **1/17/20**

■ According to the upcoming book, *A Very Stable Genius: Donald Trump's Testing of America*, the president berated leaders of the U.S. military, calling them "losers" and saying that, "I wouldn't go to war with you people," as well as calling the assembled generals "a bunch of dopes and babies." Trump reportedly made these remarks during discussions of military matters when the generals disagreed with his positions. **1/17/20**

▮ The National Archives, a non-partisan federal agency reportedly alters pictures in a women's suffrage exhibit in Washington that have anti-Trump signs in them, by blurring out the president's name. The photos, some of which were licensed for use in the exhibit but not part of the National Archives' collection, were blurred, "so as not to engage in current political controversy." **1/18/20**

▮ The *Washington Post's* Fact Checkers Team reveals that since Donald Trump took office in January, 2017, he has made 16,241 false or misleading statements during political rallies, interviews, press briefings, or social media. In 2017 he made 1,999, in 2018 he added 5,689, and in 2019 the total for the year was 8,155. **1/22/20**

▮ The president downplays possible traumatic head injuries suffered by U.S. soldiers on a military base in Iraq after that facility suffered numerous missile strikes by Iranian forces. Trump repeatedly claims that no service people were hurt by the strikes, but the Pentagon acknowledges 11 soldiers (later updated to 64) required medical attention as a result. Donald Trump tells reporters that soldiers suffered "headaches," but the military proceeds to examine whether or not the wounds are far more serious traumatic brain injuries. Trump's comments draw fire from numerous veterans' groups, including the U.S. Department of Veterans' Affairs. **1/22/20**

▮ The Trump administration finalizes a rule that prevents certain safeguards against polluting U.S. streams and waterways. The new rule, which was constructed by the Army Corps of Engineers and Environmental Protection Agency (EPA), replaces President Obama's 2015 Waters of the United States regulation, also known as the Clean Water Rule. The new regulations are designed to make it easier for land owners and farmers to dump chemicals and other chemical waste into formerly protected U.S. federal waterways. **1/23/20**

▮ Donald Trump has an interview with CNBC's Joe Kernan at the World Economic Forum in Davos, Switzerland, in which he seems to claim that the wheel was invented in the United States, not in Ancient Mesopotamia. Trump says, "We have to protect Thomas Edison-we have to protect all of these people that came up with originally; the light bulb, and the wheel, and all of those things, and he's one of our very smart people. We want to cherish these people. That's very important. He's done a very good job." **1/23/20**

■ Also, during the same interview with Kernan, the president is asked if he would ever consider cutting U. S. entitlement programs such as Social Security and Medicare. Trump responds, "At some point, they will be. We have tremendous growth. This next year I-it'll be toward the end of the year. The growth is going to be incredible. And at the right time, we will take a look at that." Trump's comments are a reversal of his position when he was running for president during the 2016 election, when he vowed, "We're not going to cut your Social Security and we're not going to cut your Medicare." **1/23/20**

■ According to a report from ABC News, Donald Trump told associates he wanted then-U.S. ambassador to Ukraine Marie Yovanovitch fired after he was told that she did not support the president, and that she was saying that he would be impeached. The report comes from audio recordings made at a small gathering with the president, Lev Parnas, and Igor Fruman. When told of Yovanovitch's comments, a voice identified as Trump's yells, "Get rid of her! Get her out tomorrow! I don't care. Get her out tomorrow! Take her out. OK? Do it!" **1/24/20**

■ In a story filed by CBS News, one of Donald Trump's associates threatens U.S. Senators not to vote for the president's removal from office during the impeachment trial, with a violent warning. According to the report, the associate told Senators, "Vote against the president and your head will be on a pike." **1/24/20**

■ Secretary of State Mike Pompeo is involved in a contentious interview with National Public Radio (NPR) reporter Mary Louise Kelly, in which

Pompeo abruptly cuts off their session, and angrily berates her for continuing to ask about his lack of defense of former Ukrainian ambassador Marie Yovanovitch from attacks by Rudi Giuliani. The secretary reportedly says to Kelly. "Do you think Americans care about Ukraine?" He then asks the reporter to point out Ukraine on a world map, which she does correctly. Donald Trump weighs in on the incident by retweeting a social media post from Conservative radio host Mark Levin questioning why NPR still exists, by adding, "A very good question." **1/24/20**

▌ Former national security adviser John Bolton, in a soon-to-be released book, makes a claim that the president told him directly that military aid to Ukraine would be withheld until President Volodymyr Zelensky agreed to begin an investigation of Joe and Hunter Biden. Bolton has agreed to appear before the U.S. Senate's impeachment trial, and the new revelation in his book creates increased pressure from Democrats to allow his testimony. **1/24/20**

▌ White House religious adviser Paula White calls for the termination of certain pregnancies by divine intervention. White, while delivering a sermon to a congregation, asks God to take authority over the marine kingdom, the animal kingdom, and all "satanic pregnancies" that seek to harm Donald Trump, or the church. **1/27/20**

▌ Donald Trump mocks NPR reporter Mary Louise Kelly, following her dustup with Secretary of State Mike Pompeo during a news conference featuring Trump's Middle East peace proposal. The president praises Pompeo for his work on the plan, and then says to him in front of the assembled media, "that reporter couldn't have done too good a job on you yesterday, huh?" Trump continues, "I think you did a good job on her, actually." MSNBC host Nicole Wallace responds to Trump's comments, saying that it shows the "complete and total rot" in the White House." **1/28/20**

▌ Following the explosive exchange between NPR reporter Mary Louise Kelly and Secretary of State Mike Pompeo, the U.S. State Department announces the removal of NPR diplomatic correspondent Michelle Kelemen from an upcoming trip to the U.K., Ukraine, Belarus, Kazakhstan, and Uzbekistan. Despite numerous inquiries to the State Department about the reporter's removal, no explanation is offered. **1/29/20**

■ A Trump-aligned group called the Urban Revitalization Coalition, begins to run events in black communities that award cash to attendees under the auspices of a 501(c)3 charitable organization. The events, reported by Politico, are run by Trump supporters, and raise questions as to whether they are actual charities, or a political action group designed to sway black voters in key swing states. **1/29/20**

■ During the questioning phase of the Senate impeachment trial, Senator Rand Paul (R-KY) tries to expose the Ukraine whistleblower by including the person's name in a question to Supreme Court Justice John Roberts. Upon reading over the question, Roberts states, "The presiding officer declines to read the question submitted." Paul then proceeds to storm out of the Senate chamber. **1/30/20**

■ U.S. Commerce Secretary Wilbur Ross makes a stunning statement about the Chinese coronavirus being good for business in America and could "help" bring jobs back to the country. The virus, which has killed over 170 people and infected more than 8,100 others, might help bring additional commerce to the U.S. as businesses consider moving their operations out of infected areas of China, according to Ross. **1/30/20**

■ E. Jean Carroll, a writer who has accused Donald Trump of sexual assault years before he became president, asks for a DNA sample from him in order to compare it to semen samples on the dress she was wearing when she was allegedly raped by Trump in a changing room of Manhattan's Bergdorf Goodman during the 1990's. **1/30/20**

■ Donald Trump orders the Department of Defense to roll back restrictions on the use of land mines. Use of landmines is banned in more than 150 countries due to potential harm to civilians, but the Trump administration claims that banning them would place the U.S. military at a "severe disadvantage" during conflict. **1/31/20**

▋ In a 51-49 vote, Senate Republicans vote to block additional witnesses in the impeachment trial of Donald Trump. The vote, which included defections from Republicans Mitt Romney (R-UT) and Susan Collins (R-ME), prevents former National Security Adviser John Bolton from testifying at the trial, before a final vote on conviction or acquittal is taken. Bolton alleges in an upcoming book that the president told him of plans to withhold military aid from Ukraine in exchange for an investigation of Joe and Hunter Biden, and of attempts to have Bolton assist Trump attorney Rudy Giuliani with setting up a meeting for that purpose. The vote to block additional testimony all but assures Trump's acquittal on the Articles of Impeachment scheduled to be voted on in early February. **1/31/20**

Note…Donald John Trump, 45th president of the United States, is acquitted of two articles of impeachment by the U.S. Senate on 2/5/20

EPILOGUE

I HAVE LABORED WITH this book for three long years. It started out as a way for me to deal with the election of Donald Trump, and grew into a near-obsession (my wife would disagree with the "near" part). As I continued to write and research, the sheer volume of Trumpian-inspired insanity became at times, overwhelming. Day after day, notebook after notebook, re-write after re-write, it trudged on. I wrote while at work, at home, on vacation, in airports. You name it; I was always ready, armed with pencil, paper, and perseverance.

As I recorded details from the Trump presidency, one fact seemed to emerge. There would be no "evolution" of his ability to govern. Those who were holding their breath waiting for Donald Trump to become "more presidential," could have died of asphyxia, because change was not-a comin.'

Say what you will about the 45th U.S president (hey, keep it clean), but even though he is a lying, egomaniacal, self-obsessed, dictatorial pompous cur with the morals of a gutter snipe, he understands two things; the media and propaganda. And he understands them well.

Donald Trump's "evil-lution" (see what I did there?) began with a masterful use of Twitter, and expanded to framing the free press as the "enemy of the people." Once he had these two elements in place, it was easy to add bombastic claims and outright lies to his legion of true believers. "Day is night, night is day, and Donald Trump is now the way!" After his propaganda methodology was in place, he went after "The Swamp."

The Swamp is a wonderful metaphor for anyone in Washington who challenges the president in any way. President Obama is in the swamp. Nancy Pelosi, a very swampy person. Hillary Clinton? She is the scum that lies on top of the festering swamp. It's all so easy. Find someone in D.C. who is in your way and "swamp-itize" them. One odd corollary about the swamp however, is that Republicans are never in it until they fail to kiss Donald Trump's ring and fall prostrate to him. Then they are relegated to life-long swamp residency. See Sessions, Jeffery and Cohen, Michael.

Trump's presidency continued to become the cancerous growth on the American carcass as he slowly and systematically began to energize his base of minions at circus-like rallies across the country, where he spoke in a stream of consciousness that allowed him to bash his opponents, and insure that maximum pressure was placed on Republicans in Congress to stay in their lane, lest they be skewered by the president on Twitter, and threatened with bodily harm by his followers. The takeover of the party was complete.

So at the end of my book, which cover years 1-3 of Trump's reign of terror, we find a president with a growing grip on power, emboldened by his escape from a special investigation (Mueller), and an impeachment (acquittal). Although I believed when I first started this book that Trump would certainly be a controversial leader, I never fathomed that he would morph into the demagogue he has become.

I hope that *Chronology of Chaos* emerges into the kind of book that enables readers to study the kind of president Donald Trump was, and begin to understand that this is not "normal" by any stretch of the imagination. I also sincerely hope that opponents of this stain on our Republic's fabric can use information in its chapters to have truth-to- power conversations with like-minded citizens in order to right the American ship, and guide her through the choppy waters ahead.

www.ingramcontent.com/pod-product-compliance
Lightning Source LLC
Chambersburg PA
CBHW060313030426
42336CB00011B/1019